M000008376

FISH OF A LIFETIME

MEMORIES AND REFLECTIONS SPAWNED BY A LIFE LIST OF FISH

AL VAN VOOREN

Copyright © 2019 by Al Van Vooren

All rights reserved. No part of this book may be reproduced in any manner without the express written consent of the author, except in the case of brief excerpts in critical review and articles.

Published in association with:

Keokee Co. Publishing, Inc.
Sandpoint, Idaho
ww.keokeebooks.com

Cover: Author with fish and older brother Ron.
Green Lake, Wisconsin, 1949. Photographer unknown.

ISBN: 9781074585495

For Dad and the boys

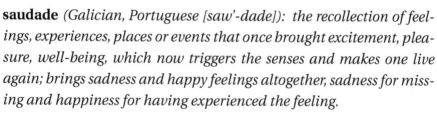

saudade *(Galician, Portuguese [saw'-dade]): the recollection of feelings, experiences, places or events that once brought excitement, pleasure, well-being, which now triggers the senses and makes one live again; brings sadness and happy feelings altogether, sadness for missing and happiness for having experienced the feeling.*
   - Wikipedia

CONTENTS

Prologue   9

Introduction   13

Part 1 Temperate Freshwater Fishes   19

Part 2 Temperate Saltwater Fishes   159

Part 3 Tropical Fresh/Brackish-Water Fishes   195

Part 4 Tropical Saltwater Fishes   207

Afterward   243

Index of Fishes   247

Acknowledgments   251

About the Author   253

PROLOGUE

I never really knew my Dad. He died when I was 23.

We lived in the same house until I turned 18 and went away to college, but we didn't connect much. For one thing, I didn't see him very often. Dad always worked second shift at the plant; he had already left for work when I got home from school and was still in bed when I got up in the morning. Weekends were the only time our schedules overlapped, but our worlds still didn't connect.

Dad wasn't a very open or demonstrative person. The old sepia-toned family photos of Dad and my aunt and uncles as kids, somberly posing in front of a stark, stone house on the Minnesota prairie, said a lot. That upbringing in a stoic immigrant family sur-viving the Depression on the southern Minnesota prairie, combined with living through the nightmares of WW II in the South Pacific, left Dad encapsulated in a shell impermeable to the visible flow of emo-tion or feelings.

I know Dad loved me and was proud of me, even though he never said the words and it was hard for him to show it. What both-ers me to this day, though, is that I never said the words to him.

But fishing opened some doors between us, and afforded a special bond.

I vividly remember the day that Dad pulled up behind me in our '57 Chevy while I was fishing down at Prospect Park lagoon in a pouring rain. I was kicking butt on bluegills. He leaned across the seat, rolled down the passenger window, and shouted, "Come on, haven't you got any sense?" I put my bike and a nice stringer of bluegills in the trunk and climbed in. We rode in silence.

But instead of going home Dad pulled up behind Champ and Joe's. "I just want to stop for a quick one. You can come on in and have a soda." When everyone made the obligatory pivot on their stools to see who was coming in the back door of the tavern, Dad put his hand on my shoulder and announced/asked, "You boys all know my son Allan?" He pointed me to the back room, which was really just the back end of one big room with some pillars between it and the bar. Without a word he put a bottle of cream soda, still dripping with water and small pieces of ice from the pop cooler, down in front of me and went back up to the bar.

I sat there by myself at that back table, surrounded by the odors of stale beer and fresh rain, and for the next hour listened to my dad brag to his buddies and anyone and everyone in the room who would listen about what a helluva' fisherman I was.

When I got old enough to drive and strike out on my own fishing adventures, I discovered there was more to fishing than the bluegills, catfish, and yellow-bellied bullheads I'd been raised on. And when things fell together and I was able to put Dad into some pretty good bass or walleye fishing, he couldn't help but let some emotion show. When he would set the hook on a good fish he would suck in a breath through clenched teeth, making a hissing sound. When he'd boat the fish, he'd invariably hold it up toward the sky at arm's length and exclaim, "Man!" For really nice ones, or when the action was really fast, he'd hold the fish aloft and exclaim with an uncontrollable grin, "Man-de-long!", whatever that meant.

Dad had his first heart attack when I was in high school, and after I left for college his second and third. He didn't get out fishing much himself after I left home, but when we talked or saw each other he always wanted to hear about my fishing. I was still thinking that one of those days, out on the water somewhere, we would be able to tell each other what we meant to one another. But before that day ever came, I got a call from a half a country away that Dad had suffered his final heart attack.

I've read a lot of essays over the years on why we fish: solitude, communing with nature, connecting to a mysterious underwater world, restoring our souls. That may be the pull for some.

As for me, I think the reason I fish, and the reason I momentarily hold every nice fish I catch up, is so I can connect with Dad......

so Dad can see how good the fishing is. And when it's a particularly nice one, I involuntarily hold it up a little higher and suck in a breath through clenched teeth. And I imagine and hope that wherever Dad is he's saying, "Man-de-long!", and telling his new friends "That's my son Allan."

# INTRODUCTION

Who can know what drives our passions in life. Whatever the factors might have been, I was dealt a passion for fishing. It goes back as far as I can remember, to the early years growing up in Moline, Illinois, a town sandwiched between the Mississippi and Rock rivers: the anticipation of summer family fishing trips to Minnesota, pestering Dad to take me fishing around home, the excitement of being old enough to drive myself fishing, taking dates fishing. The passion led me to a career in fisheries, researching what makes fish populations and fish communities tick and managing factors like harvest and habitat to make populations healthier and fishing better. My career took me to Ohio in 1968 and the lakes and streams of the southeast Ohio hill country, the Ohio River, and up to Lake Erie. Then on to Iowa in 1978 to work with Mississippi River fish populations in the stomping grounds of my youth. And finally in 1985 to the mountain lakes and streams, the wild rivers and working rivers, and the natural lakes and big reservoirs of Idaho. Throughout, the passion for fishing never faded.

And my best job of all, retirement, has brought me to the lake country of Northern Idaho and a home on huge 85,000-acre Lake Pend Oreille, my boat down at our dock on Perch Bay just waiting to go fishing. And the free time of retirement has allowed me to travel and experience new fishing holes. Now, looking back at 70 fading behind me like a trailing wake, I feel blessed to have had the opportunity to fish in so many different places and have so many wonderful fishing experiences.

This project had its genesis shortly after I retired in 2006 on the way home from a trip to a new fishing hole. During a layover in the Atlanta airport, one of the anglers who had been on the trip with me casually commented about adding some new species to his life list. I'd never thought of it before then. A fish life list. Hmmm.

The project started out simply as that – compile a list of the fish species that I've caught. But a simple journey of compilation opened so many creels full of memories that the list became an annotated list, which then grew larger into a collection of memories and reflections from a lifetime of fishing – merely organized by fish species caught. For some species, it's remembering an individual fish: maybe the first one of that species, or the biggest one, how one was caught, or how one got away. For some it's about a fish that someone else caught. In other instances, rather than an individual fish, it's a special place or experience. As I got into it and reflected, it quickly became apparent that, even though over the years I've done a lot of my fishing alone, the really special experiences and best memories involved fishing with other people.

It's been a blessing to have lived a life surrounded by people who loved to fish and to have had so many wonderful fishing companions, both family and friends. I still get to fish with some, time and distance make it less likely with others, and too many have passed away. Being taken fishing by Dad made some sweet memories and probably started me down my fishing path, and I'm so thankful we had the chance to transition from dad-taking-son fishing to father-and-son fishing companions. College led me to a career dominated by like-minded fisheries workers and some wonderful fishing buddies. My college years also led me to my close fishing partner of 37 years, Margie. We went bass fishing on our honeymoon. Margie had some of her own treasured memories of fishing with her dad, and I always thought that our fishing together made her feel in some way close to her Dad, who passed away just before we were married.

Our marriage also afforded me the opportunity for my own Dad-taking-sons fishing experiences, and now two very special fishing companions in my "boys," Colby and Clark. Distance – and the fact that they have to make a living – means our opportunities to fish together take a little more planning now. But that makes those opportunities all the more precious.

Today I feel so lucky and fortunate to have found and been able to marry Sue, my life and fishing companion for the last decade. And as a bonus in the bargain, I gained a daughter and another fishing partner in Anna. Sue always enjoys the time we spend together on the water, but if it doesn't work for her she genuinely encourages me to not miss an opportunity to go fishing.

So the project evolved in large part into a collection of memories and reflections about fish, family, and friends. And it's a large collection. It quickly became apparent that one memory per fish species wasn't going to work. There are just too many memories that I hold dear. And some reflections wander off a bit into adjacent waters before they end up back where the fish was caught.

The highlights and favorite memories associated with any one species sometimes span many decades, so organizationally a chronological ordering of species doesn't work. Bird life lists and identification books always have the same species order, starting with loons and ending with finches. Likewise ichthyology books – at least those for North American species that occur in freshwater – have a consistent phylogenetic ordering of species, beginning with the most primitive and moving through the more "advanced" species. So that is the order I've used to list fish species and organize my memories, at least for temperate freshwater species. Other species are lumped in no particular order under headings of temperate saltwater fishes, tropical fresh/brackish-water fishes, and tropical saltwater fishes.

Memory is a wonderful, unique, and mystical thing. It enables us to hold onto wonderful times, to accumulate a mental store of pleasant (and unpleasant) experiences, and to pull them back up at will to re-experience. It's unique in that our memories are ours and ours alone. Two people can share the same experience and come away with a different memory. More than once I've had someone recount their memory of an experience we'd shared and it had variations and nuances that my memory lacked. I've even had someone refer to their memory of a shared experience from years prior, adding that it was something they would never forget, and none of it even rang a bell with me.

Our memory is mystical in how it works, in what it selects to highlight, and even enhance with clarity, and what it chooses to ignore or let fade. I read recently about a study which suggests that the mind actually tweaks a memory every time it's revisited.

Some of my memories that follow, spanning over 65 years, have morphed no doubt. Decades of detailed fishing logs and countless photos have helped anchor my memory to events and times and details, but the most valued components of memories are the associated feelings and emotions, not so easily documented. Be that as it may, in reflecting and retelling I've tried to be as true to occurrence as my current memory allows.

The primary intent of all this is to provide something tangible that will help me retain and cherish my memories from a lifetime of fishing experiences – to preserve what I can before the waters of my memory muddy up. I suppose those who shared those experiences and helped make the memories might enjoy a story or two. Beyond that, I'm not qualified and it's certainly not meant to convey fishing tips or advice. There's not a story that plays out beginning to end, no connecting thread or recurring theme, other than fishing, family, and friendship. My good friend Dan Herrig would call it a "bathroom book," one that can be read five minutes at a time. My hope for those that do read it is that they might find it fun or interesting, or that it stirs and brings to mind their own wonderful memories made in the pursuit of fish.

"If there is magic on the planet, it's in the water."
-Loren Eiseley:
Collected Essays on Evolution, Nature, and the Cosmos

Artic Char

PART 1.
Temperate Freshwater Fishes

White Sturgeon

Sturgeon generally head up the list of fish species in the various compendiums of freshwater fish, being among the most "primitive" fish. And the white sturgeon is an appropriate lead-off for my collection of fishing memories. A fish that made my arms and shoulders ache for two days – the biggest fish I've ever caught – is understandably hard to forget.

White sturgeon are really something, with a life span approaching that of humans, armor plating on the outside of their body but no backbone on the inside, and a big protractile "Hoover" on the underside of their snout-like head that fondles and tastes things they find on the bottom to see if it's lunch. I'd read and been told about the big lake sturgeon that tore up commercial fishing nets on the Great Lakes in the old days, before their populations were decimated, and I'd handled a few of the much smaller and still abundant shovelnose sturgeon while I was working on the Mississippi. But it wasn't until I moved to Idaho that I caught my first sturgeon, a white sturgeon, hook and line.

Brent Mabbot, the fish management biologist in southwest Idaho, called one day and asked if I'd like to join him the next day to go check thermographs on the Snake River south of Nampa. Of course there were things I should've been doing the next day, but I hadn't been in Idaho that long and hadn't had a chance to see much of the Snake River. It's a working river – literally an on-again, off-again river. You might say it's kind of a dyslexic river, with half of the thousand-mile long river being slack water impoundments behind dams. And the Idaho State Water Plan even has a stated goal of zero discharge below Milner Dam during the irrigation season, the entire flow diverted into irrigation canals about half way on the river's journey across Idaho. Large springs enter the river below there and the river starts over again. While much of the river and its fish habitat has been severely altered, the part south of Nampa is still fairly intact.

I'd been involved in hiring Brent and was anxious to spend some time with him in the field. He was a person who was always positive and enthusiastic, yet calm and unflappable (which I suspect comes with having eight kids). And he was so passionate about "making fishing better" that he'd applied and competed with three dozen other candidates and given up a career as a conservation officer to take this job in fish management.

Brent added that we could throw a line in for sturgeon while we ate lunch. That made it a no-brainer.

It was one of those amazing sunny spring days when we launched the Fish and Game Department jet-boat at Walter's Ferry Access south of Nampa the next morning. The flat river near the launch site, with adjacent corn fields and pastures, was not that different from rivers back in the Midwest where I'd been working until fairly recently. But within the first couple of miles heading upstream, the river, kind of like my career, changed dramatically in some exciting ways. The river entered a canyon and sprung boulders and rapids. I'd seen parts of it before from the top of the north rim, but the experience of being in the jet-boat as Brent roared up through chutes and around boulders and looking up at canyons walls that were the home to ancient pictographs and the highest density of nesting raptors in North America was awesome.

Checking the thermographs, small-battery operated instruments submerged in the river that made a continuous recording of water temperature, didn't amount to much, but the run up the river was sure worth it.

We pulled up on a little beach on the south side of the river just a couple miles below Swan Falls Dam to have lunch. Brent said that this was the "trot-line hole," a spot where people had historically set trot lines for sturgeon. There was a car-sized flat rock straight across the river with an iron rod driven into it that had served as a tie-off for the lines. There was primitive road access into the canyon on the north side, and actually the remains of a couple old homesteads on the bench between the river and the canyon wall.

Brent pulled a two-piece, nine-foot "broomstick" with a big free-spool bait-casting reel out of the side storage compartment of the jet-boat and put it together. It was already rigged with a five or six-ounce pyramid sinker (a lot of sturgeon fishermen use railroad spikes) on a sliding dropper and a god awful big hook. He reached into a little cooler and, instead of lunch, pulled out a dead six-inch trout – the best bait there is according to Brent – and hooked it through the head and then back through the back.

The Snake River was about 100-125 yards across right there. According to Brent, from where we were pulled up on shore the bottom sloped out for maybe a fourth of the width of the river, then abruptly dropped into a 30 to 50-foot deep hole that ran down through the quarter mile long pool. That's where the mort needed to R.I.P. – hopefully just temporarily. With nine feet of leverage and that much lead, Brent had no trouble wanging that mort out to the middle of the river. I didn't think it was ever going to splash down. After a couple of minutes the big pyramid sinker found enough purchase to hold against the pull of the current on the line, and Brent propped the big rod up on a forked stick like we were fishing for bullheads. We plopped ourselves down a little further up the bank and I asked Brent about the chance of a big sturgeon ripping the rod and all into the river. But he said, "Nah, they just nibble."

I started in on a piece of fried chicken, visiting with Brent and keeping an eye on the tip of the big rod. And I don't think I was done with that first piece of chicken yet when I noticed the bow of the heavy line between the tip of the rod and the water surface do a brief little jig. Brent calmly just said, "Sturgeon mouthin' the bait; might want to get over by the rod." I did.

Rather than immediately pick up the rod and potentially have the fish feel something unnatural and reject the bait, we just watched for a little bit longer as the fish mouthed the bait. He liked it. Sitting behind the rod, I carefully got ahold of it. The line quit jigging, and while the fish didn't take off with the bait or really even pull, it just seemed like I was connected to something alive. I glanced over to Brent. He nodded and said, "He's got it." I dug my heels into the sand, leaned forward quickly reeling the rod down to point at the fish at the same time, and reared back for all I was worth. Whoa! I'd never felt anything as unyielding as that on a hook set. He had me!

I am definitely not the one in charge at this point.
(Brent Mabbot photo)

He took off across the river, and there wasn't a thing I could do about it. He didn't race off in a burst of speed but rather just went. He moved a short distance up and then down the pool, and after a bit came right back to where he'd started and just parked. Nothing was happening. I had a lot of leverage with that stiff nine-foot rod but I could only move the fish just a few feet before it would move back to its parking spot.

I wasn't making any progress, and Brent was a little concerned that the line might abrade on the rocky lip of the hole, so I got in the boat and Brent motored out to the fish. Brent got me right on top of the fish. Now when I really torqued on him, rather than just pulling him sideways as I was from the beach, with the hook in his mouth on the underside of his snout I was rolling him over. He didn't like that. The fish took off and moved to the head of the pool and Brent took us back in to the beach. We had a fair fight for a while, the fish moving around the upper part of the pool as I hung on and tried to make him work. But then he came back to his original spot and parked again. We went back out in the boat and got over him again. This time he again took off, but headed downstream. I couldn't stop him, and we were afraid he'd drop through the little rapids below us. But he stopped at the lower end of the pool, and then headed back upstream. Brent beached us and I got out and dug in again. I was getting a workout. I hoped the fish was too.

And he was. I could actually move the fish now. When it would move away it wasn't as far. I started to make some progress. It wasn't all over but I started to feel in charge. An hour and 25 minutes after I set the hook I had him in the shallow water in front of the beach and Brent managed to slip a rope around its tail. While "who had who" had run through my mind a number of times earlier, we had him.

We rolled the fish over, a position which calms and almost immobilizes these big powerful critters, and got the hook out of its leathery lip.

Because of their slow growth rate, the number of years it takes for them to mature and reproduce, and their long life span, sturgeon populations in the Snake River just can't do well with even a small amount of harvest. Fishing for sturgeon in Idaho has been restricted to catch and release for decades. It's unlawful to even remove them from the water, a discouragement to long photo shoots out of the water that might stress the fish.

Before releasing the fish, though, Brent waded in and took some

Sturgeon in hand. (Brent Mabbot photo)

measurements and made some notes on the fish's condition, as he did with all the sturgeon he was able to examine. He wrapped a flexible tape around the fish to measure the girth. Then I held one end at the tip of the fish's snout and Brent stretched the tape to the tip of the tail. Eight feet six inches! We set a tripod up in the shallow water, clipped a big dial scale to it with a block and tackle attached, and then slid the fish into a canvas stretcher. I cranked and Brent watched the scale. When there was daylight between the surface of the river and the bottom of the stretcher Brent called out "285!"

As my years in Idaho added up I've been fortunate to have a lot of other sturgeon experiences and memories to file away: watching my son Colby fight and land a five-footer; by myself at night following a seven-footer around the Snake River arm of C. J. Strike Reservoir in my boat, and then hanging over the side trying to get him unhooked; double headers at the Billy Creek hole; the fish that jumped in the dark one night and sounded like a washing machine falling back into the river; watching my friend Virgil Moore struggle to get a rod bent double by a downstream bound sturgeon out of the rod holder only to have the weld break before he got it done. But none have, and none will stand out like that first "lunch hour" (OK hour and a half) sturgeon with Brent Mabbot.

Paddlefish (Spoonbill)

My memory of catching a paddlefish is as disappointingly vague as the memory of my first sturgeon is wonderfully vivid. These crazy looking primitive fish with the long flat proboscis are found only in the Missouri and Mississippi rivers. When I was working on the Mississippi in southeast Iowa back in the early '80s I got an invitation from Maury Anderson to come upriver and join him and some of the fish research crew on a trip to try to collect some in the tail waters of Lock and Dam 12 near Bellevue. I probably would've accepted an invitation from Maury to spend a day with him doing anything. The big guy was always either smiling or laughing, and seemed genuinely interested in everything and everybody.

This was actually a "work" trip though. Paddlefish have the unenviable distinction of having eggs essentially identical to sturgeon eggs. At the time, there was a lot of concern throughout the paddlefish's range about illegal overharvest for the black market caviar trade, and Iowa was trying to get a better handle on the status of the population.

There's not a lot of technique involved in fishing for paddlefish. It's not all that sporting. But they do get big, the largest topping six feet and one hundred pounds. Landing a big one can be a tussle. These fish feed only on plankton, holding up in the water column facing the current and sieving for food. The only way to "catch" one is to snag it. Techniques might vary a little, but universally involve a big treble hook, some lead, heavy line, and a broomstick rod. The drill is to cast out as far as you can across the current, let the hook sink a ways down in the water column, then with repeated hard sweeps of the rod retrieve it back. Then do it again. And again.

Paddlefish fishing can leave your arms and shoulders aching for two days, even if you don't hook a fish. My clearest memory is the casting and retrieving over and over. But I also remember a rather small paddlefish maybe three feet long, snagged back by the tail, coming into the boat. I might have hooked it. It's just as likely that Maury hooked it and insisted I take the rod. That was the kind of guy he was. Regardless, I do have the recollection of reeling in my first – and to date my only – paddlefish.

Bowfin (Dogfish)

The bowfin, or dogfish as I knew it before my ichthyological enlightenment, is another primitive fish with some unusual adaptations. Among them is its ability to breathe through its air bladder as well as its gills. This allows it to live in very warm water with little dissolved oxygen by coming to the surface and gulping air. Young dogfish have even been observed surviving in mud, with no standing water, for 21 days! They are a fearsome toothy predator, preying on small fish, frogs, or anything they can catch. They'll take most any lure you'd use to fish for bass, and they put up a hard fight. I've caught bowfin fairly consistently while largemouth bass fishing in the slop (thick aquatic vegetation) on shallow Florida lakes. Some have pushed five pounds or so, and every time I thought I had a bass until I got a look at it.

But the bowfin that left the biggest impression with me was the first one I ever caught, fishing with a worm for bullheads in a shallow slough off the Mississippi. I remember it being one of those stifling hot, humid summer days in the Midwest. I don't recall now who I was with, but we were fishing from the bank in the shade of huge silver maples which dominate much of the riverbottom. The narrow, shallow slough put off the odor of decaying vegetation. I had cast my bait almost across it to the edge of some aquatic vegetation. When the fish took the worm it was obvious it wasn't a bullhead, charging off through the weeds, boiling and splashing. As bowfin go it wasn't a big fish, maybe 14 inches, and I horsed him in pretty easily with my heavy bullhead rig. But what a memorable fish to look at – after I rinsed and wiped all the mud off. I remember the long dorsal fin that ran half its length, the large black spot on its upper tail fin, and the overall green color. They were things I'd never seen on a fish before. But the thing that sticks in my mind the most was the vivid, bright green color of its fins.

Longnose Gar

Gar are primitive, rather nasty looking fish with an armor plated body and a snout full of teeth. While some anglers actually target big alligator gar found in the lower Mississippi, no one actually fishes for the smaller gar (longnose, shortnose and spotted) in the upper Mississippi. But if you pull a tiny minnow imitation lure through enough water in the upper Mississippi, sooner or later a gar is going to try to eat it. Nearly always the result is a sharp hit and then retrieving your line with no lure on the end, because it was cut off by all the gar's teeth, or retrieving your line with just the lure and no fish, because a gar's jaw is covered with such hard armor plating that the hook didn't stick. But sometimes…

I was casting a tiny little yellow crappie jig – probably a 1/16th or 1/32nd oz – around a "wing dam" at the head of Andalusia Island in Pool 16. This wing dam – an underwater wall of rocks extending perpendicular to the shoreline to direct water toward the mid-river navigation channel – came closer to the surface than most. There was turbulence where the water flowed over the top of the rocks, but quiet water below the surface on the downstream side. It was high summer and I figured there ought to be some crappies there that had moved out from the shallow backwaters in the middle of the island where they'd spawned.

I didn't catch any crappies. But on, I think, my first cast I had a hard hit right near the end of my retrieve and on the reactive hook set ripped a small 18-inch gar right up out of the water and into the boat. It was a blur of flopping around the bottom. My jig was dangling from the end of my line. The tiny hook evidently got just enough purchase for me to launch the fish into the boat. It was a longnose gar.

Mooneye • Goldeye

I doubt that mooneye, or goldeye, show up on the life list of many anglers, especially if they didn't grow up next to a large Midwest river and fished for anything and everything they could catch. Mooneye and goldeye are kind of foot-long shad look-alikes, except they are brighter silver and have huge eyes that seem to take up most of their rather small head. And if you throw enough dead grasshoppers into the river they might show up.

Before getting into mooneye catching though, a little dead grasshopper background is called for. For three years during junior high I had a job helping Mertz Pobanz commercial fish on the Mississippi where it flowed past my hometown, Moline, Illinois. Mertz, a buddy of my Dad, worked in a foundry during the week but on weekends set out "jump lines" for catfish. A jump line is basically a trot line, except instead of being tied off to big anchors it has fairly small weights all along it to hold it in place against the current. And instead of working the boat along the main line to take fish off of the droppers, or "stagens," leaving the line in place like a trot line, a jump line is picked up, taking fish off the stagens as the main line is pulled in and piled on a piece of plywood. Mertz had 15 jump lines that he kept in a big locked storage box on the river bank off River Drive between 34th and 41st streets that we set out on Friday and Saturday nights, and picked up on Saturday and Sunday mornings, from April through October.

The 15 jump lines collectively had 1,250 hooks. That meant 1,250 baits each time we set them. And from late July until first frost we baited with the best catfish bait going, according to Mertz – grasshoppers. "Red-leggers" to be more specific. The big green-brown grasshoppers, and those big dark ones with the yellow wings that make that clack-clack-clack noise when they fly – no good. To get 1,250 red-leggers, Mertz had a system. He had fabricated a heavy duty butterfly net of sorts with a long handle and a deep fabric "bag." He had also fabricated a footrest that hooked over the front bumper of his late '50s model Dodge sedan. Mertz would sit on the right fender in the little dip between the headlight and the nose of the hood, hang onto the big chrome flying V hood ornament with his left hand, and hold the net down alongside the car so the hoop was just above the top of the vegetation. Then the junior high school kid with no driver's license would get behind the wheel, push the "D" button on the Dodge's push-button transmission, and start driving. Mostly we were on backroads and I just had to keep the right tire going down the edge of the gravel and weeds. Sometimes we might go right down in the borrow pit, and sometimes we'd go across a fresh-cut hayfield.

We had to go fast enough that the grasshoppers were forced into the end of the bag, but not so fast that Mertz fell off the car or couldn't hang onto the net. And when it was time to stop, it had to be done quickly enough that the grasshoppers didn't fly back out of the bag. There was a learning curve.

There will forever be pictures in my mind of Mertz letting go of his grip on the hood ornament and giving me a subtle "cum'on" hand motion to get me to go faster, and of him instantaneously letting go, getting in two or three rapid "down-down" hand motions, and quickly re-gripping the hood ornament when I was going too fast. I also have a mental picture of Mertz rocketing forward off the fender and stumbling to keep his feet under him when my quick stop was too quick.

After a quick stop Mertz would grab the end of the net bag, shove it inside-out down into a burlap bag, and shake the hoppers, together with assorted vegetation, out into the burlap bag. Tied-off burlap bags would be hung from the clothes hooks in the back seat of the Dodge, and by the time we got down to the river where the jump lines were stored, along with a Lone Star aluminum boat chained to a big cottonwood, the hoppers would've all crawled out of the vegetation in the bottom and up to the top of the bag. At the river Mertz would grab each burlap bag just below the ball of hoppers, give it a twist, and put it in a bucket of water with a rock on it to hold it down. After a short wait we had 1,250 easy to handle fresh hoppers to put on 1,250 hooks.

In the morning we might have 100 to 150 catfish. There'd also be lots of bare hooks with no fish too. But big picture, when we got back to shore with the lines piled up on sheets of plywood, there would be hundreds and hundreds of grasshoppers still on hooks. It took quite a bit of time to get the lines back into the "boxes" – one by three-foot shallow wooden boxes with notches all around the outer edge. The main line was laid into the bottom of the box and the hook on each stagen was hung on the outside of the box in a notch. Point being, all the grasshoppers still on hooks had to be stripped off. So for a couple hours a steady stream of grasshoppers were tossed into the river.

I remember bending down on the edge of the river to rinse off the sheet of plywood that the lines had been stacked on and seeing fish rising only a few feet downstream from me and grabbing dead hoppers that had been on the board as they floated away. I pointed it out to Mertz, and he said "Yep, they're just mooneye." Well I'd never heard of a mooneye, but I was pretty impressed. At the time I don't think I'd ever seen fish come up to the surface and grab food like that in the river. I figured I could catch them.

Mertz was a pretty business like guy, and I didn't figure he'd be too keen on waiting around watching me fish when he had lunch, a beer, and a quick nap to get home to. But next time he picked me up to go down to the river I was discreetly packing some fishing line and hooks.

I typically had a small window of time right at the end of our morning before we loaded up the day's catch to take to the fish market. Mertz had to take the old maroon Evinrude off the boat and lock it and the jump lines in the storage box and make up individual packages of smaller dressed catfish that he delivered directly to customers rather than sell to the fish market down River Drive. It was all the time I needed to cut a six-foot willow pole, tie on six feet of line and a hook, thread on a dead grasshopper, and catch a mooneye. What a blast – the anticipation watching the hopper float on the surface, the excitement of the take, and the flashing, splashing silver mooneye.

The willow-pole rod found a permanent leaning spot against a big cottonwood, and the repetitive work of putting all the lines in boxes and skinning catfish became just a prelude to a few minutes of catching mooneye. I had no experience with fly fishing back then, but I think back now at what fun it would have been with a little 3 or 4-WT rod and a Joe's Hopper.

They weren't there waiting to play with me all the time, but over the three seasons I fished with Mertz they showed up enough that I caught a lot of mooneye, and I suspect goldeye. At the time, I didn't know there was such a thing as a goldeye. They look essentially just like a mooneye, except for a small difference in the location of the anal fin in relation to the dorsal fin. I didn't know an anal fin from a dorsal fin from a Mickey Finn at the time, and sure wasn't looking for subtle differences. But both species are found in the Mississippi there, and with the number of "mooneye" I caught during those three grasshopper catching/catfish catching seasons with Mertz I'm going to believe I caught both mooneye and what I later learned to be goldeye.

Kokanee Salmon

Fishing for kokanee, a landlocked sockeye salmon, like fishing for a lot of other sack-some-up-for-the-freezer species, isn't likely to leave you with memories of individual fish. On any given body of water they're all about the same, though from one body of water to another there can be quite a difference in abundance and size (typically the more abundant the smaller they are).

And the way you fish to catch kokanee – trolling, with downriggers – is not a type of fishing I generally find very exciting. Especially when the fish may not be big enough to trip the release! But oh do kokanee taste good, either cooked fresh or smoked.

I'd never lived anywhere where there were kokanee until I moved to Idaho. Tracey Trent, a co-worker, friend, and occasional fishing companion, piqued my interest and first gave me pointers on trolling for kokanee. He suggested typical depth ranges to try, generally how fast to troll, and several good choices for lures and attractors (bright flashing blades). As for bait, there were no options: you had to bait your hook with white Shoepeg corn. You could experiment with one versus two kernels, but it had to be white Shoepeg corn.

Over the years I've had kokanee "fish-offs" with the likes of Bill you-have-to-use-pink-Fireball-corn Hutchinson, and others who insisted garlic soaked corn, or maggots, was the only way to go. But I've never been inclined to switch. Tracey was right: you can't beat white Shoepeg corn right out of the can.

Lucky Peak Reservoir, right outside of Boise, has kokanee that will definitely trip your release, and the 17 to 19-inch fish would strip off line on light tackle. Catching kokanee at Lucky Peak was like catching small salmon. Literally.

But the most amazing kokanee fishing I've experienced has been on Anderson Ranch Reservoir, about an hour and a half drive from Boise. It was really exceptional. For a time Anderson Ranch had both abundant and good sized kokanee. There was a 25-fish limit, and though they weren't as big as in Lucky Peak they were 15 to 16 inches, very nice for a kokanee. One year I got wind of the fishing and made a trip over by myself. I left home way before daylight, made the hour and a half drive, and launched the boat half way up the reservoir at the Curlew Access around daylight. As I idled out from the dock I got one rod set up and dropped the ball to 40 feet. I turned and started to get a second rod set up to drop off the other side when a fish jumped behind the boat. The first rod was going crazy. Fish on! Well, it took quite a while to get a second rod down. It was non-stop action. I boated my 25th fish in a little less than two hours – less time than it takes to drive there and back.

Twenty five 15 to 16-inch fish is a pile of fish. Some people can-up their kokanee. I like to smoke them. Regardless, there is a limit to how many kokanee a person really needs. But after that trip I had a hard time staying away. And I had to share the experience.

Dave Parrish, a work colleague and friend, joined me for a day. It wasn't quite as fast as that first trip but we were busy. At one point, in the excitement of two of us working downriggers, grabbing rods, and netting fish, I knocked my prescription sunglasses off the gunnel where I'd set them after a face splashing. And it wasn't "off" into the bottom of the boat. Bummer. What a dumb place to lay my glasses. But no sense crying over spilled sunglasses so we kept trolling. And to this day, whenever I see Dave, he brings up that day on Anderson Ranch when I lost my prescription sunglasses.....and shortly after reeled in a kokanee and retrieved the sunglasses which were draped on the line.

These days I can have good kokanee fishing mere minutes away, with my boat waiting at the dock. These Lake Pend Oreille kokanee aren't so big – they won't trip my releases – but one fills Sue up and two is all I generally want to eat at a sitting. During recent good years a couple hours might put a 15-fish limit in the boat. Sue, who has never been exposed to much fishing, has become pretty adept at downrigger operation and trolling.

We'll go for limits sometimes, until we have what we figure is enough smoked kokanee put up in the freezer. Generally though, six or seven fish is all the two of us are after – just enough for a fresh grilled kokanee dinner and a few left over to warm up for lunches.

Our favorite kokanee fishing, and some of our best memories, are going out in the boat on Lake Pend Oreille with friends on a summer afternoon, sharing the fun of catching – and losing – a "mess" of kokanee, and then beaching the boat at the foot of the Green Monarchs and having shore dinner.

Shade might feel good when we first pull in, and a cold beer or glass of cold white wine is definitely good before we do anything else. Then a short rally while we get a fire started, set up the roll table, put on the red and white checkered table cloth, get serving stuff out of the old wicker picnic basket that was Mom's, and prep the fish.

I've got a vintage little "Foldaway Grill" that was my Dad's that fits nicely behind the passenger seat of the boat. I can fit just enough kokanee for four people on it. About the time the kokanee are done it's time for a second (or third) beer or a glass of wine. And with four folding beach chairs lined up facing west, we look out across the lake toward the Seven Sisters in the distance, eat kokanee, and watch the sun sink toward the mountains. It's a memory maker. Good times with good friends.

Westslope Cutthroat Trout

Westslope cutthroat are a very special fish. That's not just my opinion. When a couple of fisheries co-workers, Bruce Reiman and Bill Horton, put together a proposal in 1990 to have the westslope cutthroat officially designated the State Fish of Idaho it easily sailed through the Legislature. Westslope cutthroat are special because they live in special places. Places where just getting there is an adventure. Places you'll never forget, whether you catch a westslope or not. They thrive in wild mountain rivers and streams like the Middle Fork Salmon, the Selway, Kelly Creek, the Upper St. Joe, the Lochsa. For me, catching westslope cutthroat goes with raft trips: rapids, clear water, bighorn sheep, hot springs, pictographs, Dutch oven cooking, star-filled skies, and friends.

My most treasured experience fishing for westslope cutthroat was a trip to Kelly Creek, a tributary of the North Fork Clearwater that we could drive to ("we" being Marge and the boys and I). It was the summer of 1993, the summer between Colby's freshman and sophomore years at Oregon State. Colby managed a long weekend off from his summer job, and we picked him up there: a one-man chinook salmon trap and holding ponds on Crooked River near the Gospel Hump Wilderness in Central Idaho. He'd applied for and gotten the job all on his own, but it was a prideful moment pulling in and seeing him in the same Fish and Game uniform that his old man wore, and then to watch him as he took his mom and younger brother around the facility and explained how he trapped and handled and cared for the big salmon.

And then to go set up camp on a gravel bar alongside Kelly Creek and watch my two sons fish together, a short distance apart, laying out their fly lines and working an elk hair caddis over cut-throat holding in front of them, is a scene to remember. I think they learned a lot about fly fishing that trip. They'd both had their intro-duction to fly fishing throwing bright streamers from a boat toward the bank on Oxbow Reservoir. The plentiful smallmouth bass in Ox-bow were always eager to reward a good cast thrown close to shore.

Cutthroat trout, because they live in unproductive waters, generally can't afford to be as choosy about their food compared to other trout species. But the cutthroat in Kelly Creek see a lot of flies. It's a drive-to catch-and-release fishery (one of the first catch-and-release fisheries in North America, established in 1970) that gets a lot of use. So Colby and Clark learned about line drag and getting a natural drift. Dad coached a little, but the westslope cutthroat in Kelly Creek taught them.

Though the setting and situation was very different, westslope cut-throat are also part of many wonderful family memories of horse trips in the high country. During the late '80s and early '90s, nearly every weekend in July and August after the snow was out found us loading up our horses – Flint, Twister, Penny and Joe – and heading for the mountains, and mountain lakes.

Fish occur naturally in very few mountain lakes. Where there are fish, they are generally introduced hatchery fish. And westslope cutthroat, because they are native to the watersheds, are a com-monly stocked species. We never knew what we were going to find in a mountain lake though, and on any given horse trip we might fish a half dozen lakes or more. As my friend Bill Goodnight says, part of fishing mountain lakes is the thrill of discovery.

On one July horse trip, Marge and the boys and I bush-whacked into a lake up in the White Cloud mountains that we had seen on the topo map and found a pretty little gin-clear circular lake with a steep snow bank still reaching to the water on the uphill side, and very big westslope cutthroat cruising around the shoreline like they were on a carousel. It was tight-quarter fly casting because of all the timber around the lake but when I could manage a roll cast without spooking an approaching fish I did OK. Colby and Clark really spanked 'em though flinging a Panther Martin way down the shoreline with a spinning rod. What a memory, watching big 18-inch cutthroat try to dive for the deep in that clear water, with a son of mine on the other end of the line holding a doubled-over fishing rod and trying to crank.

Hatchery-stocked cutthroat rarely reproduce in mountain lakes but are generally restocked from a helicopter every three years. That meant that going back another year we might, and did, find small fish instead of big ones, the old ones having died out. It also meant go ahead and grill up some cutthroat over the campfire for dinner – Fish and Game will stock more.

On another horse trip, this one into the Cat Creek Lakes above Lowman, Marge and I found a great camping spot on a boulder-ringed little lake that I could see cutthroat in. They weren't that big, but I could see a bunch of 'em. We unsaddled the horses, set up the tent,

The author and Twister making a quick check of the fishing in an Idaho high mountain lake.
(Marge Van Voorern photo)

36

and got camp organized, me thinking about getting after those cut-throat all the while. I put my little 4-WT fly rod together, got the reel out of the saddlebag, threaded the line through the guides, and then, without even looking for it, I realized that I hadn't packed my fly box. Damn. We'd driven two hours and ridden six to get there. Well I wasn't going to give up. I rummaged around in my jacket and shirt pockets and the saddlebags. I came up with a little plastic sleeve that had some Aberdeen hooks in it. I had tippet material. And I had shiny, black baling twine. And a tan rubber band. And a horse.

I used the tippet material to tie a baling-twine beetle on one hook, wrapped the rubber band around the shank of another hook and tied it off with tippet material to make a chironomid of sorts, and tied some of Flint's sorrel-colored tail hair to the shank of an-other hook to make a streamer. The streamer wasn't so much of a hit, but cutthroat tried to eat both the baling twine beetle and the rubber band chironomid. You gotta love cutthroat.

Colby watches as younger brother Clark fights a mountain lake westslope cutthroat.

Yellowstone Cutthroat Trout

To me, Yellowstone cutthroat are synonymous with the South Fork Snake River. They're found elsewhere in the upper Snake River, but the South Fork is where my Yellowstone cutthroat fishing memories have been made. And Chip Corsi and Virgil Moore have been a part of nearly all of them.

Virgil was the Idaho Department of Fish and Game fish manager for the Upper Snake region and Chip was his biological technician back in the early '80s. At that time Virgil did an assessment of Yellowstone cutthroat population dynamics in the South Fork, which was followed by an extensive effort to involve and inform the public about what he found, which led to a change in management regulations. And that has led to a world class fishery.

You might say that the South Fork is in Virgil and Chip's blood. And fishing for its cutthroat is one of their passions. So much so that they started getting together in October and spending a week floating the South Fork and fishing for Yellowstone cutthroat, and they've done it every October for 30 years!

They have welcomed others to join them, and there is a diverse set of real characters that have become regulars on the annual trip. I've had the pleasure of being part of it a few of the years.

Just spending time on the river leaves indelible memories: the roadless canyon reach, moose walking through camp, deer, grouse, waterfowl, raptors, clear water and clean gravel bottoms, and one of the largest intact cottonwood riparian ecosystems in North America. In October the yellow cottonwoods are just breathtaking. Standing shin deep on a riffle at the head of one of the islands with 15-inch cutthroat packed in all around me slurping emerging mayflies is a permanent picture in my mind.

I can't say this for all fishing companions, but this group of guys that get together for the October Male Bonding Trip would do anything for each other. Everyone pitches in to set up camp, cook, haul gear, find firewood, get you a cold beer, or hand you the bottle of Baileys for your morning coffee. Until the last day.

**Relaxing with a beer on the South Fork Snake River after
a day of fishing on the Male Bonding Trip.**

The last day on the South Fork is the team competition. From breaking camp and shoving off in the morning until the rafts touch the ramp at the takeout (generally well after dark) the three-man team that catches the most fish is the winner. They are the winner for a whole year. And they don't let anyone forget it.

Any kind of fish counts, and at times a pod of whitefish might get worked over to up the head count. But winning the competition is all about catching Yellowstone cutthroat; finding a good riffle or run with rising fish and enticing them with a size 16 or 18 PMD, Blue Olive, or Adams.

Over the years, Team Doc (Chip's brother Chris and two long-time friends from med school, Jim and Sam) and Team Fish (Chip, Virgil, and Steve Elle – or sometimes a second string fill-in like myself if Virgil or Steve hadn't made the trip) have generally been there at the wire together.

On this last day, personalities transform. Verbal taunting, intimidations, and braggadocio are constant. Everyone is pretty much immune to that stuff. But cutting someone off as they work a good run, floating over rising fish that are being worked, or racing to beat another raft rowing across to a good stretch of shoreline is not unheard of.

Now for the purposes of this competition, the definition of "catching a fish" includes getting the fish in close enough to touch the leader. And the touch can be with your hand, or a team mate's hand........or a dip net.

For the last team competition I was involved in, instead of the normal trout dip net that the other rafts had, Chip had equipped our boat with a dip net with a four-foot handle. Nothing wrong with that, it was just intelligent. Still sporting. All within the rules.

But to illustrate how cutthroat (no pun intended) and un-sporting the competition can be, while Team Fish did a last policing of camp, Team Doc shoved off and headed downstream with our net! We had to row like hell to catch up and wrestle it away from them.

Team Fish was the last to pull in at the take-out that night. We'd fished until we couldn't see anything. Sue had come to pick me up and was there with everyone else when we climbed out of the raft. She was ready to help us unload and pack up. But first things first. How many?

Team Fish had beaten Team Doc by one fish.

Now no one likes to lose. Jim on Team Doc may like it less than anyone I know. I walked over to him and said something along the lines of "Man that's too bad Jim. Lost by just one fish. Did you have any fish that you missed today?"

Of course we had all missed fish over the course of the day, and he acknowledged that he had missed several.

I left him with, "Gee Jim, you'd have won if you hadn't missed so many fish."

When we drove off later Sue was very quiet. When I asked if something was wrong, she said, "Well I heard what you said to Jim. Don't you think that was an un-kind thing to say?"

She was right, it would've been a cruel kind of thing to say to a friend on a fishing trip. On any day except team competition day.

Snake River Fine-Spot Cutthroat Trout

I'm not sure I've caught a Snake River fine-spot cutthroat. I don't think I could say for sure even if I was holding one in my hand. And the taxonomists have gone back and forth on whether it actually is a species, a sub-species, or a variant. But I've fished in the Upper Snake drainage and caught a fair number of cutthroat. Some had finer, more abundant spots. So they are tentatively included on my life list, with no particular memory attached.

Lahontan Cutthroat Trout

I've only fished for Lahontan cutthroat, a lake dwelling cutthroat that can get pretty big feeding on smaller fish, one time. That was just a few years ago with John Carlisle, a fellow Board Member for the Idaho Fish and Wildlife Foundation. It was mid-April and I was at home actually about to head out smallmouth fishing when John called and asked if I'd like to go with him to fish for Lahontans over in north central Washington on Omak Lake. Omak is a long, narrow, out-of-the-way lake, actually a remnant of an old channel of the Columbia River, on the Colville Indian Reservation. John had been making a spring trip to Omak for quite a few years to coincide with a pre-spawn movement of Lahontan cutthroat into the shallows.

John lives almost three hours south of me, so we met up kind of in between around Spokane. It's a long haul over to Omak. But it went quickly listening to John's stories of growing up in the Midwest, his time in the service, and his medical career. I got to know John a lot better.

We grabbed a motel room in the town of Omak to crash in after we were done fishing, then headed out to the lake. We launched John's boat off a gravel beach at the south end and ran a short way to a little inlet where John had done well in the past. We didn't see fish cruising the shoreline like John was hoping to, but he had confidence in the spot so we dropped anchor about a good cast offshore in about six feet of water. Our fly rods were rigged up with wooly buggers and leaches on sinking line. We could make out the bottom on the shore side of the boat, but not on the deeper outside. Not seeing any fish inside, we started blind casting out to deeper water. I was focused on my casting, but John was keeping an eye on the shallow water inside, and it wasn't long before he said, "There's some!" A group of four or five big cutthroat were swimming by part way toward shore. It was pretty exciting casting to cruising fish, and we had lots of other opportunities. I'd like to describe seeing them turn and take the fly, but I'm not sure we actually caught any of the cruising ones we sight cast to. But in between throwing to cruising pods of fish we could see inside, we (read John) did pretty well blind casting out to deeper water. John, along with about everyone else, is a much better fly caster than I am and he really got into the Lahontan's laying a purple wooly bugger way out there and letting it sink. I caught some.

Like other cutthroat, the Lahontans weren't acrobatic. And they didn't really make significant runs. But they were gorgeous in their fancy red spawning colors. And they were big – up to 24 inches – heavy fish. They were fun. On that trip I caught my first, my smallest, and my biggest Lahontan cutthroat. And......John introduced me to Pendleton whisky that night in the motel while we replayed the day's fishing. It's become a favorite, and a staple in my cabinet. Every time I pour some I think of John Carlisle and catching Lahontan cutthroat.

Rainbow Trout

I don't think I'd caught a rainbow trout before coming to Idaho in 1985. And now, over 30 years and a lot of rainbows later, I've ended up living on a lake that produced a world record rainbow, a 37-pounder back in 1947, and still produces 20 to 25-pound fish every year. I catch a few small ones each season incidental to fishing for other things. But the people who consistently catch the big rainbows from Pend Oreille are specialists that know what they are doing. They also put in hours and hours of trolling – with as many as twelve lines out – to catch a fish. Sometimes it's days between fish.

It would be a thrill to hook into a big one, but I've not been willing to learn the fine points or put in the trolling time. I'd never suggest that trolling is necessarily a passive or random way to fish, but I've been drawn more to actively fishing for rainbows in streams. Working up a tributary or the upper parts of the Boise and South Fork Payette Rivers, reading the water, making a good cast with an Elk Hair caddis or Adams, and getting a natural drift down to a feeding rainbow has made most of my favorite rainbow fishing memories. And regardless of what others may think, for me, in scenarios like that, size doesn't matter; small streams may mean small fish but also more solitude.

One very sweet memory involving rainbow trout is not so much about fishing for them as eating them. It must've been in 1986 or 1987. Clark had just graduated from his pony, Gretchen, to Joe, a grade horse, and Marge, Clark, Colby, and I were on a multi-day horse trip up in the White Cloud Mountains west of the East Fork Salmon River. We'd broke camp that morning on Frog Lake, a truly

Colby pausing with a morning cup of coffee before saddling up, taking in the view of Frog Lake and the White Cloud Mountains.

43

magical setting with a large meadow and spectacular views of sheer rock peaks to the south and west, put in maybe five hours in the saddle exploring and climbing, and ended up stopping to camp at one of the pretty little Boulder Chain Lakes for the night.

In contrast to the openness of our camp at Frog Lake down below, the only decent spot to pitch a tent among the trees was right next to the lake near a small inlet you could step across. The particulars of how it played out have been lost to me, but it was discovered that the small inlet was literally full of small rainbow trout. And I emphasize both "full" and "small."

I think I tried fishing the lake, but whether I didn't catch any or the ones in the lake were no bigger than those jammed into the inlet it was decided that those little rainbows in the inlet would be our dinner guests.

Again, I don't recall how we approached it. I'd guess at least Colby, and probably Clark as well, initially took part in catching dinner. What I do remember with clarity is Marge sitting on the rocks next to the inlet, feeding sticks into the fire and operating the skillet, the boys saying repeatedly "I could eat another one," and me turning to catch another little six-inch rainbow, cut the head off, pull the guts out, rinse it in the inlet, and hand it to Marge. All without taking more than a step. I can't say any more how many we ate or even if we counted, but I do remember wondering if the six fish per person bag limit was relevant in that situation.

These reflections on rainbow trout fishing, and for that matter this entire project, would not be complete without sharing my most-told fishing story ever. It's found its way into conversations with fellow anglers from the Amazon to Alaska, and I share it here, not because it's a great fishing story, but because the experience was so instructive, and demonstrated so dramatically something I and others probably suspected or knew intuitively. It happened maybe 25 years ago, and involved a young girl with blond pigtails, the Governor of Idaho, a clear pond full of three to eight-pound rainbow, and TV cameras from all three network local affiliates (I'm not sure

FOX had been born yet – but they weren't there).

One of Boise's finest community amenities is the Nature Center at the Department of Fish and Game's state headquarters complex. Annual visitations run as high as 300,000. It was developed in stages, and this occasion was one of several dedications that took place.

In the middle of the Nature Center is a pond (closed to fishing) with an obscene number of big naïve rainbows in it and an elevated footbridge across it. The Governor (and former Director of the Department of Interior under Jimmy Carter), Cecil Andrus, was an avid outdoorsman. He was also a wonderful personality and politician. So the plan was that Cece would take this cute pigtailed girl down below the bridge and he would help her cast out into the pond and catch a big trout with all three TV cameras recording it from up on the bridge. Great plan.

After making sure everyone was set, Cece stood behind the girl and helped her cast a spinner out into the pond. On cue, probably two dozen big rainbow trout turned and raced toward the spinner. A fish was on essentially as soon as the spinner hit. The rod doubled over, the girl squealed, Cece helped her start cranking, but after only getting it in part way the fish got off.

The girl was crushed, but Cece said something encouraging to her as he reeled the spinner in for another cast.

And here's the lesson. On the next cast, with all the same fish scattered back out in the same spot, only three trout even acknowledged the spinner hitting the water by turning and moving toward it, only to stop short and turn away. On the third cast, with that same obscene number of trout out there, not a single fish reacted at all to the spinner hitting the water or being retrieved past them. Despite several more casts, Cece and the pigtailed girl never caught one of the trout. It was recorded by TV cameras. All three networks.

For anyone who's spent time throwing plugs, especially for bass, it has maybe registered that the first cast in a new spot often catches a fish while repeated casts to the same spot may or may not. I have sure experienced that. But I had attributed it to the aggressive feeders being eager to hit, and later unproductive casts were due to no more aggressive fish, or no other fish.

The rainbows in that pond that Cece and the pigtailed girl cast to were all aggressive on the first cast. But after one of them struggled and got off that spinner, the rest had either "learned," or the struggling fish emitted some sort of hormone or trace chemical that was a "warning" of sorts to the other fish. Research has shown that naïve bass do learn over time to avoid certain lures, or lures altogether. But two casts? And not even being caught themselves? It's also been shown that some fish in crowded, stressed situations emit a substance that inhibits spawning. I've never seen research on it, but emitting a substance that inhibits feeding doesn't seem that far-fetched.

Either way, Sam Mattise, who comes up from Boise to fish smallmouth with me on Pend Oreille, has heard the story about Cece and the pigtailed girl so much that he's gone to claiming if I catch the first fish when we pull in to a new spot that it's because from my position at the trolling motor in the bow I got in the "pigtail cast." I think he's right.

Steelhead

Steelhead were another kind of fish that were new to me when I moved to Idaho in the mid-'80s. Of course I knew about them, but had never lived anywhere close to these ocean going rainbow trout. While Idaho is by no means close to the ocean, steelhead swim up to 900 miles from salt water to get back to parts of Idaho's Clearwater and Salmon River drainages to spawn. That's impressive. They're impressive.

My introduction to steelhead came in the form of a "work co-ordination meeting" on the Clearwater River with the fisheries staff from the Lewiston Regional office. These guys had it down. They knew the "buckets" and "slots" where steelhead would hold, and they rowed the drift boats as we back trolled Hotshots and Wiggle Warts tipped with shrimp down through them. I sat in the front of one of the two boats like a bump.

The toughest part for me was not setting the hook. Put more clearly, when I had a hit I immediately set the hook and pulled the lure out of the fish's mouth. Tim Cochnaur, the Regional Fish Manager who was at the oars doing all the work, finally coached me to "Put the damn rod in the rod holder and next time don't touch it until the fish turns and really pulls the rod down." And with that coaching and Tim doing all the work I did eventually hook up on one of these Clearwater "B run" steelhead. Unlike "A run" fish in the Salmon River drainage, which average around 24 inches, the B run fish that return to the Clearwater River drainage spend an extra year in the ocean and get extra big – typically over 30 inches.

Now what I was using when I hooked up wasn't a steelhead outfit like everyone else was using – say an eight-foot rod and level wind reel spooled with 12 or 14-pound test monofilament. I'd taken a lot of crap when I showed up with one of my bass outfits: a six-foot rod and a bait-casting reel spooled with eight-pound test. I didn't own a steelhead outfit at the time, and I figured hey, it wasn't like having to horse a largemouth out of flooded timber. There weren't any snags, and the reel had a good drag and plenty of line.

It was immediately obvious that what I had on the end of my line was nothing like a largemouth bass, but I thought no worries. This is going to be fun. But geez, everyone else was intense, yelling "careful," "take it easy," "let it run." I couldn't do anything but let it run. This was going to take a while.

Tim dropped anchor near shore and the other boat dropped anchor nearby to watch the battle. My audience continued to urge me to take my time, take it easy. I was. Holding a fishing rod connected by a thin line to something so fast and powerful was and still is a feeling meant to be savored.

But as the fight wore on and on the novelty wore off for my "audience." The other boat pulled anchor and went off downstream to resume fishing. My in-boat coaches fell silent for a while, and then switched their coaching to "Get that damn fish in here so we can get back to fishing." And I did….eventually.

Since that introduction, my steelhead fishing has been sporadic, handicapped by a three to four-hour drive to partake. There have been some exceptional days though, like one March 11th when I drove from Boise up to the Little Salmon River near Riggins. Snow-melt high water had pulled a bunch of steelhead up into the Little Salmon, then temperatures dropped, the river dropped, and the water cleared up.

I got there at daylight and worked up the little river from shore drifting a tiny egg sack with one small colored bead into deep runs and holding spots behind boulders. The sky was dark grey, with huge snowflakes drifting straight down off and on. It was dead quiet except for the sound of an occasional car on the highway and the sound of the river. I didn't see another fisherman all day. I landed seven and lost seven more steelhead. It was a day to remember.

My favorite day steelheading came almost 20 years after my introduction. Like that introduction, several of us in different drift boats were backtrolling plugs on the Clearwater River, only further up-

Tom Gengerke with a Clearwater River steelhead.

stream above Orofino. This time I was at the oars of the driftboat, slipping the boat back and forth to get the plugs into what looked like good holding spots. The fishing wasn't great, but any nice fall day in a drift boat with someone whose company you enjoy is a great day.

In the front of the boat with me that day was Tom Gengerke. Tom is one of those people you meet in life that you never seem to be able to catch up with in the back and forth of thoughtful gestures between friends. With Tom, I was in the hole before we even met. Tom was a supervisor in the far corner of the state when I started work in Iowa as a biologist on the Mississippi, but I got a short hand-written note from him that he'd written from his easy chair at home just telling me he was glad I was on-board. That's the kind of guy Tom is.

Over the years since then we've shared a lot of experiences, and a lot of ourselves. Tom has two sons, Jason and Todd, who are the same ages as Colby and Clark. In motel rooms, and over campfires and bourbon, Tom and I have shared our hopes, concerns, and pride in our sons. I've stood next to Jason in Alaska as he fought and landed his first chinook. Tom sat nearby in a South Dakota woodlot and watched Colby draw his bow and harvest his first whitetail.

That day on the Clearwater was very meaningful and memorable for me to be able to spend it with Tom, catching up on life, and to just happen to put the boat in the right position to put his plug in front of a willing Clearwater River "B run" steelhead and feel that in some tiny way I'd been able to make a return payment to such a wonderful friend.

Brown Trout

Brown trout don't take up much space in my fishing memory bank. There are a few places here in Idaho, like Silver Creek and the South Fork of the Snake, which have good brown trout fisheries. I've never specifically fished for them. But I have caught a few incidentally on the South Fork and while trolling here on Lake Pend Oreille.

The brown trout catch I'll hold closest though was not mine. Colby and I were on a bowhunting trip for moose with Dan Herrig on the lower part of the South Fork several Septembers ago. It was midday. Dan was off in the willows somewhere, and Colby and I grabbed fishing rods and took the boat over to the other side of the river to a deep hole with a hard current break where a side channel came in. I held the boat in position as Colby cast a spinner to the edge of the current break. And BAM. Pretty good tussle, especially trying to get it in the boat without a net. But I have a mental recording of my grinning son, dressed head to toe in camo, yellow cottonwoods behind him, holding up his first brown trout.

Brook Trout

Brook trout don't take up much space in my memory book either. I've had some fun catching a few small eight-inch ones up in the meadows of the Stanley Basin from small tributaries to the Upper Salmon River. And on horse trips I've "discovered" several mountain lakes with over-populations of small brook trout that were eager

Marge and her horse Flint on West Mountain, with Lake Cascade in the distance and the brook trout lake in the timber just below.

to take anything that looked like food. That is a major problem in managing mountain lakes. If brook trout can find any suitable flow to spawn in – an inlet, or outlet, or upwellings around the shore – they just don't know when to quit, and the lake ends up being full of little stunted brook trout.

I have found and fished a few mountain lakes with nice-sized brook trout though, and one stands above all the others for the total experience. It's part of a horse trip that Marge and the boys and I, and later on just Marge and I, did frequently.

Seventy miles north of Boise, on the west side of Lake Cascade, there is an FAA installation atop Snow Peak, the tallest peak in the West Mountains. The main structure is a white building with a domed top that we referred to as the snow-cone. Though winding and very steep in places, the F250 could pull our loaded four-horse trailer up the 15-mile gravel road that provides access to the installation. From there we'd ride out along the long open ridge that runs north. It slopes gently down-hill to the west with vast meadows full of lupine so thick it looks like lakes of blue water. To the east it drops off precipitously into dark timber and craggy rock outcrops.

The view from up there is just breathtaking. Looking west you can see mountain peaks 50 miles away in Oregon. To the east, you look down on 30,000-acre Lake Cascade two-thirds of a mile below. And after standing together admiring the view for a while from one particular overlook, and maybe having lunch there, I'd ask if it was OK if I scrambled down to the lake that laid in a cirque below. That too would leave me breathless, but it was always worth the effort. It wasn't unusual to bump some elk or deer going through the strings of dark timber, and there would be 11 to 12-inch brook trout waiting when I got to the lake. Not swarms of them. But they wouldn't be that big if there were swarms of them. Making my way around the lake, casting from atop car-sized boulders and catching maybe just a couple, maybe a dozen, there was no sign of anyone else having been there. I know others fished the lake, but the folks who fish tough-to-get-to lakes like that just aren't the kind who pack along styrofoam worm containers or cans of Keystone Light to leave behind.

51

I wish I'd have hauled a camera down to the lake to have a picture of it now. I just never did. But I do have a picture that Colby took of Marge and me sitting on top of Flint and Twister up on top of the ridge next to a big twisted limber pine, lupine-filled meadow in the background. It's not like having a picture of the lake. It's much more. It makes me think of that brook trout lake, and also the blue meadows, the view of Lake Cascade, the horses, and how we spent our 25th wedding anniversary the day that picture was taken.

Lake Trout

Since moving to Idaho in the '80s I've had a chance to experience some amazing lake trout fishing – both in numbers of fish and size of fish. One of my first and more memorable outings was to Priest Lake in the northern Panhandle. Lake trout in Priest Lake aren't big, mostly 18 to 22 inches, but they are numerous and pretty consistent biters year-round. Catching fish didn't make this particular trip memorable as much as losing fish. More specifically, Ned Horner losing fish. Ned was the Regional Fisheries Manager for the Idaho Panhandle, and Priest Lake was one of his waters. Ned was, and still is, one hell of a fisherman. And he took considerable pride in that. This particular day there was a bunch of us – Virgil, Chip, Lance Nelson, Ned, maybe Bill Horton, and myself – ice fishing at the mouth of Cavenaugh Bay. We were scattered out on the ice, but close enough that we could talk back and forth. We were getting hits and we were putting some lake trout on the ice. All of us except Ned.

Ned was getting hits, but each time he swept his rod up and started cranking, the fish might be on for a little bit but then it would get off. I'll just say that Ned was frustrated. The fact that the rest of us were putting fish on the ice didn't help.

Back then, before superlines, we were all using monofilament, and there is a lot of stretch in 150 feet of monofilament line when you set the hook. Ned didn't ask for advice, but I graciously offered some. Now if you were to guess which sport Ned might have played in high school you might first guess wrestling. Your very last guess would be basketball. I suggested to Ned that his problem was that he was too short. He wasn't getting enough rod sweep to get a good hook set. I suggested he stand on top of his five-gallon bucket.

I wasn't at all surprised that Ned didn't even acknowledge my helpful suggestion. But I was very surprised a short while later to see him standing on his bucket fishing. And I was even more surprised to see him rip his rod skyward and crank a lake trout all the way up and out onto the ice.

Now, 30 years later and living in the Panhandle, Priest Lake has become a frequent destination for Sue and me. The scenery is right off a calendar. The blue waters of the 26,000-acre lake are dotted with small and large islands and surrounded by green, forested mountains. The rocky spine of the Selkirk Mountains towers above treeline to the east along the 19-mile long lake. For our summer visitors, anglers and non-anglers alike, a trip to Priest Lake is generally on the agenda.

Anna always suggests a Priest Lake outing when she comes from her home in Kona for a summer visit. The last time she brought along Jenna, her girlfriend who had heard Anna's stories, so going to Priest Lake was pre-determined. Jenna especially wanted to see a bald eagle, which are a common sight perched atop a shoreline tree. She got to see one.

We were 200 yards offshore drop-shot fishing in a spot that was 160 feet deep. A weight is tied to the end of the line, a baited hook or lure tied a foot or two above it, then it's dropped to the bottom and slowly jigged in place. I had caught a small lake trout and released it, but its air bladder had expanded coming up from that depth and it was struggling along on the surface trying to get back down. I decided that we better go get it. Sue grabbed the collapsible dip net and extended the handle while I motored over to the still struggling fish. We came alongside the lake trout, Sue plunged the net under it, but when she pulled back, the handle separated from the hoop. The hoop started sinking with the fish still in the netting. As soon as Anna realized what had happened she stepped up onto the gunnel, and she dove right in. (Living in Hawaii, she is an amazing free diver.) As Anna disappeared below the surface to retrieve the net, a bald eagle appeared overhead. It had been watching the struggling fish from its tree-top perch on shore. Anna popped to the surface 30 feet from the boat with the net in one hand, the lake trout in the other, and Jenna pointing and shouting "an eagle, an eagle, an eagle."

If we hadn't motored over to retrieve the fish it would have been eagle dinner by now. I called to Anna to throw the fish further out and let the eagle take it. With the fish now floating 60 feet from the boat and Anna's head bobbing half way between, the eagle wasn't so sure. We watched as it circled low. Then a second eagle appeared. The first eagle made a tight turn, swooped down, extended its talons, and plucked the lake trout from the surface. Anna watched the whole thing from eye level just 30 feet away. Jenna had video of the whole thing, which she sent off to her husband in Kona within minutes. In her words, "That was epic!"

The lake trout fishing on Payette Lake in the '90s was a truly unbelievable fishery for old-growth lake trout that generated so many unforgettable memories for me: taking Nancy Hadley, one of the Fish and Game Commissioners, and her husband Jim, and watching Jim catch big fish after big fish – two over 20 pounds – and then seeing the delight in Nancy's eyes when she caught a bigger 27-pounder; taking Chris Horton, the Conservation Director for B.A.S.S. who'd never stood on ice before, and how he taught the rest of us a thing or two about catching big, suspended lake trout; following a fish I'd hooked all around Luck's Point with my trolling motor, chasing it for so long I was literally shaking from excitement so much that I couldn't stand up (it ended up being a 42-inch lake trout that I'd hooked in the tail).

When it comes to an individual fish, however, my most memorable lake trout has to be "Lips" – a fish that Paul Janssen hooked and got up to the hole on an ice fishing trip at Payette Lake in 1995. Only a small handful of folks had any idea about the ice-fishing for lake trout on Payette at the time, and we pretty much had the 5300-acre lake to ourselves whenever we'd go those first few years. Payette is a deep lake, and doesn't freeze over until late January most years. "Freeze over" might not be the best description. The lake gets a skim of ice that is invariably followed by a heavy snow. And then more snow. This is ski country. The increasing weight of snow on the first ice is constantly causing water to get pushed up through cracks where it forms a layer of slush, then freezes. So when we ice-fished we had to drill down as far as our auger would reach through layers of frozen slush, and sometimes layers of water, before getting down to the final two or three inches of strong clear ice at the bottom. That might have had something to do with our having the ice-fishing on Payette pretty much to ourselves.

Paul and I had been catching (and measuring, weighing, tagging, and releasing) enough fish that winter that we often called out an estimated weight as we were fighting the fish. Well, Paul hooked a fish, but this time he didn't venture an estimated weight as he watched line run off his reel. He just said "We've got Mr. Big here." Rather than keep jigging myself, which we typically did while the other played a fish and got it to the hole, I grabbed Paul's video camera and recorded what happened next. It was a long battle, with a lot of give and take, but Paul finally got the fish close to the hole, which is the riskiest part. The fish was still making short runs and thrashing around the hole, all the while the line catching on the lip of ice at the bottom edge of the hole. At one point Paul got a glimpse of part of the fish as it swam past the hole and said "This is a monster!" And then he had to get the fish turned from horizontal to vertical to get it started up through the hole. That wasn't happening. Then all of a sudden Paul shoved his arm down through the hole to above his elbow and got his fingers under the fish's gill cover. But he didn't pull it up. "I can't get him up through the hole. I'm not kidding! Get a drill quick."

With the bigger fish that we'd caught, it was typical that their midsection was bigger than our eight-inch holes. But slowly inching them upward, letting their stomach and fat compress and reposition a little, they'd come. We'd gotten fish over 30 pounds up through our eight-inch holes that way. But not this fish. His skull was too big to start up the hole!

If you've ever taken a hand auger and tried to drill a hole that overlaps one that's already there, you know it doesn't work. But I tried. Paul let go of the fish, pulled his arm out of the hole and hung onto the line. With my boot I pushed the line to the side and covered half the hole while I tried to drill at the other edge. I chipped some ice away, but the auger jumped all over. At one point I suggested we put another hook and line on the fish, but we didn't for some reason. While we were trying to come up with some way to chip at the ice I grabbed the video again to at least get the fish's lips recorded. And that's all it was in the viewfinder – a big set of lips down in an ice hole. And then in the viewfinder I saw a big set of lips slowly sinking down an ice hole, and heard Paul yelling "Shiiiiit!" Paul flopped on his belly and stuck his arm in the hole up to his armpit but couldn't get a hold on the fish before it was gone.

Evidently the line got nicked with the auger while I was trying to open up the hole, or it just broke at the knot.

I tried to

A 32-pound younger brother of Lips', that did fit through an eight-inch hole in the ice on Payette Lake
(Paul Janssen photo)

console Paul. He'd actually caught the fish, we just couldn't get him to our side of the ice to weigh and measure him. It was no consolation. I want to believe the fish was a 40-pounder. And I really do. I've got video of some mighty big lips to back me up.

Bull Trout

My fishing introduction to bull trout occurred in 1987 on a work trip floating the Middle Fork Salmon River with Mel Reingold, the Regional Fisheries Manager for that part of Idaho. Mel was kind of a legend. Bigger than life. He'd been pretty consistent in finding reasons to make two or three raft trips a season down the Middle Fork. He knew the Middle Fork well and was protective of it like few others.

I was quite honored to be invited along on this coveted ten-day, 100-mile float trip down through the Frank Church Wilderness. I was fairly new to Idaho, and I suppose Mel thought that anyone who was going to be part of the program needed to appreciate this amazing resource, to see the ancient pictographs, see the country where the Sheepeater Indians War took place, to camp at Soldier Bar, to soak in the hot springs at Hospital Bar.

The reason for this trip was to conduct snorkel transect surveys at 25 or 30 sites where we got in the river and floated downstream from Point A to Point B, counting cutthroat and juvenile salmon and steelhead. It's not exact science, but done the same way every year it provides a pretty good index to what's going on with the populations. Along on the trip were Gene, who worked in the shop that made screens to keep young salmon from being diverted down irrigation ditches on the Main Salmon River, and Jim Davis, Mel's new biologist.

Most days I teamed up in one of the rafts with Jim. Mel wanted Jim to learn how to row the river. Sitting in camp in the evenings Mel described the next day's challenges, how each rapids had to be run just so, all the rocks that the current wanted to wrap a rubber raft around, the holes that rafts liked to flip over in, and how many people had died in various rapids. Mel might have overdone it just a bit for his new biologist. Jim was very quiet and cleared his throat a lot. I think the second evening on the river I asked Mel what the "C.D.A." that was inscribed on all the rafting and camping gear meant. When he replied "Cheated Death Again," I don't think that helped Jim any.

But except for one swim it all went well. We survived and had a great time. We got the "work" done, and rafting between snorkel transects there was some fishing. That's where I got introduced to a bull trout.

I'd been fishing a Joe's Hopper or Elk Hair Caddis and catching westslope cutthroat, along with an occasional four to six-inch juvenile steelhead. Our two rafts were floating along through a tame stretch, close enough to talk to each other, when I hooked a little steelhead. I started quickly stripping in line to take the little guy off, but then it hung up. I clamped down on the line as we continued to float downstream, figuring it would either come loose or the tippet would break.

It came loose. Again I started stripping in the little steelhead, which was now trailing straight back upstream from the raft. We

The Middle Fork Salmon River – bull trout country.

58

were floating sideways to the current, Jim just holding the oars and watching. When the little steelhead was close enough for me to see, a big dark shape came up from behind and grabbed it. My fly rod jerked down and when I instinctively reared back, the little steelhead flew out of the water and almost into the raft. Jim and I looked at each other and I don't remember whether I actually said or just thought "What the hell was that?" about the same time he said "Big bull trout!"

Up to that point there had been nothing I'd done to affect what had just happened. But when, without thinking, I flipped the little steelhead, still on my hook, back upstream and let out line Mel shouted from the next raft something that could have been interpreted as 'get that fish in or you're getting a ticket.'

Mel was pretty protective of the fish as well as the river. The fishing regulation on the Middle Fork was and still is catch and release, and all I wanted to do was catch and release that big bull trout. Catch and release regulations, though, only allow fishing with artificial flies and lures, not juvenile steelhead.

The bull trout in Lake Pend Oreille are protected just like in the rest of the state and doing quite well. They spawn in small tributaries and the adults drop back to the lake and feed on kokanee. Trolling an Apex or jointed Rapala, I've been just as likely to hook a bull trout as anything. I've never caught a really big one, but the three to six-pound fish I've caught have been healthy and fought like little bulls. Nelson Higgins did catch a big one out of Lake Pend Oreille, though. The 32-pound fish he caught in 1949 still stands as the world record.

Dolly Varden

I contend that I've caught Dolly Varden. Not too long ago I was catching Dolly Varden in Idaho, but then taxonomists said I was actually catching bull trout. Bull trout spend their entire lives in fresh water; Dolly Varden migrate to salt water and return to freshwater to spawn. Dolly Varden, bull trout, and arctic char can be just damn hard to tell apart. But in the course of a half dozen float trips down Alaskan rivers I've caught quite a few less colorful, slimmer char along with the robust and colorful fish that were obviously Arctic char. Outfitters and float plane pilots I've talked with have mixed opinions on whether they are Dollies or female Arctic char. Fisheries books aren't very definitive. Dolly Varden were supposed to occur in some of the rivers I fished. But catching what I felt were Dollies wasn't any different of an experience than catching Arctic char. Find a run with spawning salmon in July or August and it's almost certain there will be char and/or Dolly Varden in there eating eggs and waiting for an egg sucking leach.

Arctic Char

I've caught Arctic char on most of the half dozen Alaska float trips I've been fortunate enough to be able to do. But thoughts of Arctic char always elicit memories of one mid-September afternoon on the upper King Salmon River in 2002. It was actually a caribou bow-hunting trip. With me were Colby, Dan Herrig, and a college friend of Dan's, Bob Lindsey.

The weather was nice, too nice to make caribou think about moving down out of the hills to the river valley, and we were kind of dragging our feet at our first camp on the upper river, just reveling in being where we were. We played with some moose and a curious young caribou, shot some Ptarmigan, took pictures, and enjoyed some Dutch oven meals. One morning Dan had the rare chance to watch a wolverine at close range, and one afternoon we all watched a sow grizzly with two cubs grazing on the blueberry-laden hillside above camp. The next morning there was a grizzly bear track over the top of Colby's boot print in the sand between our tent and the water!

We also fished. Grayling were waiting right in front of the tents. Maybe a half mile down from camp there was a long run with a high bank on the west side, a low gravel shoreline across from it, and hip-deep water down through the deepest part. I don't really

Colby's boot print, with an over-night visitor's track on top of it.

remember anymore who hiked downstream and discovered it, but the run was full of Arctic char. From the high bank you could see redds, or nests, and fish chasing other fish.

At the time, even though we didn't actually see them spawning on the redds, we figured it was a big spawning aggregation of Arctic char. Looking back, I suppose the redds could've been salmon redds and the char were just concentrated in there feeding on salmon eggs. Regardless, they were aggressive and would take an egg sucking leach drifted past them, and even chase it down as it was being quickly stripped in to make another cast.

Colby, Dan, Bob, and I were spaced apart along the low gravel shoreline. And much of the time all four of us were fighting fish. Basically we were either fighting a fish, releasing one, or getting our line back out there.

I don't know how long the four of us fished that run that afternoon and caught char after char. But it was long enough to get in a zone. Time stood still. It was an experience that I'll never forget: yellow willows around us on the gravel bank, brilliant red crowberry bushes across on the high bank, clear water, good friends, and the breath-taking gaudy spawning colors of the male Arctic char.

Lake Whitefish

To think of lake whitefish, or Lake Superior whitefish as they're called where I live now, is not so much to think about the fish as it is to think of Russ Smith. Russ was the retired manager of the old federal fish hatchery on South Bass Island in Western Lake Erie. Russ, along with a few hundred others, was a permanent resident on the historic island where Admiral Perry went to battle with the British. I was a young 25 year old fish research biologist out on the island for a few days with my supervisor, Carl Baker, doing some planning for a smallmouth bass research project. Carl said there was someone he wanted me to meet. We drove over to the east side of the island and pulled up in front of a small house in the shadow of the tall Perry's Victory Monument. It was a century-old faded red brick home with flowers out front and a grape trellis attached to the side of the house like the classic old homes in the Amana Colonies.

Russ Smith greeted us, and right away made me feel like an old friend rather than some young buck he was meeting for the first time. He was a white-haired, spritely man with a constant twinkle in his eye and story at the tip of his tongue. And he loved company. I heard a lot of stories that afternoon over some of Russ's sweet homemade wine about the old days on Lake Erie back in the '30s, '40s, and '50s. He talked about the huge lake sturgeon that tore up the cotton nets of the commercial fishermen, and the piles of dead lake sturgeon that the commercial fishermen doused in kerosene and burned on the beach. And he talked about the robust commercial fishery for lake whitefish, what wonderful eating they were, and how sad it was that they were nearly gone. And in talking about them he said something that stuck with me: that lake whitefish smell like cucumbers.

Though they were nearly gone from Lake Erie, while I worked there doing fish sampling, we did eventually catch a couple in a gill net off the north-east side of Kelly Island. I put one up to my nose. And it did smell like cucumbers!

Fast forward 40 years. I didn't fish anywhere where there were lake whitefish until I retired and moved to northern Idaho on Lake Pend Oreille. Lake whitefish had been introduced into Lake Pend Oreille from the Great Lakes back in the '40s. They had taken ahold and done well, and even supported a commercial fishery in the '50s. They're maybe not as plentiful now, but I've caught a few whitefish by jigging in 80 feet of water during the late summer and while trolling for walleye in 12 feet of water during June. I've also caught a few through the ice in three feet of water right out in front of the house in Oden Bay. It's kind of exciting watching small perch eyeing your little jig, then having a three-pound lake whitefish zoom in and grab it. I've baked them and I've smoked them, and they are good eating. And though not as vividly as I remember, they do kind of smell like cucumbers. And they make me think of Russ Smith.

Mountain Whitefish

Mountain whitefish, though generally not considered a "prized" fish, are part of many of my prized memories. They're a fish that often save the day when there is no hatch and you can't seem to buy a rainbow or cutthroat. Find a whitefish run and slide a hare's ear nymph down through it and the day goes from fishless to "fish-on!" And I can't think of mountain whitefish without thinking of Virgil. Virgil put me on a whitefish run on the South Fork Boise River and coached me into my first ever mountain whitefish.

Virgil looks at flowing cold water and just knows exactly where a pod of whitefish will be lying. It comes from countless days sampling rivers with electrofishing gear, doing snorkel surveys...... and fishing. One of my favorite whitefish fishing memories is from a float trip down the Selway River with Virgil when he tried to combine snorkeling and fishing.

We'd just snorkeled down through a short reach counting juvenile chinook salmon and steelhead and were about to call it a day and go set up camp. At the lower end of the snorkel transect where the river dropped into a little deeper run Virgil had seen a pod of whitefish. He could've gotten out of his wet suit, dried off, got dressed, rigged up his fly rod, and sunk a nymph down to the whitefish (it was a given he was going to try to catch one). But he skipped several of those steps. He just rigged up his fly and got back in the river. Not standing in the river – lying face down in the river. I had to see this.

Virgil got positioned shoreward and upriver from the bunch of whitefish, close enough to see them well through the water. All he had to do was let out line, inch his nymph downriver, and guide it right into a whitefish's mouth. I'm glad I was next to him with my face in the water to witness just how easy it wasn't to catch a white-fish that way.

For one thing, trying to hold a 9-foot fly rod underwater per-pendicular to the current requires a new skill set. And just guiding a nymph down to the mouth of a waiting whitefish takes a little trial and error. Then having to clearly see a nymph being totally ignored is disheartening. But getting past all that, trying to set the hook under-water will do you in for sure.

People don't generally think of mountain whitefish as trophy fish, but my other two favorite whitefish fishing memories involve just that. Trophy fishing.

The first involved Steve Elle, another Fish and Game colleague who became much more than just that. We've had a lot of adventures together on the job and off. He is the kind of friend who is always there for you. For example, after Sue and I sent out invitations to our wedding reception Steve called to ask what he could do to help. We were planning to grill hors d'oeuvres and my grill was on its last leg, so I asked Steve if I could borrow his grill. He said of course. When I went over to get the grill the morning of the reception, I commented that it was so clean it looked like a brand new grill. Steve said it was. He'd gone out the evening before and bought a new grill for me to borrow….and was up till midnight assembling it.

Steve takes a backseat to no one when it comes to catching whitefish. He's a fisher of trophy whitefish, and has caught whitefish that were longer than the 22 ½-inch Idaho state record fish. Some people say that Steve even looks a little like a whitefish. I only repeat that here knowing it makes Steve smile when someone says that. (I think he looks even more like a whitefish when he smiles.)

Steve took me under his wing one October on the last day of one of the Male Bonding Trips. The group had taken off of the South Fork and most of the rest of the crew were going into Yellowstone to fish for grayling for the day. Steve and I were going for the "Shaft." More than once the "Shaft" – the annual traveling award for the longest fish of the trip – has gone to Steve for a whitefish from his secret spot on the Henry's Fork. In the fall, whitefish that have grown exceptionally big feeding in Island Park Reservoir downstream run up into Coffee Pot Rapids on the Henry's Fork.

We hiked a couple miles from the highway down old logging roads and scrambled down a steep rocky bank to "the rock" – a 2-foot x 3-foot flat rock next to a deep run in Coffee Pot. I was the guest and insisted that Steve take the rock first. Amazing. I'd never seen whitefish the size of what he caught. This many years later, with the Male Bonding Trips kind of running together, I really don't recall whether Steve nailed the Shaft that morning or not.

I do remember my turn on "the rock," and the pull of those big three to four-pound whitefish, and scrambling downstream over and around boulders trying to land them. They were by far the biggest whitefish I've ever caught. True trophies.

The other trophy fishing memory I'm keeping for good that involved whitefish occurred on the "Millionaire's Hole" of the Henry's Fork in front of the old ranch house in Harriman State Park. We'd put together a multi-day training session for the fisheries biologists from around the state and were all staying in the bunkhouse. It was June, and there was a lot of daylight yet after the day's activities and dinner was done. Which means of course, when you have a group of 30 fisheries biologists on the bank of the famous Henry's Fork, people are going to fish.

There was a brown drake hatch coming off – big dark mayflies – and the smooth water of the Millionaire's Hole was dimpled with fish rising. The hole was soon full of fisheries biologists scattered around. It didn't take but a couple minutes before someone was hooked up and, instead of a nice rainbow, landed a big whitefish. Not Coffee Pot Rapids big, but very nice, and very fun to catch. And then another. And another. Seems the feeding frenzy we were seeing was essentially all whitefish taking big brown drakes off the surface.

Whitefish? Rainbow trout? I don't think anybody cared. Everyone was having a blast – those out in the river catching fish, and those of us lying in the grass on the bank cheering them on.

If you're not staying at the ranch as we were, the Millionaire's Hole is a bit of a hike from the closest public access and generally a pretty peaceful spot. A couple anglers that were in the vicinity when our gang started fishing had vacated when the cheering started. But about the time our gang wound up and got out of the hole a couple came working downstream into the hole. I suspect they had seen from a distance fish being caught. There was still an occasional rise.

Lying on the bank we could hear some of their conversation. I guessed it was an out-of-state couple on a western trip, stopping to fly-fish for the famous Henry's Fork rainbow. The man seemed to be mentoring her, quietly offering suggestions as she cast. But when something sucked in her floating mayfly imitation and she hooked into a solid fish the tone definitely changed: "Keep your rod up, don't horse it, let it run, take your time, keep the pressure on." She was squealing and nervous and scared and excited and exclaiming how this was so awesome.

It took her quite a while to get the fish close enough that her husband got the net ready. And then he saw the fish. "It's a damn whitefish!" He turned and wasn't even going to net the fish and help her unhook it until she pleaded for help. After he got it unhooked and released it, we could clearly hear her say in disgust, "I hate whitefish."

Hmmm – it sure looked to me like she'd been having fun.

Grayling

I'd read a bit of hype about grayling, but had never had an opportunity to fish for them until well into my angling career. There are opportunities to catch grayling in the lower 48 – a few isolated remnant native populations and some scattered high mountain lake "novelty" introductions. But grayling essentially mean Alaska.

In the summer of 1997, I had a chance to go to Alaska to attend a meeting of fisheries managers from around the Northwest at a place called Chena Hot Springs east of Fairbanks. The hour drive from the Fairbanks airport to the lodge in my rental car took me along the Chena River, which had been mentioned as a popular grayling fishery in the pre-meeting materials that had been sent out. I really don't remember now how I caught my first grayling, whether it was on a nymph or a spinner or what. I do remember being impressed by the big dorsal fin on it, but somewhat underwhelmed by the experience of catching the 12-inch fish while standing in street shoes along the edge of the highway.

Since then I've had a chance to fish several Alaskan rivers, and grayling seemed to be a ubiquitous part of the fish community in all the

A grayling with its outsized dorsal fin. (Colby Van Vooren photo)

smaller ones. Grayling seem to hang in spots in a river much like where you'd expect mountain whitefish to be. They're shaped like a whitefish, have a similar small mouth for feeding on insect larvae, and like whitefish they will also rise to take an insect off the surface. Were it not for their spectacular sailfish-like dorsal fins, I suspect grayling would be regarded much as mountain whitefish are.

But oh, the wild remote places where I've caught grayling. On float trips down the Kwethluk River out of Bethel, Alaska, my raft mate for the day and I would have hook-up after hook-up on grayling to 18 inches by bouncing an egg imitation fly along the bottom as we floated between salmon holes or rainbow runs. My fondest grayling memory though is of watching Colby catch his first one. It's such an indelible memory because it was the beginning of an unforgettable father-son adventure.

It was mid-September, 1999. We'd just been dropped off by float plane on Tick Chick Lake 100 miles north of Dillingham, Alaska, to start a ten-day float trip down the Tick Chick River bow-hunting caribou. I'd done the very same trip three years earlier with Dan Herrig and we'd had such an amazing trip. A couple years later Colby said he'd really like to do a trip like that, so after a year of planning we did. I wanted more than anything for Colby to have a great time.

After getting the raft set up and the gear packed I rowed over to the lake outlet and started down the river. We didn't go 100 yards though before beaching the raft at the head of a deep run. I suggested to Colby that he get out and make a few casts with the spinning rod that was stowed along one of the tubes and already rigged with a Panther Martin spinner.

I stood by as Colby made the first cast on the first day of our adventure. I watched the spinning rod bend over, saw the huge smile on my son's face the whole time he fought, landed, and then marveled at the big dorsal fin on that 16-inch grayling. Regardless of the rain, windy weather, and other challenges that plagued us the rest of the trip, that grayling kicked off a treasured time together.

Muskellunge (Muskie)

It takes a special kind of person to be an avid muskie fisherman. I'm not that special. Where "success" is sometimes measured by how many follows you have – rather than fish caught – in several days of casting a big heavy lure all day long, I've never been able to muster much enthusiasm. I suspect when/if you finally did hook a really big muskie it would be wild, and all the casting worth it. But I favor more action.

I had handled a lot of muskies on the job in Ohio, including some real monsters over 40 pounds. But I'd never caught one sport-fishing. I'd never fished for them.

That said, back in the early '80s I was intrigued enough by a friend's stories of fishing on a "secret" muskie lake in southern Ontario that Marge, Colby, Clark, and I made a little detour on our way back home to Iowa from what was our annual fishing trip further north. My friend, who was the head of an In-Fisherman group that I worked with in the Quad Cities, got word through one of his contacts about this lake with a largely undiscovered muskie population. He made a trip there and came back with stories of muskies so anxious to hit a bucktail spinner that they spent evenings tying more "bucktail" (using shocks of their own hair) back on stripped hooks.

The "secret" lake was not hard to get to. It was right off a major highway, and actually right next to Eagle Lake, a rather famous muskie lake. The lake wasn't secret because people didn't know it was there. Rather, Lake Wabigoon was secret because very few people fished it for muskies. It was just assumed, at least by adventuring muskie fishermen, that it was polluted. It had a big pulp mill on the west end and the water was continuously very murky. As it were, while there may have been some impacts in the west end from the pulp mill, the murky water was the result of wave erosion of banks that contained a localized very fine clay material that stayed in suspension and kept the lake murky.

Margie and the boys and I had just spent a week in the bush several hundred miles north canoeing and fishing, which they had

69

loved. I'll just say that they didn't have near the enthusiasm that I did for stopping on the way home to check out muskie fishing in Lake Wabigoon. They were wonderful sports though, and up for adventure, so we pulled off the highway down to a little reed-lined bay and slid the Grumman Sport Boat in to fish for just a few hours.

The bay had a lot of submerged pondweed and just wasn't conducive to fishing a straight spinner without getting weeds hung up on the lure right away. We'd just come from a lake with spots like this and had done well on northern pike throwing a more weedless spinnerbait, so that's what I went with. And it worked for northern pike here too. I think I caught two pike by the time we got out toward the mouth of the bay where a strip of reeds came out from one side and ran two-thirds of the way across the mouth of the bay. I threw the spinnerbait back into the reeds on the point and right away started it back to keep it high in the water. As I worked it back it kept sliding up out of the water on reeds and then plopping back in. I was really expecting the water to explode. But it didn't. When I got the spinnerbait to the open water at the outer edge of the reeds I stopped retrieving and let it sink. Bam!

It wasn't a real big fish. I figured it was another northern pike. A few runs and a few minutes later it was in the net. About an eight-pound fish. And instead of a pike, I'd caught my first – and still my only – muskie.

Northern Pike

I haven't caught a lot of northern pike compared to other species that have been more available to me over the years. I do catch the occasional one here on Lake Pend Oreille. And I hooked the rare one during the years I fished Lake Erie. One of those was especially memorable. It prompted an inquiry from the Coast Guard.

Marge and I were fishing for smallmouth from our little red and white 16-foot runabout one breezy May morning. I didn't feel comfortable making the five-mile run across open water out to South Bass Island where we typically fished, so I pulled in to fish a protected boat harbor on Catawba Point. It happened to be the boat harbor for the Coast Guard station.

I had climbed over the windshield of the runabout and was sitting on the deck with my legs hanging over the bow, alternately sculling the boat with a long canoe paddle and casting a purple Mister Twister. I caught a couple smallmouth right off. And then I hooked something that definitely wasn't a smallmouth. It was a very big fish. I got excited.

I fought that fish for quite a while, with it making powerful runs which stripped line off the reel before I got it close enough to see what it was. It was about a 10-pound northern pike. Then I was even more excited.

I don't remember if we even had a dip net. It would have been in the back of the boat anyway and Marge couldn't have done much to help me up on the bow. What I do remember is looking down at that pike from my perch on the bow and seeing it turn to run again and the line going slack. Its teeth cut the line.

I wasn't happy. I got up and stood on the deck, gesticulating with the rod in one hand and the canoe paddle in the other, and yes, making loud exclamations. I had climbed over the windshield back into the back of boat, had just slammed down the canoe paddle, still making loud exclamations (and I think Marge was urging me to calm down) when an officious voice boomed out from a loud speaker up at the Coast Guard station, "Attention red and white runabout. Does your vessel need assistance?"

I sheepishly hollered back "No, I just lost a fish." I never did know whether they actually thought I was having boat problems, or had watched me lose the fish and were razzing me. Regardless, Marge loved to tell that story.

Northern pike were the focus of a couple trips that Marge and little Colby and I did in the '70s from our home in northern Ohio to the area around Wawa, Ontario, on the northeastern shore of Lake Superior. The first trip was a lot of exploring and sightseeing, but we did catch some nice pike. We had our best fishing using live six-inch suckers that we were able to buy at a little gas station/cafe/store. We fished them below big bobbers along steep rocky banks. It didn't take too long or too many suckers to figure out we had to wait quite a while after the bobber disappeared before setting the hook. Colby's favorite part was watching the suckers in the minnow bucket.

Relaying our experiences on that trip to a friend we'd met when we lived in southern Ohio outside of Athens, he said he'd like to join us on a return trip the next year. I'd like to be able to communicate what kind of a friend Ted was....and still is, but I doubt I could. Instead, I'll diverge a little with a story about our northern pike fishing trip.

We drove separately, each of us bringing a car-top boat. In addition to a car-top boat, Ted also brought a new girlfriend. I don't remember her name (I'll just call her "Me-me"), or really much about her other than she didn't like to fish all that much..... and she was a little clingy.

We spent days exploring in search of "undiscovered" remote lakes full of northern pike. Ted had just taken delivery on a new Ford Bronco, but his enthusiasm for pike fishing and adventure overshadowed any concern for the fin-

A 1978 Van Vooren family portrait taken by Ted Reed on our trip together. In our early marriage, I wore the pants....Marge wore everything else.

ish on his new vehicle. As we pushed down grown-over old logging roads that were more like tunnels, the tree branches from opposite roadsides met in the middle to brush and scrape against the side of the car. But the pike fishing we discovered was worth it. Just trolling Rapalas and red and white Daredevil spoons around the shorelines we all caught pike as long as our legs. We caught pike as long as three-year old Colby. Ted and Marge and Colby and I had a great time. I'm not so sure about Me-me.

On our last night we camped in a big clearing on the south end of No-Name Lake. The clearing was the result of an old logging operation, which meant unlimited firewood and a campfire well into the night. After getting Colby tucked into his sleeping bag, we sat around the fire recounting fish caught, reflecting on favorite moments of the trip – and our friendship, and finishing off the last of the LaBatts beer.

Me-me was not that engaged, and at one point suggested to Ted that it was time for them to head for their tent. Ted told her to go ahead and he'd be right there. Time passed. The fire and conversation continued.

Then from the confines of Ted's tent we heard a slightly muffled voice inquire of Ted if he was coming. There was just a short pause before Ted replied something to the affect that he would be there in a bit. The fire blazed and the conversation continued. More time passed. Then, instead of an inquiring voice, a demanding voice told Ted to come to bed. There was an inferred "or else." Ted looked at the tent out on the perimeter of light, looked back at Marge and I sitting across the campfire, then turned back toward the tent, hesitated a little, and told Me-me to just go to sleep, he was staying up with his friends. Ouch!

It was very "cool" in camp the next morning as we packed up to head home. First time I talked to Ted after we went our separate ways and got home, I asked how the trip home had been. He said very few words were spoken on the long drive home. When he pulled up to Me-me's place he helped her get her things out of the Bronco, and without any suggestion of seeing each other again, drove away.

Sometime after that, Ted brought another girlfriend, Judy, with him when he came up from Athens to visit us in our little farm-house in northern Ohio. While they were there Marge and I intro-duced them to Reverend Shelley, the minister of the country church we attended. The next day Marge and I stood as witnesses as Rever-end Shelley, after a brief ceremony, pronounced Ted and Judy hus-band and wife.

Ted and Judy are still in Athens. We stay in touch, and I know that Ted and I could climb in a boat or sit around a campfire togeth-er and it would be just like the 40 years never passed. I'm pretty sure Me-me was never heard from again after the northern pike fishing trip.

After Clark was born and we moved to Iowa, northern pike were the catalyst for some poignant family memories. They were what drew my young family 1000 miles north into the Ontario bush for a string of summers. Now, more than 40 years later, Marge is gone and the "boys," Colby and Clark, are middle-aged men, but the memories of those summer adventures remain one of my most cherished pos-sessions. I think that's true for Colby and Clark as well. We each remember those times from our own perspective, but a piece that Clark wrote for a college writing assignment years ago takes you there so well that I won't attempt to describe our experiences. Rath-er I'll just share his essay with you.

Season Opener

Summertime icons arrived every year. On hot and sticky July nights, lightning bugs would float above our pasture, flash-ing florescent skin on and off. Smells of freshly harvested mint and backyard barbecues mingled with the foreign sounds of adults. Im-ages of summer came and went every year: the feel of a cold wet river surrounding my body, ripe cherries in my hand, or beads of sweat trickling down the valley of my back. Only one occasion had the type of regularity that could be planned on. Every summer of the early eighties, my family loaded the old truck with a mountain of supplies and left our small Iowa farm for the mystery of Canada. Years later, the individual trips blend together in my mind with the surreal quality of a dream - a unified memory of sounds, smells and laughter.

Three days of traveling down blue highways became an adventure rather than a chore. My brother Colby and I built a nest of comfort in the back of the truck and lost ourselves in a world of imagination and sleep. The road hummed an irresistible lullaby that transcended time and space; the same music keeps truckers at the wheel and Hell's Angels running in packs.

When restless, I crawled through the wind-rustled window that separated us from the truck's cabin with its atmosphere of A.M. radio, parental conversation, and smells of engine heat. The window between those two lands was roughly twelve inches high and eighteen inches wide, an impossible border for many adult but a portal of adventure for a dexterous child of six. A two-inch gap in the middle of the window brought the sounds of the road to a high-pitched roar, enticing and taunting me to reach for the moving cement below. I always paused in the middle of that crossing, transfixed by the deafening hum of movement, while the axle below turned and turned in a ferocious blur.

The road slid quickly by the underside of the '72 Ford. We ended our journey at a gravel two-track overlooking the wave-less waters and pine-covered islands of Pashkokogan Lake. The lonely sounds of loons floated past me and a black invasion of mosquitoes rose from the grasses of the shore, charging towards the walking feast that entered their territory.

This was our destination year after year - a small island, no bigger than a house, set in peaceful waters while the loons called the night in around them. To get there involved hours of backwoods trekking across land bridges, marshes, and rivers. My father shone like some Roman immortal as he hauled the canoe up a raging, waist-deep river. Mom led Colby and me along the bank as we watched in amazement at our father's strength. I remember seeing his body surrounded by floating tufts of willow, tossed in the air by the river winds, dancing in and out of the fading northern sun. He paused to catch his breath, as I stood transfixed with that surreal sight - a combination of man and light; I wondered how I would ever be able to match the strength I saw before me.

Once the land bridges were crossed, the low purr of the outboard motor pushed our boat across the murky blue-green waters. A realm of fish lay directly beneath that restless surface. I could only imagine their foreign world of blue adventure as I slept with my cheeks next to cool metal. The nose of the boat was my private area; I crammed life jackets and blankets into the pocket of space allowed to me, arranging a den of safety clear from wind and stray water. From my position, I watched my father as he steered past islands of stumps and weeds. The excitement I could see in his eyes was intoxicating. He was fish mad, and the time he spent with us on the lake helped satisfy his drug-like addiction to the sport.

Time slowed to a crawl during those summer days. We lost ourselves in the teeming hours of relaxed play and fishing. At dusk, the sun turned the water into a golden fabric as it withdrew into the night. The stars that filled the sky danced above our heads and illuminated the landscape around us; trying to count them made me comfortably dizzy. With meals finished and the fire diminished, we crawled into the sad green tent amongst the trees and wedged against each other for warmth. '

Mornings brought the smell of dew and fire-cooked eggs. As a reward for our backwoods maturity, Colby and I were given a special breakfast treat each morning: Frosted Flakes and Sugar Smacks gave a sugary escape from the normal routine of bran and health. Any grogginess residing in the corner of our eyes quickly dispersed. An excitement, genuine and strong, welled up at the thought of the long day ahead.

Once amidst the calm of boat and water, Colby and I assumed the regal air of elderly fishermen and withdrew into a rich silence. Northern pike, walleye, and occasional bass all found their way into our boat. Everyone was a successful fisherman. At times it felt like the fish were bored, just waiting for a hook to play with. We kept some and released most. The fish took a backseat to fishing; it was the action itself that was loved and appreciated.

Each fish held a promise of a future story to tell. Fishing atop a small rock a few feet off shore, my child's frame was once hauled into the water after catching a fish that weighed as much as I. Dragged into chest deep water, the shrieks that carried across the waters were loud enough to alert my dad, the savior of drowning children. Another exceptionally greedy pike once took the bait on my brother's hook and then circled around for mine, causing us both to reel in one fat fish.

At the end of our stay, the anticipation of showers and beds made the boat skim farther and the truck speed faster. While we looked forward to the comforts of civilization, there was always an air of concern and worry around our departure. The island in the lake was our untouched home in the wilderness. We couldn't help but wonder if the next time we made the journey we might find some other family enjoying it. This concern diminished with every mile that was put between the island and us, though, and we were soon left with only the comforting stories we had collected.

Slides pulled from my parents' closet serve as illustrations of the times we shared. The images they show are heartwarming yet seem slightly inaccurate. In my mind's eye, the pictures are more brilliant, the sounds crystal clear, and the smells rich enough to inspire a hunger.

Our little island destination on Lake Pashkokogan.

Tiger Muskie

Tiger muskies, the hybrid cross between a musky and a northern pike, have the northern pike's aggressiveness and willingness to take a lure, can get big (Idaho's state record is 38 pounds!), and are sterile. That mix of characteristics makes it a viable choice for fisheries managers to stock in waters where there is a surplus of smaller fish to feed a big predator, but a permanently established big toothy predator is not wanted.

Such was the case at Lake Geode in Southeast Iowa. It had a crappie population on the verge of over-population, and tiger muskies had been introduced to hopefully "take a bite" out of the crappie population and provide a new trophy fishery. The second season after five to eight-inch fingerling tiger muskies were stocked, my supervisor, Steve Waters, called and said I needed to meet him at Geode to fish for "tigers." I said "OK." It hadn't been in the form of a question.

After spending 11 years working for the Ohio Division of Wildlife where fishing on company time was frowned upon, I was still getting used to the idea. Steve had even put a note in my last performance evaluation that I needed to fish more often as part of my work. After all, that was the business we were in: making fishing better.

So on that rough day at the office my supervisor and I convened our meeting at the public boat ramp at Lake Geode, equipped ourselves with bait-casting tools with chartreuse and white spinner baits, and after a brief conference with some interested anglers to discuss our agenda, we moved the meeting a short ways south to the opposite shoreline where Potomageton (floating-leaf pondweed) extended out from shore. A couple hours of working the outer edge of the weed-line was successful in documenting a good return and growth (24 to 26 inches) on our earlier investment and left us optimistic about future performance.

And yes, they really are aggressive.

Chain Pickerel

Chain pickerel made it onto the life list with a fish caught from a small lake in southeast Ohio where they'd been introduced. Years later they were a frequent part of the day's catch when fishing in the slop for largemouth in Florida. However, the catching of one chain pickerel in particular stands out. More precisely, it was the circumstance and the events associated with catching that one particular chain pickerel that generated treasured memories that I hold especially dear.

In September, 1973, with the end of our binary family less than four months away, Margie and I wanted to do a road trip together. I don't remember how New England became our destination, but I do recall that what I'd heard about smallmouth fishing in Maine was a factor in my mind. It was a wonderful trip wandering our way up through New England: the White Mountains, the fall colors of course, the spectacular scenes along the Maine coast, the fascinating life of the tide pools, sitting at a wooden picnic table with bibs on eating lobster bought and cooked at a coastal roadside stand.

We did have one specific destination on the trip – Grand Lake Stream. It was, and still is, a tiny end-of-the-road resort town in northern Maine on 14,000 acre West Grand Lake. It also happened to be the town closest to the Machias Lakes that I'd read about for smallmouth fishing.

We'd been making the trip and our schedule up as we went and hadn't made any arrangements for a place to stay, but I guess I'd read that there were quite a number of resorts and cabins to rent in the vicinity. When we got to the area I don't recall now whether we first drove by some resorts that were closed or just stopped initially in town to ask, but we were told that fishing for landlocked Atlantic salmon on West Grand Lake is what brought people to the area and the season had just ended. With no salmon fishermen, the resorts had closed for the season. But there was one small lodge with cabins that might still be open.

I don't remember the name of it anymore, but it was easy enough to find out toward the end of a peninsula, and the owners were still there. There were no guests and the owners were starting to button the place up for the winter. But they said between doing that and hauling supplies in to a remote cabin where they spent the winter they would be around for several more days, and yes, they would let us rent a cabin for a few days.

The cabins weren't much more than a place to sleep; one small room with a wood-burning stove. But the lodge, the couple's home, was such a wonderful place. It was a classic old massive-log structure set in the trees with a spectacular view of the lake. Coming in the front door you walked into a big elongated room with dark wood and leather furniture, a wall of books to the left, a big field stone fireplace in the wall opposite the door, and a heavy dining table and chairs to the right. An open doorway to the kitchen and their bedroom further back was to the right of the fireplace near the dining table. With artwork, fishing rods, and a couple of mounted salmon adorning the walls it was a room that just said 'welcome, come in and relax.'

I wish I still remembered the couple's names. Marge would. They were such wonderfully welcoming and engaging people. Spending the evenings with them was so comfortable, like time with old friends. We learned how much history and tradition there was in the area. Grand Lake canoes, large classic wood-frame canvas canoes designed to fish the big lake before outboards came on the scene, were still hand made in town. People from down in the cities had been coming up since the mid-1800s, initially setting up summer camps, and later as owners of classic summer homes or guests at the various lodges that had been developed. We learned from our hosts that one of the private cabins in the bay around the point was where Edgar Rice Burroughs wrote *Tarzan*.

When it got late enough that we thought we were imposing we would excuse ourselves and head for our little cabin. The September evenings chilled off quickly after the sun went down and we would be chilled by the time we made the short walk to our cabin. I remember how it seemed that it took so long to get a good fire going in the little woodstove, Marge imploring me to hurry, and how the little cabin seemed to go all of a sudden from cold to toasty. I'm sure there were at least a couple of beds in the cabin, but I only remember the one single bed that Marge and I squeezed close together on.

Wandering through a little book store in Bar Harbor days before, a book with a sketch of a guy with a shotgun, a lab, and a fireplace on the cover caught my eye. I'd never heard of Gene Hill. This was his first book: *A Hunter's Fireside Book.* I read a little of the first of what was a collection of short stories and bought the book.

In that little cabin, warmed by the woodstove and each other, Marge and I took turns reading stories of dogs, sunrises, mishaps, friendships, and reflections and alternately laughed, cried, and fell silent between stories. Gene Hill had the ability to communicate feelings and emotions that most of us silently carry. We reflected on each story and rationed them out over two evenings, not wanting it to end. In 37 years together you make a lot of memories, but I can't come up with an adequate adjective to communicate how precious the memory of those evenings in that little cabin is to me.

But chain pickerel. We did go fishing. With directions from our host, accompanied by surprise that anyone would come way up there to fish for black bass, I remember a long winding dirt road that ended at a small lake surrounded by forest, sliding the canoe in through shoreline vegetation, and paddling across dark tannin-stained water. I don't remember what I was casting, but I fished a long time without catching anything. I do remember feeling that it wasn't coming together the way I'd visualized and feeling selfish for even having made fishing a part of our trip. I eventually did hook a fish, the only fish I caught. It was a chain pickerel about 20 inches long.

Rather than a memory of disappointment though, Marge's marveling at this fish with the unique markings that she'd never seen before and her insistence, to the point of my believing, that she was having a wonderful time made catching that one chain pickerel another part of a larger cherished memory.

And now, 45 years later, looking at *A Hunter's Fireside Book* on my bookshelf, or any of Gene Hill's other books that followed which are all there beside it, still brings back lobsters, tide pools, that classic lodge, the wonderful couple, evenings in the cabin, and that one chain pickerel.

Smallmouth Buffalofish

Buffalofish, both the largemouth and smallmouth, are targeted by commercial netters on the Mississippi, but they are not a fish that is commonly caught sport fishing. The largemouth buffalo has a terminal mouth positioned to feed on plankton and it's just not interested in anything else. But a smallmouth buffalo has its mouth on the underside of its head and feeds on crayfish and aquatic insect larvae on the bottom. It looks kind of like a carp, but is more blueish-grey in color. It is favored by river anglers for eating, probably because it prefers flowing, clean-bottom rivers.

I've only caught one smallmouth buffalo hook and line. I caught it fishing by myself when I was maybe eleven or twelve right where the Green River enters the Rock River upstream of Moline, Illinois. And though I remember it very clearly, the catching of that fish isn't as unique in itself as it is a link to some valued memories of my youth.

While summer vacations to Minnesota were wildly anticipated and paramount to my becoming an avid angler, an ongoing background of my youth that drew me to water and made me a river rat was the Foreman's Camp. Dad was a foreman at the John Deere Malleable Works in East Moline, and at some time before my knowledge the John Deere foremen collectively established this close-in spot to get away from it all. It was always referred to as the Foreman's Camp but it really wasn't a camp at all, though I suppose you could've pitched a tent and spent the night. No one ever did. It was a big building set back 500 feet or so from the bank of the Rock River, which bordered Moline on the south (the Mississippi bordering it on the north).

The building (whether the foremen built it, bought it, or

rented it I don't know) was set high on stilts to stand above spring floods. It had one big long room that paralleled the river with a large screened in porch the entire length of the building on the river side. The west end of the building was a separate kitchen with a large serving counter open to the main room. The dominant furniture in the main room consisted of a shuffleboard and card tables. A closet at the back of the room held long folding tables and tan metal folding chairs which came out to accommodate frequent group-dinners and events. On the wall, just to the left of the door to the front porch, was a round target with different colored sections for shooting "picks." The picks, or darts, were always left sticking tightly together in the ten ring.

A trip to the Foreman's Camp was our Saturday or Sunday mini-vacation from the time of the annual post-flood clean-up day in the late spring until the building was battened up and winterized in the fall. And as with summer vacations in Minnesota, mini-vacations to the Foreman's Camp meant recreation and relaxing for the adults, and recreation and relaxed rules for the kids. Dad played euchre or shuffleboard and drank Hamms beer. And maybe a boilermaker once in a while. The rest of the year at home, my brothers and sister and I were allowed one Pepsi per week, on Saturday night after our baths. Mom kept the wooden case of bottles down in the basement pantry and always knew how many should be in the case. But on summer days at the Foreman's Camp we kids could take a pop right out of the big chest cooler in the kitchen without asking. At the end of the day, Dad would just ask us how many we'd had and then stuff money into the Folger's kitty can on the counter. And if it had been a good day, he'd tell us how much money he'd won at cards while we drove home.

I have no idea how young I was when I first ran boats. But it was amid this mini-vacation atmosphere of the Foreman's Camp that Dad first told me I could go ahead and take the boat out by myself to go fishing while he played cards. And so that's how I found myself about two miles upstream of the Foreman's Camp at the mouth of the Green River by myself on a summer day, in Dad's 14-foot Larson, tied up to a protruding branch of a submerged snag, and hooked into a big fish. I figured I would lose what I thought was a big catfish by it getting caught up in the submerged tree, and was surprised when I got it to the side of the boat, and even more surprised when I managed to net and hoist into the boat what was maybe a 10-pound smallmouth buffalo.

I knew what it was, I suspect from seeing whole ones lying in the glass case at the fish market down along River Drive. Did I keep it? I don't remember, but I suspect I did. To be able to show Dad. I never missed an opportunity to show Dad.

Hogsucker • White Sucker
Redhorse Sucker • Bridgelip Sucker

There are days, especially the first warm days of spring, when you just have to go sit by the water and watch a fishing pole. These are times when you aren't really fishing for anything in particular, you're just enjoying the day and the company and letting a worm drown. In angler harvest surveys that I used to do as a biologist, what I recorded as the target species for these anglers was ATB – anything that bites.

These four species of suckers are some of my ATBs, the bridgelip coming from the Snake River in Idaho and the others from various Midwest rivers. Memories of specific days or individual fish don't stand out, just a collective memory of warm afternoon sunshine, high and cold springtime water, and river bottomlands coming to life.

Mountain Sucker

I've likely caught mountain suckers in other places, but I only think of the South Fork of the Snake River when I think about catching mountain suckers. Invariably during the early October Male Bonding trips on the South Fork, unless you stick with dry flies the whole trip, you're going to catch a mountain sucker or two or three. It's a cutthroat fishing trip, but sometimes a Hare's Ear nymph or Copper John is what the cutthroat want, and sometimes the cutthroat don't want anything so you bounce bottom to get some whitefish action. That's when you just might catch a mountain sucker.

While cutthroat are the primary quarry on the MBT, the annual big fish award, the Shaft, is most often won with a brown trout of 20 inches or so. Several years ago Steve Elle started taking the prize after we pulled off the South Fork with hog whitefish that he catches from his secret rock down in Coffee Pot Rapids on the Henry's Fork. That initially generated a little scorn from the trout purists of the group, but nothing like when Virgil took the prize with a big mountain sucker.

Largescale Sucker

Largescale suckers are abundant in Lake Pend Oreille where I do a lot of fishing these days. I've never fished specifically for them but they have stepped right up a number of times and grabbed jigs or plastic grubs that I was slow-working for smallmouth and have even grabbed a fast-cranked chrome Rippin-Rap and small crankbaits being trolled for walleye. Like all suckers, these fish are built with a mouth on the underside of their snout for feeding on insect larvae on the bottom. All fish are somewhat opportunistic, but I have a hard time envisioning the contortions a largescale sucker goes through to grab a lure passing quickly above over its head.

Carp

I was a carp fisherman. I suppose I still am. I don't go to meetings or anything to help me not carp fish anymore, I just don't have it available nearby to tempt me.

Disdained by most, carp were my trophy fishing quarry for much of my youth. With the perspective of other fish I'd caught with Dad – mainly bullheads, bluegills, maybe some crappies – tying into a carp of three, or five, or ten or more pounds was big game fishing.

The initial runs after a carp picked up the bait and the hook was set were pure excitement, and the solid power and shorter runs taught me about drags, rod position, and pump-and-reel-down.

I was, you might say, a carp specialist from the time I started venturing by bike beyond Prospect Park pond, after I started driving, and up until I got obsessed with bass fishing during my college years. I took dates carp fishing in high school (not many, most were busy on the days I suggested we go). I had my own secret dough-bait recipe that involved a slice of bread (crust removed), Skippy Creamy Peanut Butter, soaked Wheaties, and flour. I molded a small grape-sized doughball onto a small treble hook and used a slip sinker so fish wouldn't feel any resistance when they picked up the bait. And I think I got pretty good at recognizing a good carp lie in a river side channel.

Mom, bless her heart, was the product of a depression-era childhood with four siblings being raised by a widowed mother, so fish – all fish – were something to be eaten. I brought carp home, and Mom pan-fried them, scored and deep-fried them to help dissolve the bones, baked them, pickled them, and fried patties of ground carp and potatoes. We tried it all, but I don't recall anyone ever saying "Mom, you should fix this more often." Thinking back now about how my mother tried so hard to create a meal with the carp I caught, I suspect she was not just trying to utilize them. I suspect she was also doing it to validate me.

I tried smoking carp fillets. People liked that, if it was big enough that picking through the bones wasn't too much of a hassle. But then you can soak most anything in brown sugar and salt overnight and smoke it and it's pretty good.

I can call up lots of good memories of carp fishing (and not all of them involve dates). For instance: Ricky Waddel and I riding our bikes down to an old lock chamber on the abandoned Hennepin Canal outside of Milan, and dropping our doughballs down along the concrete lock wall to carp mouths sucking at the surface in patches of duckweed, the explosion when the hook was set, then climbing down the steel-bar rungs on the lock wall to get the fish;

sitting in the grass in front of the Foreman's Camp with the Kempf cousins and my brother Ron, drinking cream soda and watching our rods propped on forked sticks; fishing with my little brother Mike down in Sylvan Slough at the foot of Second Street and hooking one big carp after another; fishing with Rosie out of Dad's run-about, anchored up in a small, shaded Rock River side channel on a summer day so hot that Rosie and I jumped into the river, fish be damned.

The one experience that stands above all others in my forest of carp fishing memories is probably what got me addicted to them for so many years. It happened during one of the family summer vacations at Roberds Lake in southern Minnesota. I don't know how old I was. I'll guess maybe 10. I had started reading fishing magazines, becoming curious about things-not-bullhead.

Dad and I were in the rental boat, just the two of us, anchored over toward the east-shore summer homes north of the resort, fishing for bullheads. I was in the bow. I had read a fishing article that described something called "jigging." I don't remember the context, or what they were jigging for, but what had stuck with me was that the trick was to make something look alive and more enticing. As my memory has it, just after I started to try this "jigging" thing with my nightcrawler something very solid grabbed it. It was Chevy solid. And then it took off. I just hung on as line went out and out, and I remember Dad climbing over me to pull the anchor that was tied to the bow and saying "What have you got?" I don't know that we had ever caught anything that took line out.

Though we didn't really ever fish for big fish, Dad was a devotee of very heavy line. It allowed us to dislodge a snagged tree limb and drag it in rather than break the line. So I don't remember being concerned about the line breaking, only would I ever be able to reel this fish in. With the anchor up, we were being slowly towed around.

There were a few big northern pike and walleye in Roberds Lake. We'd never caught one, but we'd seen the pictures. We had lots of time to imagine and speculate on whether I was hooked to a big northern or walleye, because for more than an hour that fish slowly towed the boat around. A small crowd had materialized in front of the summer homes 50 yards away, some sitting in their Adirondack chairs, others on the grass. Occasionally someone would yell out "What is it?" to which Dad could only yell back "We're not sure."

We never brought a dip net with us to fish for half-pound bullheads and Dad was concerned about trying to land this big pike or walleye without one, so he yelled in to our fans that we didn't have a net. Someone disappeared and came back with a net, and then actually waded out from shore as far as he could go and stood there with it. My memory skips to Dad poised next to me with this net. Whether the fish towed us close enough for Dad to grab the net from the guy, or the guy swam it out, or maybe Dad cast in to him and the guy hooked the net to Dad's line, I don't know. But we were now one hour and thirty-five minutes into this fish. Dad had looked at his watch right after I hooked into this line-stripper and periodically announced the time. Regardless of the outcome, this was going to be a story that would be told many times over.

I was one excited, and nervous, young man. I had a fish on bigger than I think even my Dad had ever caught. I'd had spectators watching me fight the fish, though quite a few had tired of it and disappeared. And now I was making progress and getting this monster up and my Dad was excited right there next to me.

But when I worked the fish up close enough to the surface to see it, instead of a big pike or walleye it was a giant carp. I don't remember my switch flipping to disappointment, though. I'm sure it did in some way. What I do remember was how excited I got – more than I had been – seeing now how huge a fish I had on.

And I remember how my switch did flip to disappointment when Dad said "It's just a damn carp." He acted like he wasn't even going to net it, but then he at least made an attempt. The fish was way too big for the net and in the process the fish surged away and my line went limp. My memory is that the line broke, but it may have just pulled off the hook. Regardless, I'd just had an epic battle with the biggest fish I'd ever seen and then lost it.

I wish we'd have been able to get that carp in the boat and

take it in and weigh it, but Dad wouldn't have wanted to show up at the dock with a carp anyway. In the years that followed, between sport fishing and sampling fish populations for work, I handled a lot of carp. Memories can distort with time, but I'm going to believe that carp weighed well over 30 pounds.

One part of the memory that remains clear, though, is how exciting it was to be hooked into a really big fish. Another part was Dad's disdain when he saw that my trophy was a carp.

Goldfish

Goldfish are probably not included on any "sport fish" list. I would not list them there. But they are on my life list of sport-caught fish.

The Western Basin of Lake Erie had a goldfish population that would blow your mind when I worked there in the '70s. There was even a commercial fishery for them, with an annual harvest as high as 200,000 pounds. (There is still an annual harvest in excess of 100,000 pounds that brings 75 cents per pound at the dock). Now these were not your little aquarium-bowl-in-the-bedroom or dare-me-to-swallow-this-alive goldfish. These were the big swim-around-the-fancy-hotel-outdoor-pond-with-the-life-sized-bronze-heron goldfish. They came in a wide variety of gold, gold and white, white, and there were even some black ones thrown in. I don't know where they were during the other parts of the year, but in early summer they amassed by the thousands along some gravel beaches. And such was the occasion for adding goldfish to my life list of fish caught.

Carl Baker and I were fishing along the south shore of North Bass Island. The underwater drop-off on the southwest corner of the island was a good spot for walleye, and we were trolling in that direction when we came upon a massive school of goldfish between us and the beach. What small waves there were, were actually rolling goldfish in water so shallow that their backs were sticking out, the small waves cresting in gold. I'm pretty sure they had love on their mind. Group love. I got in my head the idea of trying to hook one. I don't remember now whether I reeled in the Hot-N-Tot I was trolling and cast it, or whether I picked up a rod with a jig on it and cast it into the golden sea of love. But I hooked (OK snagged) and landed a beautiful trophy goldfish of maybe two pounds.......then let it go to resume whatever it had been doing.

Chiselmouth

Chiselmouth don't get very big, 10 to 11 inches, and don't really put up a fight when you hook one and reel it in. It's a stretch to say they even put up a fuss. A chiselmouth could have been the first fish I caught after coming to Idaho in mid-March, 1985. I know the first fishing I did was from the banks of the Snake River south of Nampa, just drowning a worm and enjoying early spring sunshine.

I did quite a bit of that back then. I had a lot of time to myself that first spring in Idaho. Though I made the move in March to start work, Marge and the boys stayed in Iowa until June to finish out the school year and hopefully get the house sold. The people I met at work were all great, very open and welcoming. Virgil fast became a close friend and ultimately a favorite fishing partner, as did Steve Huffaker, who I'd met briefly during college at Iowa State. But they both had young families and busy lives. I spent as little time as possible in the bare-bones basement apartment in Nampa where I was staying. Saturdays and Sundays that spring found me south of town on the bank of the Snake River fishing for ATBs, which invariably included chiselmouth.

Peamouth

Peamouth are one of the most abundant species in Lake Pend Oreille where I fish a lot these days. Even though they have very small mouths, when I fish for walleye with a jig and nightcrawler trailer, I lose worms to peamouth over and over and occasionally one of the bigger 10 to 12-inchers gets hooked.

Losing my bait and reeling in a peamouth rather than a walleye frustrates me at times, but nothing like it did my late friend Dick Hansen. Boy could he cuss peamouth.

Creek Chub

Reflecting now on catching creek chubs back in the Midwest when I was a kid, they were to me what small native trout were to a young kid growing up in the west. Creek chubs weren't in just any small stream in the Midwest, they preferred ones with gravel or rocky bottoms and water you could see into. The bigger ones were maybe eight or nine inches. They took a piece of worm on a small hook drifted into a hole, and when you pulled them out of the water they just wiggled like crazy. And in the spring, when they were in spawning colors, the male had a red stripe down its side like a rainbow trout. The males also developed spawning tubercles, numerous little pointy nubs all over their head. I still remember holding a male creek chub that my little niece had caught out of the old gristmill pool on Pine Creek near our home in Iowa so she could feel the tubercles, and her wide eyes when she looked up at me after she rubbed her finger over the creek chub's head.

Golden Shiner

I suppose I've caught a number of these but the only one that I clearly remember was part of a Mississippi River mixed bag. I was ice-fishing in the Big Timber Area, a group of backwater lakes off the river, with my old friend Bruce Strunk who I worked with back in Iowa. We were fishing among the submerged branches of a fallen tree along a deep bank using tiny jigs tipped with waxworms. We were targeting bluegill and crappie. But with 150 or so fish species in the Mississippi we never knew what all we might catch. A six or seven-inch golden shiner was among the fish that came up out of my hole in the ice that day.

Northern Pikeminnow (Squawfish)

I'd never caught, or for that matter heard of, a northern pikeminnow until I came to Idaho in 1985. They were actually called squawfish then (women evidently had the role of harvesting them for food in Native American culture; it's been noted that Native Americans even traded cutthroat trout to early whites in exchange for squawfish). They have been part of ATB bags on the Snake River, mostly smaller fish, but the ones that leave a memory mark are the big ones that have hammered my lures while targeting bass and walleye in Lake Pend Oreille. Just like the bass and walleye, pikeminnow are fish-eating machines. I can't say personally how squawfish taste, but I do know they get big and they fight hard.

I have quite a collage of pikeminnow memories framed by throwing big hero lures – five to eight-inch swim baits – across a particular sunken weed bed in Lake Pend Oreille in July. Young perch have moved offshore by then into deeper weeds and the larger predator fish join them there for dinner. Using no-stretch 17-pound super-line and a long rod, a big swim bait on a 1 ½-ounce jig head will go a country mile, yet a hit is transmitted as if the lure was right next to the boat. That's what I like and remember about pikeminnow, the feel of them on the line. Big walleye take the swim bait, northern pike hit it, but pikeminnow smash and take off with the thing. When I go out to fish the weed bed I hope to catch a trophy walleye, and I'm not at all surprised to get a pike or nice smallmouth. But I count on catching big pikeminnow.

Pikeminnow also hold the special honor of stepping up to the plate to take part in one of this grandfather's most cherished roles: helping his granddaughter Lucia catch her first fish.

It wasn't until the 2018 summer visit to Grama and Grampa's house, when Lucia was five, that she had developed the patience and real interest to give catching her first fish a serious effort.

Lucia and Grampa started out fishing off the end of our dock with a couple of cane poles I made up from long bamboo shoots that I'd cut. But they weren't just any bamboo shoots. They came from her Uncle Colby's Portland back yard. They had dried nicely and were light but strong. I thought if the fish would cooperate and take Lucia's worm, seeing a bobber go under and then being able to swing a little perch or crappie up onto the dock all by herself with Uncle Colby's bamboo pole would be something she would always remember. And it would've worked a month earlier, but it was July and the fish that had been under the dock had moved out of the bay. I gave it five minutes or so and then suggested we try something else.

So Lucia and Grampa, along with Papa Clark, Mama Sofia, and Grama Sue, jumped in the boat and motored out to a weed bed outside Perch Bay. The two bamboo poles were deployed into rod holders and stuck out opposite sides of the boat while we drifted around for five minutes or so, but again no action.

It wouldn't be the same, but I knew we could hook some fish trolling a small Shad-Rap crankbait out a little deeper. I'd done some trial fishing the week earlier and had fast action catching quite a variety of fish. We wouldn't be able to use the cane pole, but Lucia had gotten her very own little fishing rod with a purple spin-cast reel to bring along on the trip and she was anxious to use it. And this worked. It only took a couple minutes before something grabbed the Shad-Rap on the end of her line and bent her

Lucia was thrilled after catching her five-pound pike-minnow, Grampa even more so. (Sue Van Vooren photo)

pole over. Papa helped her hold the rod up and Lucia cranked away. It was hard work, too. She said so.

Grampa was ready with the dip net when Lucia's fish came up alongside the boat, and her eyes widened in surprise when I swung her first catch – a two-pound northern pikeminnow – up over the side and into the boat. Big smiles, pictures, squeals, and replays of the battle ensued. A person doesn't get to be part of that very often. The memory deserves to be savored.

That might have been good enough, but we were out there and Lucia was all for trying to catch another fish, which she did, in short order. She caught about a two-pound smallmouth bass. It was exciting. It jumped. And then she hooked a bigger fish. She said this was really hard work. Her eyes really widened when Grampa swung this one into the boat. Another pikeminnow. I hooked it onto my fish scale.....five pounds even.

We'd accomplished what we'd set out to do. Lucia was pumped. As we idled back toward Perch Bay she shouted over and over, "I caught three fish! I caught three fish!" And when we got to the dock Lucia yelled to our neighbors on both sides, and anyone else who might hear, "I caught three fish!" She just knew they would want to know.

Common Shiner

As a creek-fishin' young kid in the Midwest, I quite often caught common shiners. They are such a distinctive fish with their outsize scales, and they grow to be outsized for a minnow. The bigger ones were six or seven inches. I caught common shiners in the same gravelly streams that I caught creek chubs in, fishing the same way, drifting a little worm I'd found under a rock or a log through a pool on a tiny plain hook.

Channel Catfish

This rather unglamorous whiskered critter has provided a potpourri of memories filled with stink baits, salmon bellies, bobbers, and bells.

The first type of fishing that really lit my catfishing fire was when I was in high school. Fishing involved drifting a night crawler under a bobber along the "lateral dam." Fishing the lateral dam, and the actual concrete structure itself, are both unique. The lateral dam runs about four miles right down the middle of the Mississippi between Moline, Illinois and Bettendorf, Iowa. It starts upstream at the beginning of a big sweeping bend and ends at an old lock chamber on Arsenal Island. It was built to "trap" water on the outer Illinois side of the bend so steamboats could navigate past the long rapids on the Iowa side. Later the modern lock and dam system raised the entire river level and left the old lateral dam just at or below the water surface at normal summer flows.

Invariably, after spring high water receded, there would be a log or snag lodged on the dam to tie my boat to. Then in tennis shoes, with a can of worms and a chain stringer tied to my belt, I'd get out onto the dam. The dam had a flat top maybe two feet wide (with broken, sunken, and raised pieces to keep you on your toes) and an underwater vertical face on the Illinois side, dropping off to four to eight feet depending on the stretch. On the Iowa side, the side that water wanted to run back toward, there was a sloping apron extending maybe eight or ten feet out which had some flow going over it except for sections where the dam was above the surface.

I fished the lateral dam by flipping a night crawler suspended under a red and white bobber just a short distance out on the Illinois side. Then I carefully shuffled and felt my way along the underwater dam, following the bobber as it floated downstream. Except where the dam was above water and I could see it, there was no way I could keep up with the bobber very long. I had to reel in periodically and cast back upstream a little, which allowed me to fish it more thoroughly anyway. From Moline's River Drive a half mile away it looks as if someone fishing the lateral dam is walking on water!

What I loved most about fishing the lateral dam was seeing the bobber go down when a catfish took it. Frequently the bobber would come to a dead stop and slowly go under, which meant that the bait was stuck on the bottom and the current was pulling the bobber down. But when a catfish took the bait, the bobber instantly disappeared. Back then I'd never heard of an endorphin rush, but that's what I got every time the bobber was jerked under, not knowing how big the fish was going to feel when I set the hook. That's the part I remember best.

More than a decade later I kind of duplicated that catfish-endorphin combo: same red and white plastic bobber, same nightcrawler. But the scene was the jagged, rocky shoreline of Rattlesnake Island in Western Lake Erie, and instead of wading I was casting into the rocks from my boat. I had the Weilnau "boys" with me. Butch and Tom were our closest neighbors at the time: Tom and his wife and two little girls lived in the house across the sometimes sugar beet-sometimes corn-sometimes wheat field south of us; Butch and his wife and young son lived in the house just a quarter mile down the road to the west at the T. We used to get together a lot, often for fish feeds at our house. The Weilnau boys were big strapping farm boys who'd just not had time for fishing, but they sure could put away a big platter of fried fish.

It was the end of June and the catfish were in the rocks to spawn. We were casting as close to the rocks as we could (and in the process went through several plastic bobbers). Using a bobber had the advantage of keeping the bait from dropping down into the rocks and getting snagged. But more importantly, it provided that shot of endorphin every time it "plooped" under. And it plooped under a lot. It was an amazing day.

At that time, catfish were harvested commercially in Lake Erie and pretty well cropped off at the 15-inch minimum commercial size. That was the size of most of the fish we caught. And we kept them all and strung them on several rope stringers (this is Act I of "Fishing to Excess with the Weilnau Boys"). It took both the Weilnau boys to lift one of those stringers. I remember as they struggled to lift it over the side of the boat, the weight of fish on top pushed down and ripped the cord through the jaws of some on the bottom so several fish dropped back into the lake. As it turned out we had just under a 100 catfish, but I remember how bummed Butch and Tom were that we lost those fish off the bottom of the stringer.

I think that was the last bobber and nightcrawler fishing for catfish I ever did. But I moved on to things like Bowker's Stink Bait and sponge worms, shrimp, salmon belly strips, and even WD-40. And I moved on to Idaho. Idaho is not known for it, but the Snake River and a couple of its impoundments have provided some wonderful catfishing experiences.

Marge and the boys and I had a spot where we liked to camp on Oxbow Reservoir. It was a spot in a small grove of trees, only accessible by boat, where a tributary came in and formed a shallow gravel delta that stuck out into the steep-sided reservoir. Catfish liked the spot too. We'd set up camp, go fish for smallmouth, then come back in the evening and build a fire and cook dinner. Then we would get the catfish rods rigged up and set out just before dark.

Catfish moved up into the shallow water on the little delta after dark searching for crayfish. We had 'shrimp-on-a-hook' there waiting for them. We would prop the rods, generally three, on forked sticks at the water's edge and clip a little bell to the tip of the rods to signal a bite in the dark. The bell sometimes tinkled just slightly, but invariably was tinkling like crazy before Clark could figure out in the dark which rod it was. I remember Clark reeling in catfish and Marge, a short ways away, still sitting at the fire, asking "What do you have Clark?" There would be the sound of the fish splashing out there somewhere in shallow water. The fish was eventually caught in the beam of a flashlight, and then Clark would back up to drag the catfish, glistening and flopping, up onto the shore.

The other part of that memory, the sweet part, is the time spent sitting in our folding camp chairs around the fire, surrounded by darkness and silence, having a beer or wine or soda, prodding the fire and quietly talking about the day, what was going on in our lives, and planning more adventures.

Upstream from there maybe 80 miles, the upper end of Brownlee Reservoir near Farewell Bend provided a late-June catfishing experience that was also a real memory-maker for me. This was fishing from a boat in shallow water among flooded willows. It got going right as the chinook fishing on the Little Salmon was wrapping up, which was good timing as strips of salmon belly were a tough, oily offering that proved to be a good bait for catfish to find in muddy water. It was great fishing for big three to six-pound fish, easy to get to, and easy fishing. It made wonderful memories because I was able to share it with so many people: Blaine and Shelly, such wonderful friends to Marge and I who supported me in so many ways after Marge died; Dan Herrig; Cal Groen, fellow Midwesterner and Idaho Fish and Game colleague; Jack Acree, who helped light the way for me toward retirement; and Chris, a frustrated single mother's teen-aged son who seemingly had no interests beyond video games and bad company. Although he went along grudgingly, he came back

Clark straining with the results of over-night catfishing on Oxbow Reservoir.

jabbering about how cool it was catching all those big fish.

One last fun catfishing experience I love to think back on also took place at the upper end of Brownlee. It was one of the few times I didn't go with another person. I went with Jackson, my yellow lab. Going with other people we'd do an over-and-back the same day, not leaving too early or getting back too late. But Jackson was up for fishing as long as I wanted to (at least he never said otherwise), so on this trip we got there late in the afternoon and intended to fish through the night.

Fishing was good, but slowed down as midnight approached. I started thinking about lying down in the bottom of the boat and shutting my eyes for a bit. I had a line cast out each side of the boat and decided I'd lie down and just wrap one line around one of my thumbs and the other line around the other. Same principal as a bell, just tactile rather than auditory.

You know how it is when you doze off, not really sure if you're asleep or not. That's where I was when I heard this huge splash next to the boat and one of my arms simultaneously jerked up off my chest where it had been peacefully resting. "What the?" It took several seconds to realize I didn't have a fish on, and a lot longer to figure out that Jackson was gone. I could hear him out there in the dark swimming toward shore. He'd evidently had to use the facilities so to speak, and he knew the boat was not a facility. I wasn't grasping the situation, so he finally jumped overboard and in the process landed on the line. Geez, I felt bad that I hadn't thought of him and his needs.

A few minutes later I heard him swimming back out from shore, and gave him an assist back into the boat. He didn't come in wagging his tail like he does when there's a duck in his mouth. I suspect he wasn't sure how I felt about what had just happened. I was pretty sure the right thing do was say "good dog" and scratch him behind his ear. I remember his tail started wagging.

Flathead Catfish

I don't have many memories associated with catching flathead catfish. Mertz and I caught a lot of them – big ones – on the jump lines, but I haven't caught many of them hook and line. I caught a few fishing the lateral dam in the Mississippi many years ago, and several small ones fishing for smallmouth on Brownlee Reservoir on the Snake River in Idaho. Nothing remarkable.

Probably my favorite memory of catching a flathead didn't involve a flathead catfish at all. I was overnight fishing by myself on the Rock River while I was still in high school, and had set out some ditty-poles – six to eight-foot cut-willow poles shoved into the bank at a 45 degree angle with a short line and a baited hook hanging down off the tip to the surface of the river. (It always amazed me the size of fish that these flexible ditty-poles could handle without getting pulled out of the bank.) Periodically through the night I'd grab my flashlight and leave the campfire and the fishing lines I had cast out there to go work up through the woods along the river bank, my feet following an oval of light that flowed over logs and branches on the forest floor. Occasionally the light darted off to the edge of the water in search of the next ditty pole. Finding one of the poles bent over wasn't unexpected, but I do remember being surprised at how much resistance I felt when I took ahold of this particular pole. Lifting the willow pole with one hand and shining the beam of the flashlight on the muddy river I saw just below the surface this very wide, flat, mossy-brown shape at the end of the line. Big flathead! I stretched my jaw, stuck the butt of the metal D-cell flashlight in my mouth, clenching it between my teeth (this was way before headlamps or small Mag-lites). It was going to take both hands to land this big boy. Lifting up on the ditty pole with both hands, my excitement switched to foolishness when in the wavering beam of light I realized that it was a big soft-shelled turtle the size of a full moon hubcap on the end of the line rather than a flathead catfish. That's the most vivid fish-catching memory I have that didn't even involve a fish.

Yellow Bullhead

I've never caught a lot of yellow bullheads, and I don't recall ever catching them when I was catching black or brown bullheads. They are a different sort of cat. And they seem to like different places.

My clearest memory of catching a yellow bullhead was on a night fishing trip with Dad and one of his buddies on a stream called Mill Creek. Mill Creek ran through the pasture of the Illinois farm where my mother was raised. It was not much of a stream most of the year, but had some pools deep enough to get wet in – and support fish. It was an easy to get to spot to take a young boy who was bugging his Dad to take him fishing. Most of the details of the trip have been blurred by the years, but I remember a campfire, Hamms beer (the bear and sky-blue waters beer), hot dogs, grown men telling stories, and walking by myself downstream carrying a Coleman lantern looking only at the ground and getting poked in the forehead by a branch. And I remember sitting on the stream bank at the edge of the campfire light and reeling in a fish. I was already a veteran bullhead fisherman from our Minnesota summer vacations and I knew right away that what I'd caught was a bullhead. But it was different. That bottom fin in front of the tail was a lot longer, the tail was more rounded, and it was lighter colored overall. At the time though, it was still just a bullhead. And not a very big one at that, maybe eight inches. I don't remember that we kept it, and I don't think we caught another fish. It wasn't until some years later, as my interest in fish grew, that I realized what I'd caught that night on Mill Creek was a yellow bullhead.

Brown Bullhead • Black Bullhead

Bullheads, the mottled brown ones and the olive-black "yellow-bellies," were the fish of my childhood. These were the fish of my father. Bullheads were the first glue of attachment for my fishing connection with Dad.

There were a few places near home where we went bullhead fishing, like the old strip mine lakes near Atkinson. I remember one particular trip there when we "jug-fished." I can still picture the "jugs" – old cone-top Schlitz beer cans. These early beer cans (before flat-top beer cans were on the scene) with a pop-off bottle cap were perfect. The line was tied around the neck below the cap and then wrapped around the body of the can. Looking out at beer cans floating all around on the surface of the small lake was a strange sight that left an impression on me.

But it was the much anticipated annual vacation to southern Minnesota during my childhood that made most of my bullhead fishing memories. And memories of days on end with my family being together, along with various aunts and uncles and cousins and friends, no one going off to work, or school, or tending garden, or delivering papers.

Our summer destination every year from 1951 when I was four up until I was in junior high was Roberds Lake Resort just outside Fairbault, Minnesota. Back then in the '50s, driving there from Moline on old Highway 218 took seven hours if we didn't get caught in an Army caravan, which happened surprisingly often. At gas stops Dad and Uncle Eddie or Uncle Bud or whoever else was driving along with us would be quick to calculate and announce their respective gas mileages since the last fill up. Dad delighted in having strangers ask him about the big roll of burlap tied to his front bumper that he was pouring water on. He would explain that we were going fishing and that the bundle was a week's supply of nightcrawlers that his boys had picked, rolled up in layers of burlap and peat moss. He'd tell them that the water would evaporate as we drove along and keep 'em cool and no matter how hot it was, they'd be in great shape. And it really did work (he'd read about it in the Tap's Tips column in Field and Stream).

When we would get to Fairbault, before we headed out to Roberds Lake, we had a stop to make. Dad had grown up in southern Minnesota near a tiny town called Walnut Grove (a setting for stories written by Laura Ingalls Wilder). During the Depression, as adolescents, he and three of his four siblings struck out for Illinois to work on relative's farms. The youngest sibling, Walter, stayed behind. He had been born with cerebral palsy, and with Dad's father having skipped town, Grandma couldn't manage Walter on her own. Walter was put in a state-run home in Fairbault, where he spent the rest of his life – except for one or two weeks every summer when he was part of our family summer vacation at Roberds Lake Resort.

Uncle Walter wasn't like any of my other uncles. It seemed to me like he had a kid inside that adult body, a very sweet and kind little kid. He loved playing shuffleboard when we all gathered together late in the day in the huge screened-in open room of the "store." Uncle Walter delighted in sending the puck down the shuffleboard table. Then at times he'd get all serious and, like a little kid, ask my dad "Ray, you suppose I could have another beer?" His expression would turn to a big smile when Dad finally quit teasing him and said that he thought it would probably be OK, and ordered two more Falstaffs.

Uncle Walter was always right there to greet us when we returned from fishing and would excitedly ask us how we did. Uncle Walter never went fishing with us but stayed back with "the women." He did like to go for boat rides though, and it just occurs to me now why he didn't go fishing. He probably couldn't handle a fishing rod and reel because of his cerebral palsy. I wonder now if it was hard for him to stay back and watch us go.

When we did go fishing, our most common destination was a spot on the Cannon River down an old two-track across a pasture where the river was backed up above a low dam just outside Fairbault. There was an old rickety "T" dock that we fished from that was just inches above the water's surface. Boy, did we catch bullheads off that dock.

Our fishing gear consisted of fiberglass rods, Pflueger level-wind knuckle-buster reels (with no clutch or free-spool, the handle spun in a noisy blur when we cast) spooled with black braided-nylon line. The black line got replaced one year with line of multi colors which changed every foot. The idea was to match the terminal line color to the color of the water, as if bullheads cared. Terminal tackle was a big egg-sinker with two drop-leaders up the line baited with nightcrawlers. Double-headers were common. Another item of fishing gear, typically acquired on location, was a foot-long little-finger-diameter stick Dad would shove down the gullet of the bullheads that swallowed the bait to dislodge the hook.

We didn't go to French Lake very often because you had to rent a boat to be able to fish the lake. But I have a particular memory of one trip to French Lake when we did rent two boats. My brother Ron and I fished with Uncle Bud, a German bachelor farmer who was a prime reason why the word "laconic" was invented. Dad and Uncle Eddie and my cousin Jim were in the other boat. The boats were anchored fairly close together and we all steadily caught bullheads until our rope stringers were full and someone said it was time to head in. Uncle Bud took ahold of the oars and started to row the couple hundred yards to the dock. The other boat started to pull away from us. Uncle Bud pulled harder. When we still couldn't keep up, Uncle Bud said he supposed that our rope stringer full of bullheads still

hanging in the water was too much of a drag and asked Ron and I to pull it into the boat. We did, and Uncle Bud pulled harder on the oars. I think the other boat was halfway to the dock before one of us, I don't remember who, noticed that the anchor was still out.

Regardless of where we went,

Uncle Walter, 1957.

104

the early morning ride to go bullhead fishing is an especially nostalgic childhood memory. Dad and Uncle Eddie or Uncle Bud or whichever other adult was with us would be up in the front seat and Ron and I and a cousin or two would be in the back. A front seat passenger would open a thermos and pour coffee, the smell flowing into the back seat, which was followed by the loud sipping sound of hot coffee being tested. Then there'd be a metallic click-click as Dad opened his Zippo, and the faint smell of lighter fluid would reach me just before the smell of Dad's first puff. Today, though I dislike cigarette smoke, the faint whiff of someone's first puff on a cigarette takes me back to my childhood and being with Dad in a car on the way to an adventure.

I have such treasured memories of vacations to Roberds Lake and the times I shared with my family and my aunts and uncles and cousins fishing for bullheads and just having fun. As wonderful as those memories are, though, they are tempered by the sad memory of the vacation's end; Dad walking with Uncle Walter up a long sidewalk that led to one of the big old brick buildings of the State Home, Dad coming back to the car alone, and then seeing Uncle Walter watching us as we pulled away.

Tadpole Madtom

Fish in the Genus of little miniature catfish that includes madtoms and the stonecat are not something you'd expect to catch. Where they are found they are fairly common, but they're just so small. Working in Iowa I handled a lot of them that were collected by electrofishing or seining, and they made quite an impression. Trying to handle the four to five-inch little shits, I got stuck by their needle-sharp venom-filled spines several times and it was like getting nailed by a bee.

I might have caught a stonecat, the big boy of this group which can exceed six inches, at some time when I was sport fishing in Iowa. But I can't really be certain. The only one of these I do remember catching was a tadpole madtom. And that wasn't in Iowa, where they are native, but in Brownlee Reservoir on the Snake River in Idaho. They probably were unintentionally introduced with a truckload of catfish from the Midwest.

I was slowly fishing a small tube jig along the bottom off a steep shoreline on the Idaho side, where there was a lot of broken rock. It was a spot with "good interstitials" – gaps in the rocks that hold crayfish, and in turn attract smallmouth. I wasn't sure I even had a fish on until I got it to the boat. He wasn't a fighter, but catching the little five-incher has stuck clearly in my memory just because of how surprised I was to catch a tadpole madtom. They must like interstitials too.

American Eel

I've caught one eel. I caught it fishing for catfish in the Rock River when I was in high school. And though I didn't catch it on a rod and reel, it has made my life list of sport caught fish because I caught it by means which at the time were permitted with an Illinois sport fishing license.

As I remember I don't think there was any restriction on the number of rods you could fish with, or limb-lines or ditty-poles for that matter. In addition to fishing rods, a person was allowed to fish a trotline (or jump line) with I think up to 25 hooks. So if a person was interested in fishing for catfish, you could put out some serious effort.

I was fishing alone at night, using a couple of rods and periodically running a trotline. I probably had some ditty-poles out as well (it might have been the same night the flathead turned into a turtle). The trotline was anchored well, one end tied to an exposed tree root on shore, the other end tied to a big anchor I'd set out in the river that had good purchase. Every few hours I pulled my boat along the trotline in the dark to check for fish. As I recall I hadn't caught much if anything yet when I felt the eel, and just lifted it up over the side into the boat, figuring it was a little fiddler (Midwest term for a small "good eatin' size" catfish). I do remember how hard it was to handle the eel and get it off the hook. I had to use one hand to try to hold the eel, one hand to grab the hook and get it out of the eel's jaw, one hand to hang onto the main trot line, and my teeth to clamp down on a metal D-cell battery flashlight hanging out of my mouth. But I got it done. That part was fairly easy compared to trying to get ahold of a loose two-foot long eel squirming around in the bottom of the boat in an inch of water and getting it into a gunny sack.

I don't recall thinking that it was so unique catching this fish. A surprise maybe, but Mertz and I had caught them every once in a while commercial fishing with jump lines on the Mississippi. I think I knew from Mertz about an eel's unusual life history: born in the Atlantic Ocean east of the Bahamas, migrating hundreds of miles up rivers, and then returning to the ocean to spawn. As with so many other recollections, it was the occasion rather than the catching that has branded an unforgettable memory in my mind.

Like most high school-aged boys I had a lot going on. There was trying to do well in my classes, extra-curricular activities, and working several evenings and weekends at the new "Turnstyle", a combination grocery-department-mega-store. And there were girls. One in particular.

Then school let out for summer, but my weekly hours working in the Turnstyle produce department ballooned to over 50. I remember feeling overwhelmed, frustrated that I didn't seem to have any time of my own. What was the point of working all those hours (yea, yea, the making-money-for-college thing) if I didn't have a life. So on one evening when I got off work early I borrowed the family car and Dad's jon boat and headed for the Rock River to spend a night alone fishing.

And here's the mental picture and memory that is going with me to the end: there is a high-water cut-bank about four feet high right behind me, an open field full of horseweed and fragrant wild alfalfa back beyond that, with river-bottom silver maple woods up-river and downriver; I've got a fire going on a little bench between the cut bank and the water and by firelight I can see two rods propped up on fork sticks at the water's edge; the boat is tied off at the first tree upriver; it's Midwest-summer warm and humid; I'm lost in thoughts about what was going on in my life and that one-in-particular girl, listening to turned-down middle-of-the-night music on a transistor radio the size of a cereal box, and looking at a half moon out over the river.........when over the radio comes Henry Mancini's, "Moon River." I've never heard that piece since without having the river, the solitude, and the smells of that night – and that time of my life – rush back to mind.

Burbot (Lawyer)

I remember catching a small burbot, or "lawyer" as it was referred to at the time by my Dad. They have a single barbell on their chin like an old-time lawyer's goatee. Dad and my brother Ron and I were bullhead fishing on French Lake in Minnesota. Actually I remember the fish being caught, and think I was the one who caught it but couldn't swear to it. The reason I think I caught it is because I do remember feeling disappointment when Dad called it a trash fish and threw the strange foot-long fish back.

I've never caught another one, but have more than once thought how ironic it was that many miles and many years from French Lake I had colleagues working on Idaho's Kootenai River in northern Idaho to restore populations of burbot, a prized sport fish that once supported an important fishery.

White Bass

As with other species like yellow perch, bluegill, and kokanee which are caught in good numbers and are all about the same size, there's no individual white bass that I've caught that stands out. It's the people you go white bass fishing with that you remember. White bass can provide crazy action and bring out the excited little kid in most anyone.

White bass are not a particularly good eating fish. They are

OK. And they're not a big fish. In Western Lake Erie they were about as big as they come – maybe one to two pounds. But man are they fun to catch. They hit like a little runaway train, and they often come in big schools. I'm talking acres of feeding white bass splashing the surface, small gizzard shad flying out of the water, and the air full of screeching seagulls diving to get in on the action. Running a boat into the orgy often puts the fish down some, but usually doesn't run them off.

On Lake Erie we just threw a white or yellow ¼-ounce marabou jig and started retrieving as soon as it hit the water. If we weren't getting hit we let it sink a few seconds first.

That was the scene for Act 2 of "Fishing to Excess with the Weilnau Boys." The set was off the south side of South Bass Island. As generally happened, we spotted the seagulls first and headed toward the school, shutting the Johnson off when we got close and gliding into the action. The opening lines of dialogue I'll never forget, and have recounted them many times. I had the first line, delivered from the captain's position as the boat came fully to rest and we were all anxiously grabbing rods: "Butch, throw the anchor out." I had the second line as well: "You didn't tie the anchor line to the boat??!!" One Danforth anchor and probably 100 feet of rope sacrificed to the lake. My fault. The Weilau boys were kind of new to boating.

They were new to white bass as well, but geez did they catch fish. We kept moving the boat and resetting our drift to stay with the fish, but it was pretty much a fish on every cast. They couldn't believe it.

With three of us catching one to two-pound fish it didn't take long to fill the cooler. But we couldn't stop. I blocked off a back corner of the boat with the cooler and our tackle boxes and we started throwing fish on the floor. When the level of fish rose near to the top of the walled-in corner I suggested we had more than enough and better stop. But the Weilnau boys kept casting and catching. So, so did I. When the fish started spilling out onto the open floor of the boat I repeated that we needed to stop. The response was the same. They are SO much fun to catch! When it got to the point that I couldn't move my feet without stepping on fish I quit fishing and put my rod away. I added this time that "somebody" is going to have to fillet all these fish. They quit casting.....but only after I started the outboard and the boat was underway.

One year in the mid-'70s when I was working on Lake Erie, white bass actually helped finance a summer vacation for Marge, Colby, and I. It was a unique circumstance.

In I believe 1970, a graduate student in Michigan did an analysis of fish flesh samples documenting methyl mercury in concentrations that exceeded the established tolerance limit for human consumption (the established tolerance limit at the time for beef was ten-fold that set for fish!?). That news set off a flurry of fish testing by states. Our testing on Lake Erie fish species found that white bass larger than 10 ½ inches had mercury concentrations exceeding the limit, which triggered a closure on commercial harvest of white bass over 10 ¼ inches (there was a minimum commercial size of 9 inches!). Two things happened as a result: the number of larger white bass in the lake increased significantly, and the commercial dock price jumped from around 10 cents to around 25 cents per pound. It was legal to sell white bass and other commercial species that were sport caught. And there was no size limit for sport anglers. So Marge, Colby, and I went out "sport-commercial" fishing.

I don't remember all the specifics any more. I know we went out twice. We put three garbage cans and a cooler of ice in the boat and filled two and a half garbage cans with white bass one of those times. I don't remember how we did the other trip, but a figure of $78 comes to mind, which must've been for both trips combined. What I remember most about the experience was little three-year-old Colby. Marge and I were each rigged with two jigs and catching fish after fish, doubleheaders much of the time. Colby was toward the back of the boat doing his version of fishing off the starboard side. He couldn't cast, but he was having fun holding a fishing rod just like Mom and Dad and "play fishing" with a short line, dipping his jig in and out of the water. And he caught several fish! He couldn't lift them up over the side of the boat, but he could hang on until he got help.

Yellow Bass

As a biologist I've handled these smaller versions of white bass a number of times surveying fish on the Mississippi, but I only have limited evidence to suggest I've caught a yellow bass hook and line. I have a mental picture of rings appearing on the calm surface of Roberds Lake in the evening which Dad said were caused by "stripers," (yellow bass). And I have an old photograph of Dad, Ron, and I, when I was maybe six or seven, with a mixed stringer of fish that included stripers.

White Perch

I saw my first white perch, a small member of the true bass family which is quite prolific in parts of the east, in 1977. It was my seventh year doing gill net and trawl sampling as part of my fish research work on Lake Erie, and it was the first one I or any of the crew had seen.

When I left to go work in Iowa in 1979 they were showing up more, getting a toe hold in Lake Erie. By 1985 I'd moved on to Idaho, but flew back to fish Lake Erie with two guys, Steve Waters and Tom Boland, whom I'd just spent six years working with in Iowa. It was, and still is, a fabulous smallmouth and walleye fishery. Steve and Tom picked me up at Chicago O'Hare with boat in tow. By the time we headed east across Indiana we were running late due to the fact that my fishing rods ended up not flying from Idaho to Chicago via Denver on the same schedule I did. They hung around Denver for a while before flying to Chicago. We were trying to time it so we could catch a morning ferry from Catawba Point near Port Clinton, Ohio, out to South Bass Island where we were going to camp and fish. But we figured we ought to stop and get fishing licenses before going to the ferry dock. So we – Steve and Tom from Iowa, and me from Idaho – pulled in to a convenience store in Port Clinton to buy licenses. You see it coming.

After a long overnight journey we missed the morning ferry out to South Bass Island and had to chill at the dock till the next one came in. (Steve Waters photo)

We told the young clerk what we needed, she pulled a pad of licenses out of a drawer under the counter, and she went to work with Steve, asking him for his information, with her nose to the pad as she wrote. It went reasonably well until she got to the address part…specifically "state." She looked up at Steve after he said Iowa, processing what she'd just heard. She put the pen to the pad, not moving it for a few seconds.

Now, over 30 years later, I honestly don't remember where she thought the "H" ought to go in "IOWA," after the "I" or before the "A." But she figured there had to be an "H" in there somewhere. It took a little back-and-forth conversation, but she and Steve eventually got it straight, I-O-W-A spelled out on the line after a couple of scratched out versions. Tom stepped up and she did well, only hesitating slightly before questioningly spelling it out loud as she wrote it down one letter at a time.

I think she was feeling pretty confident by the time I stepped up, figuring the third "IOWA" is the charm. When I said "Idaho" she straightened up from writing, looked at me without saying anything for a few seconds, then turned the pad around, slid it toward me, handed me the pen, and said, "You write it down."

We missed the morning ferry, but we had a great trip. Neither the smallmouth or walleye fishing were as good as they can be; we were a little late for bass and a little early for walleye. But I caught my first, and still my only white perch on a Hot-N-Tot trolling for walleyes on a shallow rocky bar between South Bass and Ballast Islands. It was certainly nothing remarkable – essentially a small white bass without the stripes – other than it was my first (you always remember your first).

Largemouth Bass

Where do I start with memories about fishing for bass, both largemouth and smallmouth? More aptly, where do I stop? They are only two species out of however many I've caught, but collectively they account for such a large pat of the fishing I've done....and the fishing memories I have.

A largemouth bass just may have been the very first fish I ever caught. I certainly don't remember it, but there is the old photo of a not-quite three-year-old me holding a stringer with a ten-inch largemouth bass on it while my brother Ron stands next to me with a bamboo pole. And there is a second photo of me alone holding the fish, which suggests that I was the lucky angler who caught it. Mom's writing on the margin just says, "Green Lake, Wisc. '49." These are the two oldest photos I've seen of me holding fish, and as thrifty as Mom was, there had to have been something unique about the fish for her to "spend" two frames of film to document the occasion.

My earliest actual recollection of fishing for largemouth bass is of a time when I stayed on my Uncle Bud's farm to "help him with chores" – those where my "helping" didn't cause him too much extra work. I remember riding along on the tractor, being in the corn crib by myself cranking and feeding ears of corn into the hand-sheller, and having big noon-time meals with ice cream for dessert. And I remember one morning riding with Uncle Bud in his pickup to the little lake at Matherville, Illinois, which was being drained, to help him catch some fish to take back and stock in his farm pond down in the pasture. I remember Uncle Bud's big farmer hands struggling to bait my hook with a little squirming minnow. And him casting out for me and giving me the rod, my dancing and bobbing bobber, and the two of us catching little 10-inch bass one after the other. It's probably not accurate, but my memory has evolved to recall that we caught three dozen little bass with three dozen minnows.

Another early bass catching memory is from an overnight fishing trip at one of the strip mine lakes around Atkinson, Illinois, with Dad and my older brother Ron. We were going night-fishing for bullheads. I might have been nine or ten, just old enough to help with Ron's paper route and save enough money to become the proud new owner of a Shakespeare Model 1777 push button spin-cast reel, which would actually allow me to cast something lighter than a bullhead weight. Before dark I worked down the shoreline from camp casting a silver-bladed white Abu Reflex spinner and I caught a largemouth bass. Maybe more than one, I can't recall. I do remember Ron wanting to use my new outfit to try to catch a bass. And I remember Dad, and the anguish on his face, as he worked with a pair of needle nose pliers at getting the spinner's hook out of the side of my brother's neck where he had impaled it just below the earlobe on one of his casts. It took the experience of becoming a father myself to fully understand the expression I saw on my Dad's face all those years ago.

It wasn't really until 1962, when I gained the mobility of being able to drive a car, that I was able to make largemouth bass a target species. I'd been faithfully reading Jason Lucas's fishing columns about bass fishing in Outdoor Life, and it wasn't long until I had my own car-top boat – an eight-foot Sears aluminum flat bottom boat that I purchased for $50 and named the "PAID IV" (I copied the name from Bazooka Joe's boat in a bubble gum wrapper cartoon). I could load and unload the little boat by myself and hike and carry it overhead across pastures to farm ponds. My first car – a 1957 Plymouth Suburban station wagon – was sized perfectly for the little PAID IV to just fit inside and still be able to close the tailgate. When

I was fishing out of the little boat I would sit on the bow and quietly scull with a short canoe paddle in one hand (just like Jason Lucas), holding my rod in the other. It worked great. The only drawback was I always had to look for rocks or logs to weigh the stern down enough that the bow didn't go under from my weight. I even started smoking a pipe while I fished, just like Jason Lucas. Those years introducing myself to largemouth bass fishing were wonderful times. They blend together, but I do remember when Jason Lucas retired and his Outdoor Life fishing column was replaced with one by a new guy named Homer Circle. It ended up OK, but I felt like I'd lost a mentor.

Dad wasn't much into bass fishing, but one summer when I was home from college, I talked him in to going with me to fish for largemouth in an old strip mine pit lake near Galva, Illinois. We took Dad's 14-foot jon boat. It wasn't great fishing but he caught a couple very nice bass, and let his excitement show. It might have been the first time I heard him say, "Man-de-long," and it just occurs to me as I write this that we were probably fishing with my then go-to De Long purple plastic worms (anise scented) and maybe that's what the exclamation that I've remembered all these years was about. It was a particularly memorable trip. It was the first time that I took my Dad fishing.

Bob Dodd, a fellow fish and wildlife biology student at Iowa State in the '60s, carried me to the next level of largemouth fishing. He was my first real fishing partner. We'd fish together at local farm ponds around Ames on afternoons when we didn't have class. He came home with me and fished the strip mine pits, and we made a couple spring trips with the PAID IV to the Aunt's Creek arm of Table Rock Reservoir in southern Missouri.

It wasn't so much the greater skill and knowledge that he had as it was his approach. Bob, from southern Indiana, was contemplative. He made me think about what I was doing. I was in a De Long's purple plastic worm rut back then, and I remember Bob suggesting that rather than give a bass line and let him run after he picks up the plastic worm – only to have a good share of them drop it – I ought to try just hesitating a second for the bass to turn, then rear back and "break 'em to lead." I tried it. I did better. I picked up little things from Bob that can make a big difference, like checking my line after catching a bass and re-tying frequently. When we fished the flooded timber I watched him tie on a big-lipped Bomber lure with its two treble hooks and cast it through the timber, thinking he'd snag and lose it right away. Instead, that big lip banged and bounced off and over the underwater timber and the only thing that got hung up was bass after bass.

I remember the trips to Table Rock with Bob for more than just the fishing. Bob had done a lot more camping and outdoor cooking than I had, and on those trips we lived on Bob's fried potatoes and fried largemouth fillets. We cleansed our palates thoroughly each evening after dinner, and didn't always clean up. I remember one morning looking at the cast iron skillet sitting on the outdoor grill and seeing small tracks and holes in the solidified grease where birds had been pecking on leftover bits of fish from

Young skinny white boy Clark, spankin' the largemouth on Paddock Reservoir.

the previous night's dinner. And I remember lighting a fire under the skillet, the tracks disappearing, then throwing in some bacon and eggs for breakfast. On one of those trips I recall neither of us remembering one morning how we got from the Queen of Clubs in nearby Silver Dollar City where we had gone to cleanse our palates the night before, to where we were, waking up in Bob's car in the middle of one of the campground roads.

Bob stood up for me when Marge and I got married, and I was there when he married Suzanne a couple years later. We managed to get together fairly often while Marge and I lived in Ohio and Bob and Suzanne were in Indiana, both raising young sons to appreciate the outdoors and everything in it. We've stayed in touch, but it's been decades since we've fished together. I hope to be able to change that.

Largemouth bass fishing was a part of Marge's and my early marriage. We took our honeymoon trip to Table Rock Reservoir and Beaver Reservoir in northern Arkansas. While we lived in southern Ohio as newlyweds, many spring and summer weekends were spent largemouth fishing on Burr Oak Reservoir, small ponds, or Tycoon Lake. Tycoon was our favorite spot. The fishing wasn't that great, but we were generally the only ones there and it was home to the only osprey either of us had ever seen. We would watch it and watch it, but it seemed we'd invariably turn our attention back to fishing only to hear the loud SPLOOSH, then turn to see the osprey lifting off the water, carrying a fish away.

After moving from southern Ohio up to Lake Erie in 1971 I caught smallmouth fever, which I've never shaken. I still enjoy largemouth fishing, and have good memories of catching big ones on Lake Tohopekaliga and Lake Okeechobee in Florida, and of catching some very nice ones here in northern Idaho. I have especially fond memories of fishing for largemouth on Paddock Reservoir in southwest Idaho with Marge and a then young, skinny, red-headed, white-skinned Clark. He would stand shirtless up in the bow of our little boat cranking on bass and talking trash about he and I being professionals. I wish I could go back to so many early times fishing for largemouth and experience them again, but I'll settle for savoring old memories and working on making new ones.

Finally, a collection of favorite memories about largemouth fishing would not be complete without including the 2000 spring fishing trip to Mann's Creek Reservoir with my good friend and co-worker Bill Horton. It was kind of a spontaneous trip that had come out of a phone conversation just the day before. It had been a phone call to check with each other on how the other was recovering.

I had gone into the hospital for a little laparoscopic abdominal surgery. The doctor had said it would be no big deal, I'd be able to go home a couple hours after the surgery. However, when I came out of the anesthesia I had a big incision where they had pulled my insides out to the outside so they could see what they were doing on the inside better. I went home a couple days after the surgery rather than a couple hours, and on doctor's orders wasn't to go to work or lift anything heavy for a week. While I was in the hospital, Bill had done a little facial rearrangement after passing out during a noon-hour run on the Green Belt. When he came to he realized that he had done a face plant onto the asphalt. It was never clear why he blacked out, but on doctor's orders he wasn't to drive or go to work for a while either.

As I recall, during our phone conversation it came up how the regional biologist had recently done a fisheries survey at Mann's Creek and found some nice largemouth. It also came up that the forecast for unseasonably warm temperatures the next day would make it a good day to go bass fishing, and it came up that while Bill couldn't drive I could, and it came up that while I couldn't lift anything heavy (like the tongue of my boat trailer) Bill could, and it came up that our doctors only said we couldn't go to work. They didn't say anything about going fishing.

We were quite a pair, me shuffling slowly around, half bent over, and Bill tentatively feeling his way around with a big white bandage in the middle of his up-turned face (evidently it hurt more when he tilted his head down). But we got 'er done. We caught one very nice largemouth out of real shallow water on the north bank where the sun was warming the water. We hadn't anticipated that it would hurt as much as it did though – not from getting in or out of the truck and boat or the fishing, but from laughing so hard at ourselves and each other.

Spotted Bass

I caught my first spotted bass in a stream in Southeast Ohio, when we lived down there, but it's the memory associated with one particular trip a few years later when Marge and I caught spotted bass that stands out. We had moved from southeast Ohio to northern Ohio where I started a new job with the Lake Erie Fisheries Research Unit. I had met everyone working there at various statewide meetings of the Department, but really clicked, both professionally and socially, with Dave Davies. He was a big, unassuming guy who spoke with a quiet and serious enthusiasm about everything and, as I found out, was incredibly generous.

Marge and I had been talking about going back to Beaver Reservoir in northwest Arkansas, where we had gone on our honeymoon. At some point I must've been mulling over the logistics of a trip like that around Dave, including the age and condition of my old maroon F150, because one day he just declared matter of factly that we should go and we should drive his new Chevy pickup. We wouldn't have to worry about having a breakdown, and it had a nice cap on the bed all set up for sleeping in the back.

This was not like borrowing someone's new truck to run an errand. This would be a trip of a couple thousand miles. I of course said I couldn't. But he insisted, and did so in a way that I felt he would be hurt and disappointed if I didn't accept. So I did, and Marge and I had such a wonderful, carefree adventure, just driving down to the Ozarks and back. None of that has anything to do with catching spotted bass other than it made the trip possible, and to this day it's the most generous thing a new friend has ever done.

We had fun fishing and boat-camping on Beaver Reservoir, though the fishing itself was a little disappointing. Our timing was off just enough that we missed the peak pre-spawn fishing for large-mouth in the flooded timber. But we found spotted bass on open gravel shorelines and they made the trip. I remember our last evening meal on the reservoir. We grilled spotted bass fillets in a folding grill over the campfire. And I'm sure we gave thanks to Dave for making the trip work.

We did find a way to thank Dave. Marge later invited Dave out to the house for dinner, and also invited Ellen, one of her co-workers at Children's Services. They seemed to kind of hit it off. Last I heard, over 40 years later, they were still married.

Smallmouth Bass

I certainly remember the first smallmouth bass I caught. I didn't fish anywhere there were smallmouth until I was about 12 and we started making family summer vacation trips to Woman Lake in northern Minnesota. On one of the trips, maybe the first one, I started bugging my dad to go fishing as soon as we arrived. Whoever it was that had gone with us that year felt bad for me I think. He said he needed to test run the little outboard he'd brought and asked if I'd like to come along. He mentioned that I could troll while he "test drove" the motor along the shore. I'm pretty sure it was a sham, but it sounded good to me.

After we motored out of the little boat harbor, out through a channel under a footbridge, and into the lake, he turned right and idled along a steep shoreline. I sat astride the front seat facing the open lake and held onto my rod with a lure of some sort trailing behind the boat. Down the shore only a quarter mile or so was a bay. We were going to head across the mouth of the bay, and I remember that just about where the shoreline turned into the bay I could see rocks under the boat. I guess I remember it because it was a new experience for me to be able to see that far into the water and to fish somewhere with a rocky rather than muddy bottom. Then, as we motored across the mouth and the bottom dropped away out of sight, my rod bent double. I assumed my lure was snagged on the rocks we'd just gone over, but don't recall whether I had time to actually say it or not before a big fish jumped back behind the boat. I had never experienced anything like that, a fish that jumped and fought that hard. It took a while, but I got it in. It was a smallmouth bass.

With the bass in the boat we headed back in to show it off. The owner of the lodge said we ought to take it into Longville and enter it in the weekly big-fish contest at one of the stores. I don't know if it was a grocery store or a fishing tackle store – most likely in little Longville it was an "everything store" – but inside one of the front windows there was a case, like a meat case, with whole fish laid out on display on crushed ice. I'll never forget the big northern pike lying there. And I'll never forget my 3 lb 12 oz smallmouth being laid on the ice for everyone to see.

As I recall, my fish ended up being the biggest for the week, but it doesn't matter. That first smallmouth bass couldn't be more deeply imbedded in my memory. I do wish I could remember who it was that took pity on me and took me along to test drive his motor.

There is another smallmouth that holds a special place in my lifetime of fishing memories. It was caught over a decade later by my then new wife Margie. I was working as a fisheries biologist in Southeast Ohio and spending a lot of time assessing fish populations in the Muskingham Mine Area, a big area dotted with flooded old strip mines. There were over a hundred of these long, narrow, winding lakes, and dozens of lakes where mining haul roads created dams on some of the drainages. The area was somewhat unique in that the coal in this part of Ohio was overlain with limestone, and instead of having the acidic water found in so many coal mining areas these old mine lakes had alkaline water which fish did well in. Margie and I spent a lot of weekends there with the PAID IV fishing out-of-the-way lakes. Most contained bluegills and largemouth bass, but there were a few that had been stocked with smallmouth.

On one fall work trip to the area I took a look at one of the larger streams which drained the area. Lakes in the area occasionally flooded out or got breached by new mining activities, and about anything found in the lakes could end up in the stream. In my explorations I dropped over a steep bank down to a big pool below a man-tall culvert that carried the stream under a haul road. The pool was maybe 50 feet wide, twice as long, and over 10 feet deep where the water plunged out of the culvert. Downstream from the culvert there was a vertical limestone bank on the left with a barely visible underwater shelf extending out a few feet. While I stood at the culvert looking at the pool, a big dark shape rose up just off the shelf and held facing the current for a while, then sunk back out of sight.

The next Saturday I was back standing there, with Marge standing next to me holding a spinning rod. I told her to cast the small two-inch Pico Perch Minnow I'd tied on (a lip-less crankbait that's no longer made) down the pool and retrieve it back along the outer edge of the underwater shelf. She did it perfectly, but nothing. I suggested she do it again. Again nothing. She made the same cast and started to retrieve along the shelf a third time....and the lure stopped. Like me with the Woman Lake smallmouth, she had just enough time to think she was hung up on a rock before this big shakin' smallmouth cleared the water with a small Pico Perch Minnow (which I still have) in its jaw. Marge would tell many people later how I was such an excited wreck, coaching her to do this, be careful not to do that, while she calmly fought the fish and brought it into the bank where I was standing in the water at the edge of the pool. It was the biggest smallmouth I'd ever seen. It was a wall hanger. I took off my undershirt, dipped it in the stream, wrapped it around the fish to keep it from drying out, and we scrambled back up the steep slope to head home and call the taxidermist.

It made a beautiful mount. It weighed 4 lb 6 oz and, like most stream smallmouth, was exceptionally long for its weight at 22 inches. We filled out an application and submitted it along with photos of Margie holding her fish to the Genesee Beer Big Fish Contest. And she won it. I don't remember whether it was for the month or the year, but she got a nice certificate and a little gold-colored plastic trophy with a fisherman on the top. Margie's smallmouth found a home on the wall in every place we lived after that. As I write this, nearly 50 years later, it's hanging in my shop above all my fishing gear, a little worse for the wear from all the moves, but a trigger for memories of all the early-marriage fishing adventures we shared those many years ago.

In 1971 we moved to smallmouth mecca. I took a position at the Lake Erie Research Unit in Sandusky, Ohio, and I was taken under the wing by fellow biologist and smallmouth fishing fanatic Carl Baker. I picked things up from Carl that have stayed with me to this day, including "smallmouth fever." I learned a lot from Carl, like watching in the spring for blooms on the smallmouth bushes (Japanese flowering quince) to know when the smallmouth were moving in shallow and feeding. And how to work a hair jig with short, abrupt hops timed just right to make it look like a scooting crayfish. Carl made his own hair jigs, which he shared. He was convinced it had to be black bear hair (some brownish colored under-hairs were OK). Barry Apgear, the State Research Supervisor and an equally fanatic smallmouth fisherman, referred to Carl's jigs as the "Seven Deadly Bs" (Baker's Black Bottom Bouncing Black Bass Busters). Most springs, the third week of May would find the three of us spending a few days out at the Division of Wildlife's research station at Put-in-Bay on South Bass Island. We'd do some work, assisting the biologist stationed there, but daylight each morning would find us at Terwilliger's Pond, just a short walk from the station. Terwilliger's Pond was actually a small bay that had been cut off from the much bigger Put-in-Bay by a causeway. There was a short bridge over a narrow opening in the causeway which provided a water connection between the two bays. It was bass-o-matic, if you knew exactly where to cast, the best time to cast, and how to work a Seven Deadly Bs.

The where-to-cast part was easy: I could see where Carl and Barry were casting and catching all the fish. They didn't fish the outside of the causeway or the opening. I would try once in a while but never caught anything on the outside. The smallmouth were on the inside on the rock-fill of the causeway, especially right at the corner of the mouth of the opening. The when-to-cast wasn't as immediately obvious. I did notice that Carl and Barry at times would fish very intensely, and then would kind of kick back for a while and watch me not catch anything. They soon shared that it was when water moved through the opening into Terwilliger's, setting up a very minor but noticeable current, that the smallmouth actively fed. That wasn't surprising, the bass taking advantage of food coming to them and/or concentrating at the current breaks on the corners. But what amazed me was that water movement through the opening reversed directions on a predictable rhythm, every seven minutes. I'd learned about a seiche on large bays and enclosed bodies of water in limnology class, but this was my first time witnessing one.

Carl coached me on how to work the jig, but he and Barry out-fished me time after time. Then one morning, when I happened to bring a stiffer fishing rod, I got the feel. I got rhythm. Evidently my jig started to look more like a scooting crayfish and I caught a lot more smallmouth. Carl and Barry still out-fished me, but not by nearly as much.

Don Hair, the biologist stationed at Put-in-Bay, conducted a smallmouth bass life history study over a three year period. I went out to work with him quite a bit when I had breaks in my own field work schedule. I don't remember anymore what "ah-ha's" came out of his study, but I had a personal smallmouth "ah-ha" that I and all my colleagues found pretty amazing. One spring Don had a trap net – a kind of funnel-trap net off-shore with a seine-like "lead" running from the trap to the shore – set in Put-in-Bay so he could get his hands on some smallmouth to tag and release. We knew from experience that smallmouth bass didn't go into trap nets as readily as other kinds of fish, but it was a type of gear that Don could run by himself. And he was able to catch and tag smallmouth.

From my office in Sandusky I kept up with his progress. Don commented over the phone one day that, with over a 100 smallmouth tagged and released right there in the vicinity, he was surprised that he hadn't recaptured a single tagged fish. We joked that that meant that it must be an infinite population.

I was back over at Put-in-Bay sometime later and after going out in the boat with Don to help run the net, with still no recaptures, I took off down the shoreline to go fishing. When I got to where the net was, I stood on the bank where the lead from the net attached to shore and cast out along either side of the lead. I caught seven smallmouth from that spot. Three of them were ones Don had tagged.

Well over a 100 smallmouth caught in the trap net without re-catching one tagged fish – yet three out of seven caught fishing next to the net were tagged fish? What's the saying about "fool me once?" Smallmouth might go into a trap net once and get tagged, but they sure weren't about to go in a second time. Smart fish!

It may not have been an infinite population, but smallmouth bass fishing around the Bass Islands in Western Lake Erie was just great. We didn't catch monsters, but we caught a lot of fish and most were two- to three-pound fish. Bob Dodd came up from southern Indiana to fish for smallmouth bass with me several springs. Those were some priceless days to get to fish with Bob again. And to have such good fishing. One specific instance that stays clear in my memory was a day that Bob and I had tied my runabout up and were fishing from shore around the many large docks in Put-in-Bay. The smallmouth moved into the bay in May to spawn around the docks. We would cast down along a dock, or along a boat tied up to the dock, and scoot a Seven Deadly Bs along the bottom. We caught some very nice fish, especially when the bass had first moved into the bay and the water was still in the low correspondence '50s. I especially remember when the jig would just stop dead, that second of uncertainty after I reared back on the rod, and the endorphin rush when a slow-pumping rod tip told me I had a big smallmouth rather than a snag.

There were a lot of big boats from Detroit and Cleveland docked at Put-in-Bay on weekends and we tried to be as inconspicuous as possible, but one particularly large acrobatic smallmouth that I think Bob hooked jumped and splashed right below the rail of a very expensive looking 40-foot boat with an older couple sitting on the deck. The woman stood up and looked over the rail to see Bob catching this nice smallmouth, and exclaimed, "Look George, these young men are catching fish right here next to our boat." In a few minutes George appeared at the rail with a fishing rod and whipped some kind of lure out toward deeper water. We didn't see him catch anything though. He wasn't casting to the right spot, and I doubt that he had the rhythm. I'm sure he didn't have a Seven Deadly Bs.

When I left Lake Erie to take a job in southeast Iowa working on the Mississippi I figured my smallmouth fishing days were pretty much over. And for the six years in Iowa, except for a couple trips back to fish Lake Erie, it was a smallmouth drought. I had no idea, however, about the smallmouth bass fishing ahead of me when I moved from Iowa to Idaho in the mid-'80s.

My first trip to Brownlee Reservoir on the Snake River and the incredible numbers of smallmouth it held hooked me and held onto me for the 25 plus years I lived in southwest Idaho. Marge and the boys and I spent many spring and summer weekends camping and fishing on the three main-stem Snake River reservoirs (Brownlee, Oxbow and Hells Canyon) that form the Idaho-Oregon border. They were all full of smallmouth. The bass were not big – some years only one out of ten fish would make 12 inches. But casting a brown tube jig or grub to a rocky bank was non-stop catching and non-stop fun. And every once in a while there would be a bigger fish.

Colby and Clark learned to fly fish at Oxbow Reservoir. Sitting just off shore in the boat and casting toward the bank they got the feel for the timing and laying out the fly line without having to worry about something interfering with their backcast. With a bright streamer tied on, if they made a good cast to the bank, they could actually see the streamer suddenly disappear when a smallmouth inhaled it. Nothing like being rewarded for a good cast by the pull of a smallmouth bass.

I made countless trips to these reservoirs with my fishing

buddies and had some really fun times, but taking people who didn't get to fish very much was especially fun and rewarding: Steve Barton and his elderly dad, who refused to let me put on a new grub in place of the one he had on which was falling apart, as he just kept catching bass after bass; Mark Wheeler and his teenage daughter Brie, who'd been having a little rough go connecting lately, but they whooped and hollered together catching smallmouth; Jack Acree, the recently retired husband of one of Marge's colleagues who wasn't sure what to do with himself and discovered fishing just might be it; the secretaries from my office who appreciated getting to "go out in the field" and more than held their own catching fish.

And Rob Southwick. Rob was a consultant from Florida who did a lot of great work for fish and wildlife agencies around the country conducting independent public opinion, economic, and social surveys. He was not new to fishing, but hadn't had much experience with smallmouth. As we pulled my boat out of the water after an amazing day on Oxbow when we just couldn't keep the little bass off, he asked how many fish I figured we'd caught. While I never kept track of anyone else's catch, and I never announced what I caught, I always did try to keep track of my catch for my fishing log. I had caught just over a 100, and I figured that Rob might have caught somewhere close to that, so I told him that we probably caught around 200 smallmouth. With the boat strapped down and the gear stowed I pulled out onto the blacktop that parallels Oxbow Reservoir and Rob got out his cell phone. To his surprise he had coverage down there in the canyon and called his wife in Florida. I couldn't help but hear his end of the conversation. He excitedly told her about the fantastic day he'd just had. There was a short pause. Then Rob said into his phone, "We caught 300 smallmouth!" I knew then that Rob was a more experienced fisherman than I had realized.

Over the years, as much action as there was fishing those reservoirs, it got a little repetitive and just not as much fun unless there was someone to share it with who was experiencing it anew. I'd done some fishing in the main Snake River above the reservoirs, but it wasn't until the last five years I lived in Southwest Idaho that I discovered the phenomenal fall smallmouth fishing in the Snake.

Tim Shelton invited me to join him for an opening day duck hunt on the Snake in 2006, and told me to bring a fishing rod. It was a calm, sunny mid-October bluebird kind of day, but we had a great hunt and limited out on ducks by mid-morning. With the decoys packed up and loaded, we took off running up the river in Tim's jet-boat with Tim telling me about some of the fall bass fishing he'd had on the river. We stopped at spots just below the heads of islands where the current deflected out, and cast along the current breaks and the slack water toward shore. Some spots we didn't catch anything, but when we did catch fish they were toads.

Tim kept moving and said he had one particular go-to spot. It was a little different, nothing that would've gotten my attention. It was on the outside of a long gradual bend. It was surprisingly shallow for quite a ways out from shore along the downstream part of the bend, coming up to just a couple feet deep right about where the river straightened out. And there it abruptly dropped off to four to six feet deep, then dropped again a short way below that. Tim pulled in and tied off to shore just downstream of the first drop-off. Without moving the boat, we were able to fish

Bill Horton pauses for a picture before slipping some smallmouth back into the Snake River.

everything from the first drop-off down to the deep water. We spanked 'em.

Tim was a guy who had pretty much done it all in the outdoors, including a lot of smallmouth fishing on the Snake. I couldn't believe how matter-of-fact he was. I was beside myself catching more big smallmouth than I'd caught in all my previous fishing years combined. Several were well over four pounds. As it was for me when I took other people fishing on the reservoirs in the spring, it was obvious that Tim most enjoyed seeing me experience this fall fishing for river smallmouth.

Until I moved to northern Idaho in 2012, every fall after that trip with Tim found me in my little jet-boat on the Snake River. It wasn't until the water temperature dropped into the '50s that things turned on. Mid-October was prime. I went some by myself, but it was again sharing that kind of fishing with other people that I enjoyed and value the most. When Bill Horton went with me, we took time to pose him on the bank, surrounded by colorful fall leaves, holding an impressive bunch of smallmouth that we'd held in the live-well before releasing. He had the framed photo hanging in his office until he retired. And most memorable for sure was the day I took Bobbie.

Bobbie is a fun lady that I hung around with a bit for a couple of years after Margie passed away. Bobbie was just getting interested in fly fishing. We did some trout fishing together, but when mid-October rolled around I just had to be on the Snake and asked if she'd like to join me. She said sure and asked if we could fly fish for smallmouth. And I'm glad she did.

Other than fly fishing for the small bass on Oxbow with the boys, I'd not really fished for smallmouth that way. It was a blast. We went to Tim's go-to spot. Rather than tie up on the bank with trees right behind us and try to roll cast though, we anchored out in the river and cast white and chartreuse Clouser minnows in to the shallow water and let them swing down off the drop off into the deeper water before stripping them in. The bass were vicious. What fun taking three-pound plus smallmouth on a 4-WT fly rod. Bobbie had never caught a smallmouth before and she was just giggly.

But it seemed like we caught all the super aggressive ones pretty quickly and then nothing, so I moved the boat in to the bank and we switched to spinning outfits and brown tube jigs. We were back in the game. The fish weren't as aggressive, just sucking up the jig in-place, but they were stacked in there. We fished the area below the first drop-off pretty thoroughly and caught a bunch of very nice fish. When things started to slow down there I made a long cast down to the deeper water just below and caught a nice smallmouth. Bobbie couldn't quite cast her jig that far. After casting down there again and hooking what felt like a very good fish, I had Bobbie take my rod with the fish on while I took her rod and cast her jig down to the deeper water, then switched rods back again. It took me a good while to get my fish to the boat, during which Bobbie hooked up on a fish. When I finally netted my fish and swung it into the boat I was bug-eyed. It was the biggest smallmouth I'd ever caught. I hooked it onto my little electric fish scale: 4 lb 10 oz. I wanted to get a picture of it, but Bobbie had her fish about to the boat and needed help so I put my fish on a chain stringer and hung it over the side of the boat closest to shore. Turning back to the other side I got a look at Bobbie's fish. I didn't say anything right away. I was stunned. I netted the fish, brought it into the boat, and actually slumped down on my butt in the bottom of the boat, leaning against the port side and holding the net and Bobbie's smallmouth in my lap. Bobbie, with little experience or perspective about smallmouth, asked what was the matter, was I OK. I asked her if she had any idea what she had just caught. She didn't. I told her people fished for smallmouth their whole lives without ever catching a smallmouth that big. Bless her heart, she still didn't seem especially impressed. I regained my composure enough to hang her fish on my scale: 6 lb 2 oz. We had just caught a smallmouth double that weighed almost 11 pounds! When it was all said and done, the 10 biggest smallmouth that we caught and weighed totaled over 40 pounds!

I have several pictures of Bobbie and me on various outings during the time we spent together that make me smile. My favorite, though, is the one of the two of us holding our respective small-mouths, hers dwarfing the personal best I'm holding.

I won't go on forever about smallmouth, but I can't leave out the final perspective of smallmouth bass in Lake Pend Oreille where I live now. Pend Oreille has a great smallmouth fishery. It's so relatively untouched and the fish are big (I still haven't topped Bobbie's fish though).

It's a relatively new fishery here. I clearly remember the local conservation officer, J. J. Scott, announcing at our 1992 fishing regula-tions scoping meeting in the Panhandle that he'd seen a smallmouth caught from Lake Pend Oreille. Seems he was eating lunch at a lake-side café in Hope when a fellow approached him and asked how long smallmouth had been in the lake. J. J. said he told the individual that there weren't any smallmouth in Lake Pend Oreille. The guy turned around and left. He came back 15 minutes later holding a still-alive smallmouth bass. As interesting as that is, fast-forward exactly 20 years to when I happened to recount the story to my new neighbor at the house Sue and I had just moved into on Lake Pend Oreille – turns out he was the guy who caught the smallmouth "on-demand" and brought it back to prove to J. J. that there were indeed smallmouth in the lake.

There are so many good areas on the lake to fish, but I don't have to go far for good smallmouth fishing in the spring – just walk down the hill from the house to our dock on Perch Bay. I've added some brush shelters under the dock, and it's so dependable in the spring that, like the bass fishing back on Brownlee, it can get a little repetitive and not as much fun as it should be.

But Mike and Brie who own the lot next to ours have four young kids. The oldest is especially nuts about fishing. After seeing him try to cast over to our dock from theirs one day I told him to just go over and fish off our dock whenever he wanted. And now the most fun part of smallmouth fishing at our dock is getting up on a spring morning when Mike and Brie are up from Coeur d'Alene for the weekend, looking east from our loft-bedroom window, and seeing their kids, outlined by the morning sun, catching off of our dock.

Black Crappie • White Crappie

These two different but very similar species have slightly different habitat preferences, but they've often co-contributed to a good mess of crappies and memorable crappie fishing experiences. Their flaky white fillets are among my favorites, especially from freshly caught fish. With a few exceptions, individual crappies don't stand out though; they're often all about the same. Sixty-four quart coolers filled to the top with crappies, and cleaning them, is what sticks in my memory. Crappie have provided ample opportunities to demonstrate poor judgement and indulge in excess.

Crappie populations are very cyclic, with one age of fish dominating a population and suppressing newer year classes until the old fish fade away, then a new big year class moves into the fishery and creates another population peak. Marion Conover, a fisheries classmate of mine in college who became the State Fish Manager in Iowa, had a motto concerning crappie populations and sport fish harvest: "Ream 'em while they're there." I've never forgotten that. And I've shared it with others.

Brownlee Reservoir on the Snake River had had a so-so crappie fishery that was supported entirely by black crappies until the late '80s when white crappies, which had been introduced into Crane Creek Reservoir, found their way downstream into Brownlee. The result was typical of what often happens when a new species gets established into a body of water: there was an explosive year-class of white crappie that survived and thrived and grew as fast as their skin would stretch. That year-class supported a crappie fishery for several years the likes of which few people had ever experienced. One time during this period, after a fishing trip with Virgil, Dan Schill described how good the crappie fishing had been in terms of five gallon buckets full.....of fillets.

I think my personal low point in crappie harvest judgement occurred one June morning in the mid-2000s on C.J. Strike when the crappie population there was at a peak. It's so hard to stop fishing when just as soon as a 1/16th-ounce tube jig sinks enough to tip the bobber upright, the bobber just goes down, cast after cast. I just couldn't stop until two 64-quart coolers were full.

I was by no means the only one of my friends with poor judgement. That summer, and for almost a year, every potluck gathering had a plethora of crappie casseroles, fried crappie, pickled crappie, baked crappie, crappie cheese-balls, and other unrecognizable dishes with crappie as an ingredient.

Memories of crappie excess have stuck with me involuntarily, but the memories I cling to and value most are those of days spent fishing with family and good friends when crappie just happened to be our quarry. Like the sunny June day in 1990 when my mother, out from Illinois on a visit to Idaho, went crappie fishing with me in my little 14-foot aluminum boat on the upper end of Brownlee. We slowly trolled the shoreline; I thought it would be the easiest for Mom. She had this big wide-brimmed straw hat to fend off the sun and sat in the front of the boat holding a fishing rod, gazing at the cliffs and steep hillsides so unlike the Midwest where she'd spent all of her 75 years. I had never known Mom to fish before. She really liked it and couldn't totally hide the excitement when she reeled in a crappie. It was just the two of us that day. It was the only time just my mother and I fished together.

Crappie gave me a lasting lesson on a spring trip to Brownlee with Virgil and Steve Huffaker. I don't remember a thing about the trip before boating into the bay in front of Mountain Man Lodge and my catching a crappie with a cast up next to the T on the end of the lodge's long floating dock. There were no boats tied up, so after a few more casts in toward the dock we decided to pull up and step out on the dock so we could fish along its edges. Virgil and I worked around the dock and I suppose caught a crappie or two, I really don't recall, but Steve stood in one spot on the T casting back in and retrieving his jig along the shaded side of the long part of the dock.... and caught fish after fish after fish. He was using a little chartreuse curly tail grub. Virgil and I switched to little chartreuse curly tail grubs. Nothing changed for us. Huff kept catching fish after fish. So Huff stood to the side and let me cast where he had been casting. Nothing. He stepped back up, cast and caught a fish. I said, "Gimme your damn rod!" I cast, started the retrieve along the dock and caught a fish right away. So Virgil and Huff and I stood there with our respective lures in our upturned palms trying to figure out why only Huff's little chartreuse curly tail grub would catch fish. The grubs were identical. But the little lead-head jigs that our grubs were threaded on were not. I don't remember anymore how it was – Huff had on a 1/16th ounce and Virgil and I had on 1/8th, or maybe 1/32 vs. 1/16th – but Virgil and I switched to jig heads to match the weight Huff had on and it was fish-o-matic for all three of us.

The water was off-color with maybe only 18 inches transparency, and the crappie were evidently stacked at a precise depth just below that. Huff's lighter jig stayed up and came through the band of crappies, while our slightly heavier jigs dropped through that depth, with only an occasional hit, and came in on the retrieve below the crappie.

About the time fishing had transitioned from catching fish to rote harvesting, a boat came around the point into the bay and headed for the dock. We were still catching fish as it pulled up, and one of the two guys in the front of the boat said to the big guy at the motor, "Geez Jerry, you take us all around the reservoir and we don't catch anything. We should've stayed right here!" I was quick to recognize "Jerry" from his frequent appearances on local TV advertising some product or business. Jerry Kramer, the Hall of Fame guard for the 1950s Green Bay Packers, tied up the boat and enthusiastically greeted us while his two fishing guests hopped up on the dock and started casting. We made just a couple more casts, catching fish each time, and then I said we were about done anyway, we'd get out of their way. We loaded stuff in our boat, but before shoving off I had to acknowledge to the still fishless guys that I knew how frustrating it was to not catch fish when someone next to you is. I told them our story – that it was all about the weight of the jig – and broke off the jig and grub I had been using and gave it to one of them. As I recall,

Virgil and Huff did as well. I'd like to swear that we saw Jerry and his buddies catching fish before we motored back around the point, but I really can't. Regardless, that's the way I'd like to remember the end of the story.

Two of my favorite people to crappie fish with were Lou Racine and Dick Hansen. Lou and Dick were both members of the Idaho Fish and Game Commission, and while I knew them both professionally I didn't really get to know them until I fished with them. There is a saying about breaking bread together – spending a day in a boat together is the same.

When I had presented fisheries issues to the Commission, Lou had made it pretty clear that he didn't think much of warm-water fish. He was a catch-and-release dry-fly trout fisherman from eastern Idaho, land of the Henry's Fork and the Jackson Hole One-Fly Tournament. I first fished with Lou on an outing that was put together to get the Commission out fishing on Brownlee Reservoir with Department staff and members of a local bass club. Fishing together on that outing, he and I in a boat with Dennis Udlenick, the Conservation Director for the Idaho B.A.S.S., Lou did get pretty excited about catching smallmouth bass. I remember him saying something like, "Wow, these things really jump." I also remember his response when I reminded him that we had agreed to all meet on a beach down the way at noon for lunch, that it was past noon, that I could see all the other boats down at the beach, and that we had the lunch in our boat: "Let 'em wait. I'm the chairman, and I'm catching fish."

I'd already gotten to know Dick a bit from doing a little fishing together. Dick was about as opposite from Lou as you could get. While Lou was an attorney in southeast Idaho and an Idaho native, Dick was a forester in northern Idaho that had moved to Idaho many years ago from Wisconsin and didn't think much of any fish that wasn't a candidate for filleting. Dick particularly liked perch, crappie and walleye.

As opposite as these two seemed, they became fast friends

while serving together on the Commission, to the point that some years later they even bought adjacent lots on the Washington coast and built vacation homes next to each other. After that first Commission outing on Brownlee it became somewhat of a tradition to take Lou and Dick fishing when they were in Boise for a spring or summer Commission meeting. But fishing with the two of them together, friends that they were, was like spending a day in a boat with Walter Matthau and Jack Lemon. Lou and Dick were constantly on each other about something. If we stopped at the mouth of Dennet Creek and got into crappies, Lou would complain that catching crappies was boring and we should go fish for smallmouth because they fought more. If we were working a shoreline casting grubs and catching smallmouth, Dick would soon complain that fishing for "red-eyes," as he called them, didn't make any sense when we could be catching a nice mess of crappie to take home and eat. Dick really was a helluva crappie fisherman. He had the touch, and his favorite red and white tube jig always put more than his share of fish in the cooler. He frequently pointed that out to Lou. On one outing, Virgil joined us and we fished out of two boats; Dick with Virgil in his boat and Lou in with me in my boat. It was probably early May, a nice sunny day, but the water was still cool and the crappies were scattered. Virgil and I decided to go to different areas and then check back if either of us found fish.

Virgil and Dick were decidedly better crappie fishermen than Lou and I, but I'd caught some crappie the previous weekend at Dead Cow Cove (not the official name; named that by my son Clark). The outer down-stream side of the cove had a sheer south-facing rock wall with some steeply sloping underwater rubble. Early season crappies are probably attracted to the spot on sunny days because of the extra heat radiating off the wall, or because the zooplankton they feed on stacks up there. Whatever the reason, when Lou and I pulled into the cove and started pitching little jigs up next to the wall we started catching crappies. It wasn't every cast, but it was steady. I said something about going to find Virgil and Dick to let them know we'd found some crappies, but Lou offered that they could find their own. He was putting crappies in the cooler, and there was nothing he would enjoy more than catching more crappies than Dick. I felt uneasy about not going to look for Virgil and Dick, but kept fishing for the time being. We continued to catch crappies, mostly just "nice" ones, but I did catch one of the few individual crappies that I still remember. It was a "nicer" crappie, maybe 12 inches. I remember it not so much because it stood out from the others in size but because of the mileage Lou and I got out of it.

I didn't have to fret about going to look for Virgil and Dick too long. Pretty soon we heard a boat coming. We were tucked in the cove a little tight to the cliff and they were almost past us before they spotted us and swerved to come in where we were. It took just long enough for them to get there to see Lou and I each pull a crappie into our boat, Lou sitting in the back seat and swinging his rod and fish around to me in the middle of the boat to take the fish off and put it in the cooler. Dick's red and white tube jig hit the water a couple feet from our boat before their boat was fully stopped. They hadn't found any fish, and seeing Lou catching crappies while he hadn't caught one yet didn't set well with Dick.

They did catch some crappies. But they had stopped in a little deeper water, and the crappies were

Lou Racine showing off the nice crappie to Dick Hansen, over and over. (Virgil Moore photo)

137

either more abundant or more cooperative where Lou and I were fishing closer to the wall and underwater rubble. That frustrated Dick. Lou caught another small crappie and swung it around for me to take off. After I unhooked it and put it in the cooler, I couldn't resist hooking the bigger one I'd caught earlier on Lou's jig and slipping it over the side of the boat away from Dick and Virgil. Lou waited a minute, then hauled it in whooping and hollering. That really frustrated Dick. He and Virgil got more intense. It was so much fun. We did the big dead fish thing once again, me slipping it over the side of the boat hidden from Dick and Virgil and then Lou hauling it back in whooping and hollering and asking Dick how he was doing. I even commented loudly that it looked exactly like the last big one and that the big ones sure don't fight that much. Lou and I couldn't help but laugh out loud, but Dick and Virgil just got more frustrated and more intense. I think Lou and I did the big dead fish thing two more times before I figured the fish's lip was getting so ragged we might lose the only decent crappie we'd caught. Dick and Virgil never did catch on. It wasn't until another fishing trip with Dick that I told him about the gag. He said something about sons-a-bitches, and added, "Should've known – Lou's not that good of a crappie fisherman."

Warmouth

I don't think anyone ever fishes for warmouth. Like rockbass and green sunfish, they have more elongated bodies and bigger mouths than the other sunfish, and they are more aggressive. Because of that, they are pretty catchable, but I've never found them that abundant or big enough to end up in the creel. All the warmouth I've caught have been incidental to fishing for bluegill or crappies in small Midwest lakes. They are distinctive, with dark lines radiating back from their eyes.

My friend Ken Hill caught one while fishing for smallmouth bass on Brownlee Reservoir on the Snake River in Idaho, a long way from the native range of warmouth. Like the madtom catfish that

I'd caught in Brownlee, the warmouth had probably found its way to Idaho in a truck load of catfish hauled out from the Midwest.

Rockbass

It's been many years since I've caught a rockbass, but I have fond memories of fishing for them off the dock at Knotty Knoll Lodge on Woman Lake in Minnesota.

The resort had a small boat harbor, connected to the lake by a short, narrow channel, but there was also a "seasonal" dock down the hill and a little ways up the shoreline from the cabin my family rented. It was just a straight dock, and though I can't remember wheels under it or how it worked exactly, the dock was stored up on shore for the winter. I remember that because one year Dad, my brother Ron, and I helped "put the dock in." It's odd I suppose, but for all the fuzziness around actually doing it, I remember specifically that the water temperature was 58 degrees. To this day, almost 60 years later, 58 degrees is a reference point for me when thinking about whether water is too cold to spend much time in. It is.

There was a grassy flat on shore where the dock was placed and the closest thing to a beach that the resort offered. It was actually kind of sandy for a short distance out from shore, but further out as the water gradually got deeper the bottom turned to small gravel, then small rocks at the outer end of the dock. People sunbathed on the dock. People tied fishing boats up to the dock during mid-day breaks from fishing. I fished from the dock.

I'm sure it was a relief to Dad to have the dock there, because when I would pester him to go out fishing in the boat he would just say that we'd go later and why didn't I go down and fish off the dock. Which I would, and didn't mind at all, because there were always rock bass there.

It was one of my earliest experiences fishing in water clear enough that you could actually see the bottom – and the rockbass hiding under the dock. I could catch some rockbass casting out away from the dock, but it was best right underneath it. This might have been my first real lesson in the affinity that some fish species have for structure.

Green Sunfish

Green sunfish have been incidentals caught while fishing in various Midwest lakes, ponds, and river backwaters. They don't get very big, a six-incher is a big one, but they have always impressed me with how big they thought they were. They have an outsized mouth compared to most other sunfish and are decidedly more aggressive. I've had the impression that they will grab anything they think they can get in their mouth, and then some.

I had the opportunity to attend a meeting of the American Sportfishing Association one summer when it was held in Minneapolis. As part of the event, the organizers teamed up a member of the press with a state fisheries agency representative to fish with a local member of the tackle industry on Lake Minnetonka. Considering the lake is essentially right in town, I didn't expect much in the way of fish catching, but I was really impressed. The local angler I fished with manufactured synthetic skirts for spinnerbaits. Not surprising, we fished with spinnerbaits.

The big spinnerbaits we were casting worked great in this relatively shallow lake with its many scattered weed beds. It surprised me a little that in only a couple hours of fishing, we each caught several very nice largemouth. And I caught a decent northern pike, which impressed me because I hadn't caught a northern in quite a few years. But when I caught a green sunfish, I was really impressed that he thought he could eat that big spinnerbait.

Bluegill

Bluegills weren't as big a part of my childhood fishing as they were for most youngsters in the Midwest. Dad much preferred to fish for bullheads. But we had relatives who lived on farms. And farms meant farm ponds. And farm ponds meant bluegills. So I do have some memories of sitting with my brother and my cousins on the bank of a farm pond, with a can of worms and a cane pole, watching with anticipation a cork bobber floating on the surface. I remember a lot more bobber-dancing and two-handed pole lifting than I do actual bluegill catching. In hindsight, I'm sure we were using hooks and bobbers that were too big to effectively catch the size of bluegills in the pond, but it got us away from the adults.

And I remember getting the worms I think even more vividly than the fishing. Before we would hike down to the pond we'd grab a potato fork out of the barn and go around back to the pile of old composted manure and straw bedding. My older brother or cousin would dig, and the rest of us would watch every forkful break open as it was turned over and pounce on the worms that wiggled out. And if we'd run out of worms while we were down at the pond, we'd roll over logs and old boards. Sometimes there was nothing. Usually there were bugs and beetles and centipedes or even a garter snake. Eventually, where the wood had been lying there long enough and there was the right amount of moisture, we'd hit a bonanza and find enough worms to keep on fishing.

Dad with our bluegill catch from Roberds Lake.

After I gained the independence of bike mobility, the bluegills of Prospect Park Lagoon occupied quite a bit of my time. Only a mile from my house, the park pond had a narrow road circling it, and at one point there were a few concrete steps that went down from the road to an old concrete pier which stuck out quite a ways into the pond.

The pier had metal posts supporting a locked chain link gate across it just a few feet out from the base of the steps. I never really understood why. But it was not an obstacle to young boys. We'd grab the metal pole and swing out over the water around the end of the gate and head out onto the pier to fish for bluegills in the heat of summer. I don't remember now which of my buddies I was with this particular time, but we'd just gone to Tom's Variety and bought these fishing hand-lines. They came with their own hook and weight and bobber and a wooden H-frame that the line wrapped up on. It was perfect for the back pocket of a bike-mobile angler who needed two free hands to swing around the end of gates. I remember lying on my stomach on that warm concrete pier, summer sunshine on my back, holding a handline, and peering with anticipation into the shadow of the pier at a bobber tight against one of the concrete pilings.

And I remember one very big orange-breasted bluegill which I hooked and was afraid to try to lift up onto the pier for fear it would get off. I walked it down the edge of the pier, and managed to hang onto the line and swing around the end of the gate. I went down to the water's edge and slid the fish up into the tall grass. I don't remember if I kept it, but it was the biggest bluegill I'd ever seen.

The only time I recall Dad actually fishing for bluegills, and the first time I became aware of bed-fishing for bluegills, was during a summer vacation trip to Roberds Lake. Bill, who owned the resort, said he'd heard it mentioned that someone had found a bunch of bluegills on spawning beds out along a low reed-covered island across the lake and that could be some fun fishing for us. Dad and my brother Ron and I were there the next morning. We couldn't see the saucer-shaped depressions, or the bluegills on them, because of the ever-present blue green algae in Roberds Lake, but I remember casting a minnow below a small bobber towards the reeds along the south shore of the island, seeing it disappear completely before it even settled, and then reeling in a nice bluegill. And then doing it again. And again. It was magic.

Fast forward many years and halfway across the country, and fresh in my mind is the wonderful bluegill fishing I've discovered here in northern Idaho. It's something I look forward to every year in early June. My go-to spot is a small lake just south of the Canadian border. On an early summer day when the water lilies are blooming, you might see ospreys, eagles, deer, often a moose with calf, and maybe even a bear.

The northeast corner of the lake is ringed with a wide band of thick-stemmed yellow water lilies clustered a ways off shore. There's rather an abrupt outer edge to them with deeper open water beyond, and inside of them toward the bank there is a covering of the smaller-leaved pond lilies. It's a perfect bluegill combination. In the cool morning I typically position the canoe along the outside edge of the water lilies and start with a nymph fished fairly deep along the outer edge, but by afternoon fish move inside onto spawning beds in just a few inches of water. Oh my, the fun I've had with a 4-WT fly rod and a little foam spider. I love the anticipation after the spider lands, just before the "thip" of a bluegill sucking it in.

Sometimes I anticipate it maybe a little too much. On my first trip one June I got there in the afternoon when the fish were already right in on the beds. I tied a little black foam spider with an orange stripe down the middle of the back onto my 3-lb tippet. I laid it on the edge of a little opening with the telltale sign of "humpy water" from bluegills chasing each other around. The "thip" was almost immediate. I whipped the fly rod up in excitement.....and broke the fish off at the knot. Well, I calmed down, tied on another foam spider, and put a bunch of nice bluegils from that little opening into the cooler. Then I moved down the shore and used the same tactics in several more spots over the next couple of hours. But things kind of shut down in the real shallow water after it clouded over and a little cool breeze started up. Before calling it a day, figuring the fish had moved offshore, I paddled the canoe back toward where I'd started and then worked out into the water lilies in deeper water. I dropped the spider into a bushel-sized opening in the lily pads near the outside edge – about 50 yards from where I'd started – and "thip." I managed to get the fish through the tough lily pads and into the boat. I grabbed it and got the hook out of its lip, and then noticed something down in its mouth. Something black. I reached in with my forceps and managed to get it out. Yep. A small black foam spider with an orange stripe down its back! In that lake full of bluegills, over 50 yards from where I'd broken it off a couple hours earlier! Individual bluegill don't often stand out in your memory, but I'll remember that one – and that big orange-breasted one that I slid up into the grass at Prospect Park Lagoon over 60 years ago.

Pumpkinseed Sunfish

These colorful little fish aren't very big, but they're eager. On late spring trips over to Chase Lake to try and catch the pre-spawn largemouth bite, more often than not the bottom along the shallow shoreline is pocked with pumpkinseed nests. The largemouth have been very cooperative at times, but I always get a lot more "cheap thrills" from the five-inch pumpkinseeds peck-pecking at the tail of my Zoom Lizard or finesse worm, giving me that little endorphin rush with the brief hope that it's a largemouth picking up the bait.

I've never minded little pumpkinseeds adding to the fly fishing action on early June bluegill outings. Some of the pumpkinseeds that have risen to a fake spider in Perkins Lake have been big enough to end up in the cooler with the bluegills I've been targeting.

Going back over 40 years ago now, a pumpkinseed sunfish might be the first fish that Colby ever caught. How embarrassing is that: a guy who can't say what his first son's first fish was. But I can't think of anything he might have caught before that spring afternoon outing with Bob and Suzanne Dodd and their son Quentin when the boys caught pumpkinseed sunfish. Colby and Quentin were both at an age where we held their hands to help balance their unsteady walk back to a pond on a local wildlife management area. They were small enough that their moms still held them on their hips occasionally. But they were just big enough to raise a short cane pole high enough to lift a little pumpkinseed out of the shallow water next to shore.

I'm pretty sure that Colby wasn't big enough to swing the fish all the way in and get ahold of the line though. In an old picture I have, Colby has the cane pole but someone else's hand is in the picture gripping the line and holding the pumpkinseed in front of him. Colby's arm is stretched out toward the pumpkinseed, one finger is just about to touch the colorful little fish, and I see wonder in his eyes. And I see the spark of a new little fisherman in the making.

Redear Sunfish

Redear just aren't very notable for me. I made a specific trip one time to catch redear after Larry Mitzner, a colleague in Iowa, talked up the big redear in Red Haw Lake. It was tougher than bluegill fishing. We fished deep water and I don't recall catching many, but I do recall they were nice fish.

Yellow Perch

The firm, mild, almost sweet flesh of yellow perch – or "ring perch" as Dad called the occasional one we'd catch on our Minnesota summer vacations – puts them right up there near the top of my list of good-eating fish. That's not just my opinion. At one time while I was working on Lake Erie, I noticed yellow perch butterfly fillets in the butcher's case at the grocery store which were selling for more per pound than the T-bone steak displayed nearby.

Because they don't get very big it takes two, three, or four for a serving, depending on the size of the fish and the person's appetite.

To me, an 11-inch yellow perch is the perfect size, a compromise between the increased labor of filleting to make a meal of smaller ones and the declining flesh quality of larger ones. Bottom line: my fishing for yellow perch is not sport fishing, it's meat fishing.

Many of my yellow perch fishing memories are thus, not surprisingly, characterized by excess and poor judgement. Like the time that Steve Elle and Dexter Pitman and I went ice-fishing south of Sugar Loaf Island on Cascade Reservoir in the early '90s. We'd gotten there early as the fishing typically tapered off as the morning wore on. Not this day. It was crazy. Each of us had augered two holes and were fishing two lines, two hooks per line, and alternated rebaiting and dropping one line down and pulling the other up with a double header of 10 to 11-inchers on it. And it didn't taper off. Steve and Dexter both reached their self-imposed limit of how many fish they wanted, but I couldn't stop. It finally ended up with them standing over me, with fish and gear loaded on their sleds, telling me to stop. One more!? It is so hard to quit when it's fish-o-matic. But I finally did when Steve and Dexter headed in to shore without me.

Clark with a summer time catch of yellow perch from Cascade Reservoir in the late '80s.

I had only one five-gallon bucket, but a bunch of plastic bags. I carried the full bucket of perch. The rest, tied up in plastic bags and loose, were all Colby's little plastic sled would hold. I paid for the good fishing with time in the garage filleting perch, but I sure ended up with a nice stock-pile of fillets in the freezer.

Another unforgettable yellow perch fishing experience (and the third and final chapter of "Fishing to Excess with the Weilnau Boys") occurred many years before that trip on Cascade. It was when I lived in Ohio in the mid-'70s and had invited the Weilnau boys to go ice fishing for perch on Lake Erie. Perch fishing had been red hot off Catawba Point that winter. I figured if there were ever a time they'd feel they could get away from the farm to go fishing winter was it. So I wasn't surprised when they said sure, they'd really like to go catch some perch.

Walking out across frozen Lake Erie was a first for them. Going up and over pressure ridges and hearing the cracking and booming of expanding ice made them nervous. I tried to assure them how safe this was, but I think all the people out beyond us and the occasional truck driving across the ice probably gave them the greatest reassurance.

I had gear for all of us: short rod tips from past broken rods inserted into a hole drilled in the end of 12 inches of broom handle, with two nails in the broom handle to wrap the line on. Fancy. I had them rigged with cheap fly line because it's so much easier to see and handle on the ice with gloves or mittens on. At the end of the fly line was a one-ounce weight, which we needed to be able to get our lines to the bottom 30 feet down (I'm still amazed at how much current there can be under the ice in a big lake in some wind conditions). Under the weight was a wire spreader with a short monofilament leader and snelled hook on each arm that we baited with live shiners.

The fishing was still red hot. We watched for the weight to hit bottom, lifted it a foot or so, felt the bite, set the hook, and hand over hand pulled the line in and the fish up onto the ice. Re-bait and repeat. It didn't take long to catch on that waiting a bit after the first bite before setting the hook generally produced a double. And it didn't take long to run out of shiners. We switched to perch eye-balls for bait and the fishing never slowed down.

I think that every fish that came up on the ice turned into a crisp fried perch fillet in the eyes of the Weilnau boys. We were having so much fun, it was hard to stop. But we should have stopped long before the sun got low and we were forced to leave. Oh my, we had so many fish to haul back to shore. An excessive amount.

We went to Tom's house because he had a nice bright, heated garage. Tom's wife Sandy called Marge and Butch's wife Jill, and soon the garage was full of kids and wives, the great fishermen, and buckets and buckets of fish. It wasn't long before someone asked how many fish there were and the counting began. I don't recall anymore whether it was before or after the total was determined when my poor judgement became apparent. I soon discovered that neither Butch nor Tom had ever filleted a fish. I ended up filleting essentially all 327 of those yellow perch, except for a few that Butch and Tom attempted surgery on before switching to rinsing and packaging fillets.

It really ended up to be a wonderful evening with all three families laughing and working together cooking dinner or processing fish. We didn't get them all done that night though. We ended up burying what was left in a snow drift in Tom's front yard when we finally decided to call it a night. I'll have to be honest and say that coming back the next day to continue filleting perch was not nearly as much fun as the evening before. That was the last time I ever took the Weilnau boys perch fishing.

One last notable experience involving yellow perch occurred after I moved west to work for the Idaho Department of Fish and Game. Jerry Conley, Director of the Department in the '80s and '90s, was an angling purist you might say. Fishing was purely for meat. And he loved to catch yellow perch. At one March Fish and Game Commission meeting in Boise he suggested that I join him and several Commissioners who were going ice fishing the next day on Cascade Reservoir, about an hour and a half north. I think he had heard that I'd gotten into perch really well up there on some earlier trips. I gladly accepted the invitation.

The next day's trip still sticks with me for several reasons: a power auger, a Labrador retriever, and the genesis of a new fishing partner.

At the end of the Commission meeting we made a quick plan for the next day. It was going to take two vehicles to get all of us up there so I volunteered to drive. I mentioned that the fishing was often best early, and then tapered off later in the morning, but I suspected plans for that evening would trump a plan for an early departure. I was right. Except for Dick Hanson. Dick, the Commissioner from up in the Idaho Panhandle, grew up perch fishing in Wisconsin. Dick took a backseat to no one when it came to meat fishing. Dick suggested that he and I leave early and put some fish in the bucket while the rest of them lolly-gagged around in the morning.

It hadn't been light very long when we got there the next morning. I put my hand auger, a couple five-gallon buckets, and the rest of our gear in my son's yellow plastic sled and we hiked the half mile out to a big sandy flat in about eight feet of water south of Sugar Loaf Island. I drilled a couple of holes about 50 feet apart, and by the time we saw the rest of the crew starting out from toward us from shore, Dick and I had a good start on filling a five-gallon bucket and were still catching fish. When the crew got out to us they were excited to see that we were into fish. Jim Keating wasted no time in firing up his gas powered auger and drilling several holes between Dick and me.

But when the new crew dropped their baits down.....nothing. And it didn't take long to register with Dick and me that we had quit catching fish. Jerry had brought a "Little Buddy," a fish finder on a wand so to speak, with a little LCD screen on the handle. He walked around and stuck it in all the holes. No fish showed up on the screen.

I drilled and tried a couple more holes, working my way further away from the group, and got back into fish. Jerry noticed and came over with "Little Buddy." He stuck it down in the hole while I was taking a fish off and rebaiting and the screen showed lots of fish hanging within a couple feet of the bottom.

He went back over to the group and pretty soon Jim was drilling holes all around me with his power auger. Just that quick I quit catching fish. Jerry put Little Buddy in my hole again. No fish.

With time and patience I'm sure fish would have returned, but there was a lesson here. In only eight feet of water, on a big sand flat with no structure or cover to hold fish, a gas powered auger can be quite disruptive and stop a bite cold.

We shifted around from hole to hole and continued to scratch out a few fish, leaving a fish or two or three lying on the ice at different holes. Jerry had brought his yellow lab along, and like all labs, she was everybody's friend, trotting from person to person for a head scratch. On one of her trips over to me, after the head scratch, she went behind me momentarily and then started trotting over to Jerry – with the head and tail of one of my perch protruding from the sides of her mouth. She trotted over to Jerry and put the perch down on his pile of fish!

Jerry denied training her to steal other people's fish. He said it just came naturally to her.

It was a fun and memorable day with the whole group. But I'm especially thankful that Dick Hanson decided to go early with me and we got to spend that time fishing just the two of us. It was a connection that led to many fishing trips together. Dick was so much fun to be with, with his quick, dry sense of humor, his many colorful stories, and his passion for conservation. As it ended up, for the last five years of his life we lived at the opposite ends of Lake Pend Oreille, and occasionally we were able to get together to go fishing for kokanee or walleye on the lake. I wish we'd have done it more. Dick passed away in 2016.

Walleye

I've never been real passionate about fishing for walleye (though I must admit that fishing for them on Lake Pend Oreille the last couple of years is beginning to change that), but I have some meaningful memories collected over the years of fishing for them with family and friends in various settings.

The earliest of those, and the most powerful, is of the day on one of our first summer vacations to Knotty Knoll Lodge in northern Minnesota that Dad and I found the walleyes. Until that point Dad had always been a bullhead-bluegill-catfish-white perch kind of fisherman. His fishing was the kind where you sat in one spot and waited for the fish to bite. But Knotty Knoll was on Woman Lake, and Woman Lake was about bass and northern pike and walleye, fish you had to go after.

I don't remember the name of the older man who, along with his wife, owned and operated Knotty Knoll, but he gave Dad some suggestions for places on the 5500-acre lake to try for different fish. One of the spots was a long, narrow, off-shore bar not far from the lodge that came up shallow enough that there were underwater weeds growing along the top of it. He said we ought to be able to spot the weeds, and it was a good place for walleye. And we did, and it was.

I don't know how or why we came to use them, but we trolled three or four-inch silver Flatfish, X4s I think, with a night crawler hung on the rear treble hook. I don't recall, but I suspect we had a weight of some sort crimped on the line ahead of it. Once Dad got the gist of how the bar ran, we trolled off to the side of the line of underwater weeds, and BAM, we caught a walleye. That may have been the first walleye I'd ever seen. We kept trolling, and we caught more walleye. I remember Dad's excitement, and I think pride in fishing for and actually catching walleye.

I don't know how long we fished, just Dad and me, but I remember the outboard motor kept dying. It was an old Sears Sea King that hung on a rack in our garage all year, mostly just waiting, like I did, for our annual summer vacation. It was a monster by today's standards. It was a 5 or 6 HP, but the size of a 15 or 20 HP today. It had two gears: in-gear and neutral. To go in reverse Dad swiveled the motor 180 degrees. The flywheel was exposed on top, and every time the motor died out – which it did repeatedly – Dad put the knot at the end of the starter rope in the notch on the flywheel, wrapped the rope around the fly wheel, and gave the rope a yank. And did it again. And again. And eventually the motor would start. Looking back, I suspect the plugs were fouled from a combination of months of non-use and then hours of low-speed trolling.

We didn't exactly kill 'em, but I think we ended up with five or six nice walleye. I remember when we did call it a day and motored back into the small boat harbor how proud Dad was – and how proud I felt as well when Dad told me to lift that stringer of walleye up out of the boat for my mom and younger brother and sister to see.

That evening in our cabin, after a dinner of fresh walleye, Dad started to complain about how much his chest and arm hurt from yanking on that old motor. I'd never seen Dad like that. He was in real pain, and it scared me. I had no idea at the time how much it must've scared Mom. Mom told Mike and Debbie and I that we needed to go into the bedroom we were sharing and go to bed so we didn't bother Dad. There is a visual permanently burned in my memory of standing there, hesitant to leave, looking at Dad sitting stiffly in a straight-back chair at the little dining table, gritting his teeth and staring straight ahead. The table was covered with a red and white checked oil-cloth, empty except for a small glass and a bottle of whiskey. Dad filled, drank, and refilled the glass trying to deaden the pain.

In the morning Dad was Dad again. It had passed. Sometime after we had returned home from vacation Mom sat Debbie and Mike and Ron and I down and told us that Dad had been to see the Doctor and that the Doctor told Dad that he had had a heart attack. Life changed a little after that. Dad began drinking "near-beer" instead of beer, used co-salt instead of salt, and he "took it easy." This was the early '60s, and that's about all the Doctors had for heart attack survivors. Dad survived two more heart attacks in the next decade. One ironically occurred during a trip to see Margie and I in Ohio after Dad and I had spent the day fishing together. His fourth and final one came less than a year later.

A few years after that I found myself working on Lake Erie doing walleye research, and like a postman taking a walk on his day off, I spent a lot of days-off fishing for walleye with Marge or one of my co-workers. Those were idyllic summer days on the water. We'd typically try to get out there at daylight and call it quits when the heat got too uncomfortable. In reflection, most of the days on the water blend together. Some trips stand out though. Like one trip with my boss and good friend Russ Scholl. Russ lived just a couple miles away from our place out in the country. I hooked my little runabout up to the old maroon Ford pickup and pulled in his driveway to pick him up just as the sky started to turn early-morning grey. Russ threw his stuff in the back of the truck and before climbing in asked if I'd checked the trailer lights. Now I hated boat trailer lights. And they hated me. They demanded way too much time. I think I said something like, "they're probably OK," but Russ was already on his way to the back of the trailer. I don't remember anymore what it was that wasn't working. It seems there was always something about boat trailer lights that wasn't working back then. I do remember the sun was already hot by the time we left Russ's place and headed for the lake, with trailer lights that worked all around.

We fished a couple of different ways on Lake Erie. Sometimes we trolled diving plugs – generally a Storm Hot-N-Tot – along rocky shorelines and bars. Off the old dump on the south shore of North Bass Island, and the bar between Ballast Island and Perry's Monument on South Bass Island, were go-to places. With the right speed and light line we could get the Hot-N-Tots to run as deep as 18 feet. While we were targeting walleye, we were just as likely to have a smallmouth bass or freshwater drum ("sheepshead" on Lake Erie) take the lure. Trolling as a technique can be really boring, but trolling the rocks on Lake Erie with Russ, Carl Baker, Dave Davies, Marge, and others produced lots of action and lots of fun.

The other technique most everyone used to fish for walleye was kind of unique to Western Lake Erie. Lake Erie didn't have weed beds which walleye typically move into as the season progresses in other walleye lakes. And it didn't have much bottom topography or rocky bottom areas that would hold walleye. Western Lake Erie is for the most part just a vast, flat-bottomed water area 20 to 35 feet deep. For much of the year walleye wandered the open water area and fed pelagically on schools of emerald shiners. When walleye schools were suspended like that we went to weight-forward spinners with a night crawler threaded on the hook. My favorite was the old Hildebrandt Nugget Twin Spin, a silver one. It was a hit and miss kind of fishing back then without the fish finders and side-scanning sonar that is available today. But we'd just keep moving and casting, and when we hit a school it was good. Sometimes really good.

Jim Fofrich was one of the early sportfishing charter captains on Lake Erie, and the developer of a weight-forward spinner called the Erie Dearie. Jim started chartering in the '60s when commercial fishing for walleye was still going on. A good day for Jim back then might be two or three walleye. Jim was a constant and outspoken critic of commercial walleye fishing, but it took finding mercury in the early '70s to shut down the powerful commercial walleye fishing industry. Then, combined with passage of the Clean Water Act in 1970, the explosion of walleye populations and the sport fishing industry that developed nailed the lid shut on the commercial walleye fishing coffin for good. The estimated sport harvest of walleye in 1976 was 112,000 fish. By the mid-'80s it had grown to five million!

Not surprisingly, as the walleye populations expanded so did the charter fishing fleet, and in 1977 or 1978 the first Pro-Am Walleye Tournament was held, sponsored by the Lake Erie Charter Boat Association. Jim Fofrich would of course be in it, and he invited Russ to be on his team and fish the tournament with him....and to bring another amateur who knew how to fish. Russ asked me to join him.

I was thrilled. I'd never fished with someone who took people fishing for a living, and Jim was somewhat of a legend. His son, Jim Fofrich Jr., and as I recall two other guys, one himself a charter fisherman, rounded out the team. But that day we were just a group of fishing buddies. We had loads of fun. It was clear, though, that Jim wanted to make a good showing in the tournament. We certainly didn't just randomly search for walleye. From fishing nearly every day Jim knew areas where these open water walleye were more likely to be. And when we shut down to drift and cast in an area, we were all equipped with different colored Erie Dearies. We spread out around the boat and fan cast in different directions as we drifted. Jim told us to count down before we started our retrieve, to vary our counts and to holler out when we hooked a fish. "gold on a ten-count"............."white on a twelve-count"..........."white on a ten-count"......."red and white on a twelve-count"........."white on a ten-count." Then we'd all switch to white and count down ten to twelve.

"Competition" and "fishing" are two words that don't go together in the language I speak. Typically, if I go fishing with someone and they announce during the day how many fish each of us has caught, as if it's a competition, then that is the last time we fish together. But fishing that day wasn't a competition between us. It was both fun and exciting. Without verbalizing it, we were intent on working together to show this burgeoning charter industry who Jim Fofrich was.

We had a good day. We were catching enough to be selective for bigger fish and hung quite a few in the eight pound range. Russ and I, fishing up on the bow, held our own. At the end of the day, after all the teams had weighed in, Jim's team was in first place! What a day. What a celebration that night. We had another day to fish though.

We weren't quite so chipper and excited at daylight the next morning, and the second day didn't seem the same. I think we were too serious. Now we wanted it too bad, and it wasn't as much fun as the first day. I'd like to say that the Fofrich team won the whole shebang, but we couldn't find the big fish the second day and dropped to third place in the final standings. Regardless, Jim felt good I think about how he'd stacked up against the rest of the fleet. He'd made his mark.

Jim passed away some time ago, but I think he'd be pleased to know that just last year, almost 50 years after that tournament, I ordered several colors and weights of Erie Dearies from Cabelas to try on these walleye here in Lake Pend Oreille.

Good or bad, the walleye population on Lake Pend Oreille has pretty much kind of exploded from just background levels for almost a decade, and the fishing of recent surpasses anything I experienced on Lake Erie in the '70s. Casting crankbaits, big hero-swimbaits, and pitching a jig and worm have all worked, but trolling has been the hottest and the easiest way to fish when Sue or someone else goes along. It's been fun to be able to take out my neighbor David, and get him into walleye. He's a casual fisherman at best, but a snow plower extraordinaire who keeps our lane clear. I wasn't that surprised to get his feedback on how much his wife Renee, who doesn't like to eat fish all that much, loves walleye. Bill Hutchinson (Hutch) and I had one amazing August day trolling out on the lake when it seemed like all the other predators in the lake had joined the walleye for young-of-the-year perch dinner. Along with walleye we caught smallmouth and pikeminnow, which is common, but also 13-inch perch, 15-inch crappies, a 20-inch rainbow trout, and even a bullhead! A good share of the walleye we've caught have been taken by trolling a silver flatfish with a night crawler hung on the rear hook, just like Dad and I did 60 years ago on Woman Lake. I actually still have one of the original silver flatfish that Dad and I used, half of the silver paint missing now. But it doesn't go in the water anymore. I'm afraid it would get bitten-off by a northern pike. Instead, it has a permanent home hanging on my rod rack out in the shop.

Sauger

It's been a while since I've fished a big Midwest river and caught sauger. The last time was in the early '80s when I lived near Muscatine, Iowa, along the Mississippi and went sauger fishing with my friend Denny Weiss in the tailwater below Lock and Dam 16. We did well fishing minnow tipped jigs.

The first time I fished for sauger was with Mertz Pobanz, the buddy of my Dad's who actually paid me to help him commercial fish back in the late '50s when I was in junior high. Mertz was a nice enough man, but he was pretty much all business. So it surprised me when late one fall he suggested that we take a day and go sauger fishing before he pulled the boat out for the season. I'm talking rod-and-reel-'em-in fishing. Mertz had heard that people were catching sauger in the tailwater below Hampton Dam. Obviously, I thought it was a good suggestion.

Hampton dam, Lock and Dam 14, was maybe ten miles upstream from where Mertz kept his boat and gear on Pool 15 where we commercial fished. We'd never run the boat that far up the pool and I remember it was a cold ride which seemed to take forever. We fished the current break below the last dam-gate on the Illinois side, the boat anchored in the slower back current. We fished live minnows below a big, golf ball sized plain cork float that drifted in different directions with the swirling current. The sauger hung close to the bottom, which was nasty, snaggy rocks. Mertz adjusted our big cork bobbers on the line until he got the depth that would let our minnows float around just off bottom but not get hung up.

Mertz was a commercial fisherman, but he was no slouch fishing with a rod and reel. I remember we pulled sauger into the boat pretty steadily, mostly 12 to 14 inches. And I remember looking over to guys fishing from shore off the rip-rap at the end of the earthen part of the dam a short distance away, and feeling somewhat superior.

I don't know that I could find a plain cork bobber anymore, other than maybe in an antique store. But whenever I picture one, I think of Mertz and sauger fishing.

Freshwater Drum (Sheepshead)

Not much stands out about this fish, other than I've caught a lot of them and they wear different hats in different places. My earliest memory of catching "perch," as they were called in southern Minnesota, was catching small 10 to 12 inchers as a kid and stringing them up right along with the bullheads we were fishing for on summer vacations. After I started fishing on my own, I went down to the Mississippi at the foot of Second Street in Moline and caught bigger fish and brought home some pretty impressive strings of "white perch," as they were called there.

Then after college and eventually moving to northern Ohio, I found the most impressive fishing for "sheepshead," as they were called on Lake Erie. They were very abundant and commonly five to eight pounds. But anglers on Lake Erie, with abundant walleye and yellow perch and smallmouth bass available, considered sheepshead a trash fish (only 100 miles south on the Scioto River near Columbus they were "white perch" which anglers fished for and kept).

I was generally like the other Lake Erie anglers who threw freshwater drum back, favoring walleye, yellow perch, or smallmouth. But I did bring some home several times and we used them to make a version of "poor man's lobster" that someone had told me about: fillet and cut into chunks, drop in boiling water for just a minute or so, take out before they start to flake apart and cool, and serve with cocktail sauce. We had our neighbors Tom and Sandy Weilnau over and sat around the table in our little red-farmhouse kitchen and we all liked the kind of chewy chunks. It wasn't lobster. But it was OK. It was good.

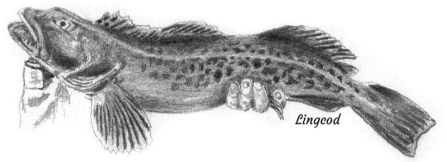

Lingcod

PART 2.
Temperate Saltwater Fishes

Chinook (King) Salmon

As I reflect on it, considering how relatively little I've fished for them, I have a disproportionate amount of special memories that revolve around chinook fishing. I guess it's because every chinook fishing experience I've had has been with special friends.

Before moving to Idaho in the mid-'80s I'd been aware of the unique runs of chinook that made it all the way to the inland state, with some fish migrating as far as 900 miles from the ocean. After arriving in Idaho, I found out that there was a sport fishery for hatchery-origin fish on the lower few miles of the Little Salmon River where it ran right next to Highway 95. Though runs were pretty low, the opportunity to catch a salmon created a combat fishery with anglers standing along the west riverbank right along the highway, nearly shoulder to shoulder, and having to synchronize their casts. Twenty hours per fish caught was considered a good catch rate. It wasn't something that interested me in the least. Then in 1992, with a big run of fish returning, a couple things made me re-consider Idaho salmon fishing. The main Salmon River was opened to fishing to provide more fishing opportunity and spread fishermen out. And a couple of buddies told me about crossing the Little Salmon at a private bridge that was closed to vehicles, then hiking a couple miles upriver and having the east river bank pretty much to themselves.

So I did fish the main Salmon, with Tracey Trent. We stayed in his camper which he left at a little campground several miles below Riggins. We did well anchoring his drift boat along a current seam and dropping back a Kwikfish with a herring fillet strapped to its belly with stretchy thread. It was not fast action by any means, but if we spotted fish porpoising below us heading upstream there was a good chance one of the rods would pull down a few minutes later.

My favorite remembrance of chinook fishing in Idaho was a late-May trip on the Little Salmon River in 2001 with Virgil. He had quickly become a close friend when I moved to Idaho. We worked together, sharing a lot of windshield and motel time together. And we played together. We just seemed to connect and always be on the same page. Virgil is one of my favorite fishing companions. He likes all kinds of fishing. He's good; I always learn from him. And his enthusiasm and obvious love of fishing is contagious and a joy to be around.

This day on the Little Salmon we'd done the thing crossing the river to the east side and hiking upstream a couple miles. We slid down a tall dirt bank downstream from a popular hole that had a line-up of fishermen casting into it from the opposite bank. The river was in high runoff and a ripping current raced down the opposite bank across from us. There was no one there. Right in front of us was some quieter water below the boulders that formed the lower end of the upstream pool. A perfect spot for a salmon to pause before charging up through the run of fast current.

I know some good salmon anglers. Laurie Janssen is probably the best. She really has the feel for it and always out-fishes everyone, including, much to his frustration, her husband Paul. My "feel" is when a snag pulls back I figure I've got a salmon. That's the way it was that morning with Virgil. We were drifting marble-sized balls of tuna wrapped in egg-sac cloth with a pencil-weight dropper about 18 inches above it. Either the weight or the tuna ball was constantly hanging up. It was generally on a rock, and we lost a lot of gear. But often enough when the drift stopped and the rod was slowly raised there would be a kind of "softness," maybe even a slight pull. The endorphin rush in that split second between when you realize it's a salmon and it realizes it's hooked and it explodes, is a rush that's addictive.

That day fishing with Virgil there was one small flat rock at the water's edge that we stood on. It offered the best drift through the best slot and we'd take turns standing there, switching after whoever was on the rock hooked a fish or broke off and had to re-rig. This type of fishing was as new to Virgil as it was to me and both of us seemed to get more excited and have more fun, whooping and hollering, as we caught more fish.

These weren't big salmon, maybe 12 to 14 pounds. They'd lost a good portion of their body weight since leaving saltwater. But they were powerful, and if they got out in the fast current they were practically unstoppable. After losing a few fish we adopted a mantra "Never let them look downstream!" and tried to keep them close to

Virgil limiting out on the Little Salmon.

our bank. It was all our gear could handle, and I ended up landing my last fish with half a rod, the top half above where it broke ending up down the line with the fish. Virgil had one more salmon to catch to get his four-fish limit and I thoroughly enjoyed just sitting back on the bank and watching him focus so intently on feeling his tuna ball down through the slot. It wasn't long before there was a quick snap up of his rod on a hook-set, a salmon circus that followed, and I netted his last fish.

After we managed to get ourselves and eight chinook up that steep dirt bank, which was no easy chore, we had two miles to hike to our vehicle. On subsequent trips we took backpacks, but at this point the best we came up with was to string the salmon on a pole and carrying it between us on our shoulders. It was quite a hike. Evidently it was quite a sight from the bank and the highway across the river too, based on the shouts from fishermen as we went by and the honks from vehicles going past on the highway. Now still, more than 25 years later, that trip and carrying those eight salmon strung on a pole between us often comes up in the conversation when Virgil and I get together.

Sitka, Alaska, is the point of origin for the majority of my memories of chinook fishing in saltwater. My first trip to Sitka was a late-April, 2005, trip that Steve Huffaker invited me on. Steve was the first person I fished with after I came to Idaho. He joined me on one of those first spring days to watch fishing rods propped on forked sticks and drown worms in the Snake River.

When Steve came by the house to offer his condolences a few days after Marge died, he told me about this trip he had coming up in a few weeks to fish with Art Schmidt from Sitka on his live-aboard boat and invited me to come along. Actually, invited is not the right word. He insisted. I was glad he did. I made a new friend in Art. We caught a lot of fish. And at night we drank a lot of whiskey, told stories, laughed a lot, and cried a little too.

A year later I returned to Sitka on a June trip, just a couple weeks before my retirement from Idaho Fish and Game. Several times I'd had conversations with Pete Hassemer, a Fish and Game colleague who worked on anadromous fish issues and a former resident of Sitka, about going somewhere and doing a hard-core salmon fishing trip. Pete still had connections in Sitka and an old friend of his had offered the use of his boat while he was away in June. Prime time for chinook fishing. Joining us on the trip was John Polenski, who worked for the National Marine Fisheries Service in Portland, and his son-in-law, Phil.

The trip was outstanding, one memorable event after another. The first one was returning to the floating cabin the first evening. We'd hastily unloaded things into the house and onto the outside deck before heading out to try and catch some rockfish for dinner. As we came back in and got close to the cabin, we saw that the lid was open on one of the two big coolers we'd left on the deck. For a minute or so we assumed we'd left the lid open. Then we got close enough to see egg shells, lettuce scraps, and plastic wrappers strewn about on the deck. What the hell?

When we got out on the deck we discovered the cooler was empty. It took a few minutes to figure this out. Peering in the water and seeing some food packaging scraps down on the bottom below the floating deck sealed it. Otters. The bastards! The other cooler with the lid still closed had some prized 15 year old Wisconsin cheddar that Pete's uncle had aged in his basement and sent him. We discovered it was also empty. The otters had just closed the lid on that one before they left.

I had not really known John Polenski before this trip. It didn't take long to see why colleagues of mine spoke so fondly of him. He had a great attitude about life and was so much fun to be with. We were there during the longest days of the year. That's really long in Alaska. We'd be heading out to the fishing grounds at four a.m. and John would reach for the bottle of McNaughton's whiskey he left on the galley table and take a big pull. He'd set it back down and ask rhetorically, "How you gonna drink all day if you don't start first thing in the morning."

Both John and Pete were experienced salmon anglers. We

were trolling and John had a particular set up for chinook that he believed in, and that is what he stuck with. I tied on a new-fangled flasher that I'd bought just before the trip. It had something new at the time called an "e-chip" and was touted to attract salmon and out-fish traditional flashers. I don't know if there is anything to that, but for some reason my rod caught the first three salmon. John was frustrated. I told John to grab my rod the next time a fish hit but he insisted his set up was tried and true and he'd catch his salmon with what he always used. He watched his rod intently. Any minute.

When John turned around at one point and took his eyes off of his rod I couldn't resist it. I shouted, "John…….." He snapped around and jerked his rod up out of the holder. Then I finished the sentenced with, "………there's still nothing happening on your rod." It took him a second to realize he didn't have a fish on. When he finally did, he just muttered under his breath. As I recall we limited out without John's rod contributing. That's just the way fishing can be, but he was frustrated. I actually got him two more times with "John…….."!

Our small cabin on the floating deck had a separate little structure that was a wood-burning sauna. It wasn't until our last evening, I think, that we fired it up. John and Pete and I sat in there and sweated and talked about fishing until we couldn't stand the heat. We stepped out onto the deck, quickly shined a flashlight over the edge into the water to check for jellyfish, then Pete and I dove into the cold ocean to cool off. John didn't take the plunge though. We went back in the sauna and John confided that he didn't jump in because he was afraid he might not be able to pull himself back up onto the dock.

OK he was carrying some extra weight, but Pete and I convinced him we'd get him up on the deck. I don't know how many times after that we repeated the cycle, with John joining us in the plunge, and all of us laughing, before we went into the cabin to call it a night. I had known it would be a great trip with Pete. Having John along and getting to know him made it special. I'm going to believe it was a special memory for him too. That fall Pete told me that John had been diagnosed with an aggressive form of cancer. John died the next year.

And one last Sitka story...

There is a group of guys who have been getting together in Sitka to fish for salmon for almost 20 years, and I've been able to be part of the group for most of the last ten years. The size of the group is set by the capacity of the resort: 30 beds and five "six-pack" boats (boats set up to accommodate six anglers). There is some shifting back and forth in the specific annual makeup of the group, but it is about as diverse a group as you could imagine. There is a district court judge, a tractor salesman, a symphony conductor, a high school principal, a proctologist, a convenience store owner, a chiropractor, a couple attorneys, some tech company guys, a state board of education administrator, a bar manager, state Fish and Game Directors, Fish and Wildlife Service administrators, and quite a few biologists. I've gotten to know and appreciate a diverse group of real characters over the years of fishing together and socializing at the lodge. I've managed to get both Colby and Clark in on a trip as part of the group.

The fishing consists of mooching with herring: six anglers spread out around a 32-foot custom walk-around boat repeatedly dropping a herring on a six-foot leader behind a sliding ball weight and then reeling it back in. When someone hooks up on a chinook, the fish often runs off a lot of line, sometimes going deep and sometimes going way out on the surface. It's pretty much unheard of to land a chinook at the same spot around the boat as where it was hooked – unless it just happens to end up there after a lap or two around the boat. It's pretty much chaos. A fish is hooked off the stern and heads toward the front of the boat with the angler following, squeezing past the other anglers, passing rods over or under each other to try and keep from getting tangled up, bending over the bow and passing the rod under or over the anchor line if we're at anchor, and on around the boat or right back the same way depending on the whims of the fish. Dan Diggs, a friend from Portland, seems to always get the wildest fish. But maybe it just seems that way – Dan gets very excited when he hooks a king, doing an animated narrative the whole time. I think Dan does have the record, though, with three laps around the boat before one exceptionally wild chinook was netted.

Watching that kind of excitement as other people hook and catch fish is a big part of the Sitka adventure. But I have to admit a fish that I just happened to catch generated my favorite memory. There is some minimal skill involved in catching fish like this I suppose, but the boat captain is the one who really makes it happen. In my opinion, Guch is the best and definitely my favorite captain to fish with. All five captains from the resort certainly work together, but Guch has more of a tendency to strike off on his own in the morning on a hunch and try for the home run. I like that. Guch knows the spots, finds the balls of bait fish that hold the salmon, keeps the boat in position, and watches the fish finder. He lets us know when he sees salmon and how deep they are. That's precisely

Colby, braced in front of the captain's cabin door, just
hanging on as a Sitka king peels off line.

what happened one calm misty day in 2008 when I was mooching off the starboard side right next to where Guch was sitting in the cabin in his captain's chair watching the fish finder. The fishing was kind of slow. The side slider-door was open and Guch and I had been talking, when Guch said kind of matter of factly to me, "There's a salmon down there at 70 feet that's about to take someone's bait."

It took mine.

Guch really prides himself in getting his fishermen into fish and is genuinely happy when we do. But he does this every day, all summer long. Nothing much was going on around the rest of the boat so Guch just stayed in his captain's chair and shouted back to his deckhand that I had a fish on and for him to come up front with the net. It didn't seem like a very big fish the way I was able to just bring it right straight up. Guch got up and stood in the side doorway and watched while the deckhand stood by the railing with the net. Then we saw the fish. It was huge.

The fish immediately dove deep, stripping off a lot of line. Guch jumped out of the cabin door, grabbed the net from the deckhand, and started excitedly coaching, "Let him run. Don't horse him. Keep the rod tip up. Keep the pressure on." The fish stayed deep and started going under the boat to the other side. I shuffled up to the bow, passed the rod under the anchor rope and started down the other side following the fish with Guch shouting to the other guys, "Reel up, reel up. Move, move, move," as I squeezed by to the back of the boat. The fish never did make a run out away from the boat. It took a while but I got him back up. Guch was poised and ready, leaning over the rail with the net when the fish got to the surface. Guch made a jab and got part of the fish in the net, but not enough. The fish flipped out and took off. Guch cussed a little. Luckily the hook in the fish's jaw hadn't caught in the net and pulled out of the fish, and I got it back to the boat pretty easily. The fish presented itself better and Guch made a perfect scoop. When he managed to get the net and fish up and over the railing he turned to me and just stood there with a big grin. He was happier than I was. It was the biggest chinook he'd ever gotten on his boat.

Of course I had my picture taken with the fish, but the picture I have of Guch with that 48-pound chinook is the best. It brings a smile to my face whenever I look at it. Almost as big a smile as the one on Guch's face.

Guch (right) and his deckhand were all smiles after getting the big king aboard.

Besides the pictures, I've got a keepsake of that experience. It's a cook book put together by the resort cook, Mama Kate, which I bought before we flew out. She'd been there at our last night's dinner when it was announced that the 48-pounder won the big chinook derby that the group does every year, and was also the biggest one caught out of the lodge so far that season. It wasn't until I got home and opened the book that I saw an inscription she had written: "Big Al! Whoever says size doesn't matter...didn't catch the big fish!"

And a sweet footnote to that story: that "boat record" for Guch was broken a couple years later when he invited his dad up to Sitka for a visit and some fishing – and his dad caught a 55-pound chinook!

Coho (Silver) Salmon

Coho, while not achieving the size and bull power of king salmon, more than make up for it with their eagerness to hit and their wild and crazy antics once they're hooked. They are a mainstay of the great memories I've accrued fishing with the gang at Sitka. Trolling for them out of my own boat with Margie out of Port Hardy at the north end of Vancouver Island, and years later with Sue off La Push, Washington, have left some wonderful memories as well. Things like cranking up the cannonball and having a coho locked to it as it came up, staring at a chrome patch on the ball from a couple inches away until the ball finally broke the surface. Or dropping a herring and flasher over the side and starting to explain to Sue the fine points of trolling like how far back from the boat the bait needs to be before you clip the line to the cannonball and lower it, only to be interrupted by a coho taking the lure on the surface next to the boat and ripping the line out of my hand.

And coho have been the catalyst for some truly wonderful times on Alaskan float trips. It is an unforgettable experience to be dropped off on the upper end of a river 100 miles from nowhere and spending 10 days floating and fishing, catching acrobatic coho with good friends and the occasional grizzly or moose or caribou. The coho fishing can be just crazy good.

The best of those times was a trip down the Kwethluk River with Colby and Clark. Doing an Alaskan float trip with my two sons had been on my bucket list, and we finally put it together in 2012. I can't describe how special it was to share an experience like that with my sons. For someone who's a parent themselves, there's no need to try.

The coho fishing actually wasn't great on that trip. Until the last day. It had been raining for days before Steve, at Papa Bear Adventures flew us out of Bethel up to the upper end of the river to start the trip. The river was high and off-color, but just starting to drop. It had come down quite a bit by the last day of our trip and we were hooking fish here and there as we floated toward the pick-up point. We were pulled over fishing the lower end of a side channel when we heard a power boat coming up the river. We hadn't seen a human let alone a power boat since Steve dropped us off 10 days earlier. The boat dropped down off plane and idled over. In it were three guys that manned a salmon weir we'd floated over back upstream. The guy driving asked if we were trying to catch silvers. I said yea, we're trying. He suggested we head downstream to an old oxbow. He said it was full of silvers, we'd catch one on every cast.

We fished our way downstream, casting into every quiet side water we passed without much action. I was beginning to wonder if we could've floated past the spot. But when we got to it there was no mistaking it. I don't remember whether it was Clark or Colby who pointed it out as we approached a quiet marshy channel off the main current. All through the flooded grass and across much of the open water there was movement – salmon dorsal fins and tails cutting the surface everywhere. I worked the raft so Colby and Clark could fish. Colby was using a fly rod with a big streamer and Clark was using a spinning rod casting a Pixie spoon. And the guy was right. It was a fish on every cast. At first, whole pods of coho would charge a lure, creating converging wakes in the shallow water that culminated in a big boil. On hook sets the shallow water would explode. Eventually the pod of fish started spooking and began to disperse a little. At one

The boys, Clark (left) and Colby, with a new-dime-bright coho on the Kwethluk River.

point a wall of salmon pushing a wave in front of them charged past the raft headed for the main river. But the boys continued to catch coho after coho until I reluctantly said we had to head downstream to get to the pick-up point in time. Colby might have taken the oars for a while to let me fish, but most of the time I just enjoyed keeping the raft in position and getting ahold of salmon to unhook them for Colby and Clark. That was a full time job – the best job I ever had.

My most cherished memory of a specific coho, though, is Margie's fish. Margie caught a fair number of coho on various trips, but the very first coho that she ever caught was on a trip to Ketchikan. It was one she never forgot and neither will I.

The whole trip was wonderful. It was the first adventure like that we'd ever had, staying at a place called Silver King Lodge on an island up the coast from Ketchikan. We saw whales and otters and eagles, and pink salmon jumping at a falls. And we caught lots of fish. Dan Herrig and Dan Diggs were with us, and we fished on our own out of open, low-sided, 15-foot Livingston boats (kind of Boston Whaler wanna-be's), with Marge and I in one and Dan and Dan in another. The owner of the lodge wasn't the most helpful in offering advice on spots and techniques, but the cook was married to a local fisherman and she dialed us in: a hoochie with double slider hooks baited with the length-wise half of a herring fillet, 18 inches behind a flasher, with a two-ounce banana weight ahead of the flasher. The spot was an underwater "wall" across an inside passage that created an upwelling and concentration of bait. The pink salmon were thick. That's what we were catching. They weren't big, maybe three pounds, but they were scrappy and lots of fun.

On our next to the last day we were fishing the wall and already had several pinks in the boat. Then Marge hooked up and it obviously wasn't a pink. It peeled line off her reel making a fast run out from the boat, then abruptly turned 180 and came right for the boat. I was telling Marge to reel fast. She was sitting on the front seat looking down at her reel when the coho jumped right next to her, as high as her head. I saw the whole thing, this beautiful salmon, bright as a dime, hanging for a split second next to Margie. She saw enough of it to squeal. The fish continued to go co-ho-crazy darting from one end or side of the boat to the other. Dan and Dan were close enough to watch the whole thing and cheered when we got it in the net. I've got a perma-nent mental picture of that coho hanging in the air. And I've got a photograph that I'll cherish al-ways of Margie with a huge smile sitting in that little boat holding up that bright coho.

Marge and her acrobatic coho.

Sockeye Salmon

With sockeye not much interested in eating herring or taking salm-on lures, I've never caught one while fishing for salmon in saltwater. It's no better once they start their spawning run up freshwater rivers. But in the course of floating rivers in Alaska I've seen a lot of sockeye spawning aggregations and always make a cast at them. Hutch and I were working up a side channel/slough off the Kwethluk River in Alaska with our fly rods when we came upon a pod of sockeye. I had an egg-sucking leach on and cast it into them, let it sink, and caught an Arctic char that was there gobbling up sockeye eggs. Bill, always positive and always full of BS, cast into the bunch of sockeye and immediately started to retrieve. I really don't remember what Bill had on his line, but I was surprised to see one of the sockeye turn and take it. The fish was pretty well worn out after the rigors of migrating and spawning and it came in not unlike a wet towel. But it was the first one I'd ever seen caught. And not at all unlike Bill, as he unhooked and released the fish he said, "There, that's how you do it Van Vooren."

On a later trip on the Kwethluk with Virgil and his son-in-law Josh and friend Nate, we actually all caught several sockeye. Nearly all were the more aggressive males, with their bright red hump-backed bodies and green heads with the bizarre looking big kipe (the big hook-shaped form their upper jaw takes during spawning season). They are worth a picture.

Pink Salmon

The first pink salmon I caught stands out from the many that followed. I was in Anchorage for a summer meeting, rented a car afterward, and drove down the Kenai Peninsula to see the country and try some fishing. Someone in Anchorage had suggested I try the

A male pink salmon from the Kasilof River that
has transformed into a "humpie" during spawning.

173

Kasilof River. There was good access and there were some coho running up the river. It was pretty memorable for one of my first trips to Alaska. I shared a campsite with a cow moose one evening. I shared the river bank with a black bear one morning. And something big took the white clouser minnow I was working with my fly rod. When I finally beached it I saw that instead of a coho it was a male pink with the long hooked jaw and huge misshapen spawning hump.

Humpies, as pinks are often called, are rather disdained when salmon fishing out of Sitka, kept only to be used for halibut bait. But they have been the target and basis for some great times fishing and catching them with Marge, and Paul and Laurie Janssen, at Port Hardy on the outer tip of Vancouver Island. My first trip there was my first experience of self-outfitted fishing for salmon in saltwater. Some days Marge and I fished with Paul and Laurie in their boat and some days Marge and I fished out of our boat. We caught some coho and a few chinook, but the smaller pinks were the constant action and so much fun to catch.

We did some other things. Marge really liked crabbing. And she enjoyed seeing whales and sea lions and all that comes with being around the ocean. But it was cool, and it was misty, and the water got a little rough at times. I always felt a little guilty taking Marge on vacations that revolved around fishing.

On our last day of that trip I figured we could fish until noon before we had to pack up and start the five-hour drive down the island to catch the ferry at Nanaimo. But I woke up at daylight to the sound of steady rain hitting the tent. It had already been a great trip, and I wasn't going to ask Marge to go out and fish in the rain. I was lying there on my cot just thinking about how good the trip had been when I heard Marge say from her cot, "Well we better get moving if we're going to get any more fishing done."

Paul sent me a framed picture after Margie passed away that he had taken of Marge and me from his boat that morning. I'm at the back of our boat doing something with one of the rods. Margie is at the steering wheel driving the boat, kind of hunched over. Her head is turned slightly toward the camera, and under the hood of her wet raincoat you can see a smile on her face.

Chum (Dog) Salmon

Chum salmon is not a fish that I or many people would specifically fish for (other than native Alaskans putting up a supply of food for their dogs). I haven't caught many, and the one that provides the clearest memory for me was the first one I caught.

I was fishing with Marge on the trip to Ketchikan. It was early in the trip, before the cook dialed us in, and Marge and I were trolling along the north side of a bay that had a stream coming in at the upper end. There were lots of pinks staging. I was fishing with the fiberglass casting rod that Margie's dad had made. It had his name, Warren Lilgegren, inscribed on it. I hooked a good-sized fish that fought well and, though I'd never caught a chum before, when we got the fish in the boat the characteristic vertical bars were unmistakable.

What I remember most about the experience, though, was Marge hooking a fish after we took off trolling again, me propping her dad's rod – with the line still out – against the seat next to me while I reached forward for the net, and the sound of that rod hitting the water when a fish pulled it overboard. I was sick. I even talked with someone at the lodge about hiring a diver to look for it, but realistically with a salmon on the line we decided it could've been anywhere. There was nothing to be done.

Over the years I've lost a number of fishing rods. Some were pretty expensive rods. But the only one that mattered was the one that Margie's dad made, and she inherited when he died the year before we were married.

Halibut

I've got fond memories of fishing for halibut on trips out of several Alaska ports. I always love the anticipation and not knowing whether you'll hook a "chicken" (the good-eating 10 to 20 pound fish) or a big "barn door."

My favorite incident of catching halibut is from a trip with Dan Herrig to the little town of Coffman Cove on the north end of Prince of Wales Island. Dan and I had been on a lot of great adventures and had made some wonderful memories together. A passion we share, bowhunting, has taken us to the tundra of Alaska, peaks of the Idaho high country, sage brush deserts, and Midwest river bottoms. We've shared a tent more nights than I can count.

At some point, probably in a tent or on the road, Dan and I got it in our heads to go on a serious do-it-yourself saltwater fishing trip. Several people suggested that Prince of Whales was the place to go. We ended up going to Coffman Cove after doing some on-line research and making some phone calls. The whole stay in this tiny village was a unique experience. Our host, Barb, owned and operated the town liquor store and market, which had an apartment of sorts in the back. That's where we stayed. Barb told us to help ourselves to whatever we'd like from the store if it was closed and she wasn't there; just keep track and let her know at the end of our stay (we had a king's meal one evening after fresh shrimp and oysters appeared in the store cooler case).

Barb also owned a 14-foot open aluminum boat with, as I recall, something like a 25-horsepower outboard on it. That's what we fished out of. The boat worked fine in the protected inside waters around Coffman Cove and we caught some silvers and pinks and a little bit of a lot of things, including quite a few weird looking bottom fish that neither of us had ever seen before. At the time, neither of us had ever caught a halibut either. Barb set us up for that. Neither Dan nor I owned a halibut rod at the time so Barb loaned us the halibut rods we used. She also provided a harpoon. She said if we hooked a big halibut, the last thing we would want would be to have it thrashing around in the 14-foot boat with us and our gear. The harpoon had a detachable point with a length of rope tied to it and a very big round orange rubber buoy tied to the other end of the rope. The idea was once we got the halibut up and alongside the boat, we would throw the harpoon, preferably hitting the fish in the head, and drive the point all the way through. The fish goes wild and pulls the point, with the rope attached, off the harpoon shaft, thus stringing itself up. And be ready to throw the buoy over.

One calm morning we went out a little deeper than we had been fishing to a spot that Barb suggested we ought to try for halibut. It was a great morning. The water was like glass and the tide was slack. We pretty much held in place bouncing heavy jigs baited with strips of salmon belly on the bottom. The action wasn't fast. There wasn't any at first.

But we were entertained watching whales blowing and breaching, and at one point witnessed some whale group-feeding behavior I'd only read about. It was dead quiet. We were watching across the smooth, dark ocean surface for spouts and more whales breaching. All of a sudden, less than 200 yards away, the ocean burst open and four whales, belly to belly, shot straight up over half way out of the water, then simultaneously fell backward in a huge white splash. From the depths, the whales had cooperatively created a vortex of rising bubbles to concentrate krill, then simultaneously shot up thru the vortex with mouths open, scooping in krill. It was spectacular. But it was also a little unnerving, sitting that close in our little open boat. It was also unnerving when one of the whales reappeared and swam right at us on the surface. He went under about half way to us, but he didn't breach like they do when they dive deep. He just slipped under while still swimming our direction. It took a while after that to re-focus on fishing.

We hadn't caught anything yet or had even a bite, when I felt a few light pecks on the salmon belly. I figured it must be a rockfish or something small. If the halibut weren't going to cooperate I wanted to at least catch something, so I cranked up the big halibut jig real fast and dropped down a 7/8 ounce jigging spoon. It was tied to 40-pound test super line on the light rod that I had been using to fish for rockfish. It took a long time to reach bottom. As soon as it did I started jigging it with a short quick lift, then letting it flutter back to the bottom. I don't recall how many times I made the quick lift – not many – before I tried it and the jig wouldn't move. It was solid. Figuring that I was hung up on a rock I snapped the line a few times trying to free it. Still solid. Then I just pulled hard to try and break it free. That's when it moved.

Oh my! I had hooked something really big. And with that light rod I was definitely not in charge. The next half hour or forty-five minutes or hour – I really don't remember anymore how long it was – was exciting. I remember that at one point I was actually shaking. I was just putting as much pressure on as I could and hanging on. The fish would come up off the bottom a ways, I'd gain a little line, and then it would go back down taking out the line I'd just gained. There was nothing I could do about it. But Dan and I had nothing but time. After a while the fish tired a little pulling against what pressure I dared put on it and started coming up a little further off bottom before abruptly diving back down, stripping off line against the drag. Eventually I did get it to the surface. Big isn't an appro-

priate adjective. I was comparing it to the size of the boat. The halibut was surprisingly docile stretched out alongside the boat. Until Dan hit it with the harpoon that is. It exploded and dove and Dan threw the big buoy over. Dan had hit it in the head per- fectly. When the fish got to the end of the line the buoy partially went un- der then came back to the surface. We watched the buoy

We were glad when Dan caught a good eating-size halibut, but even this one raised hell in the bottom of our little boat.

178

for a few minutes. It jerked and bobbed only a short while before it was still. We motored over to the buoy and Dan pulled it into the boat, then hauled up the rope and the fish. The fish was basically done for. I was still hanging onto the rod through all this, the lure still in the fish's jaw. I remember vividly that at one point after Dan hauled the harpooned halibut up to the side of the boat he let loose of the rope to grab something and the fish started sinking backwards. I panicked watching the dead weight of the sinking halibut pull line off the reel before I thought to grab the rope.

Barb had been right. Looking at all 4 and 1/2 feet and 80 pounds of that halibut there was no way we would've wanted it in the boat with us alive. And we saw no reason at that point to have it in the boat dead. We tied the rope off near the bow with the fish's head pulled partway up out of the water, and looped another rope around the tail and snubbed it off back by the stern with the fish's tail pulled up out of the water.

We stayed out and kept fishing and Dan caught a nice 15 to 20-pound halibut, the perfect size for eating. I harpooned it for Dan, repeating the drill. Except that when we pulled the "done-for" fish back to the boat with the rope we evidently thought he wasn't that big (relatively speaking maybe) and we pulled him up over the side and onto the bottom of the boat. He wasn't done for. He made enough flops and thrashes to throw gear around and make us scramble….and appreciate that we hadn't tried that with the first one.

Arrowtooth Flounder (Turbot)

On that same trip to Coffman Cove with Dan we caught several arrowtooth flounder, which Barb and others call turbot. Dan and I didn't know what they were. We were bottom fishing for rockfish when we caught them, and at first we thought they were small halibut, only a couple feet long. They kind of looked like a baby halibut, except their head was more pointed and they had longer, more pronounced teeth.

When we described the fish to Barb, she told us what it was that we'd caught, and that turbot weren't very good to eat. We had to judge for ourselves though, and brought one in and cooked it up. Barb was right.

Interestingly, I've since learned that there is something in the flesh of turbot that causes it to break down and get mushy when cooked, but that turbot is excellent as sushi.

Starry Flounder • Rock Sole

Dan and I caught these fish while we were rather randomly bottom fishing with smaller bait-tipped lures around Coffman Cove. I've caught sole in other places as well, and I think they are just fine to eat. But when you're hoping for a rockfish of several pounds, or something bigger, it's never been all that tempting to keep these small flatfish. There's really nothing very remarkable about these little guys.

Great Sculpin

During the course of my job I'd captured and handled quite a few sculpin. They are a pretty cool fish. The few species I had captured pulling a short seine net down through gravelly riffles in freshwater streams were all just a few inches long, big headed, with big pectoral fins. They lie motionless on clean gravel bottoms, and with their dark, mottled coloration they are essentially invisible – a perfect example of the old adage among hunters, "stillness is the best camouflage." The only chance of seeing a sculpin is if you happen to catch their occasional dart – almost a hop – to a new position. They are an "indicator species", only found in the best quality streams.

So at the time I never dreamed I would ever catch a sculpin hook and line. But I'd never heard of the "great sculpin."

Along with the other odd fish I caught for the first time fishing around Coffman Cove with Dan, I caught a sculpin about 10 inches long. It looked pretty much just like the little sculpin I knew, with the big head and big pectoral fins. It wasn't until I compared the picture I took to photos in reference books that I determined I had indeed caught (actually snagged on the top of the head with a jigging spoon bounced off the bottom) a saltwater "great sculpin."

Ratfish

I caught a ratfish up at Sitka, and as with a lot of the different kinds of fish I've pulled up off the bottom of the ocean for the first time, I had to ask what it was. It was one of the weirdest looking fish I've ever caught. When Guch said that the fish, about 14 inches long, was a ratfish I remember thinking what a perfect name. Its head and pointed snout looked so much like a rat's, and it had a long narrow rat-like tail.

Spiny Dogfish

Marge caught the first dogfish (not to be confused with the fresh-water bowfin which is commonly called dogfish also) I'd ever seen on the fishing trip to Silver King Lodge north of Ketchikan with Dan Herrig and Dan Diggs. Marge and I were trolling for salmon with

Marge showing off the first dogfish we caught, when it was still quite novel.

flashers and hoochies on the outside of the island when she hooked it. It was the biggest thing we'd hooked so far on the trip and it was a pretty exciting fight. Then we saw it, two and a half to maybe three feet long. I didn't identify it as a spiny dogfish. All I knew was it was a shark! Cool. I got enough of it in the net to get it in the boat. The Dans were off fishing somewhere else and I remember thinking they wouldn't believe this, catching a shark. We took lots of pictures and released it.

We started trolling again and it wasn't long before one of us, I don't remember who, hooked another big fish but it got off after just a brief fight. When the line came in there was the flasher but there was only a leader behind it. The hooks and hoochie were gone. I tied a new leader – with hooks and a new hoochie – to the flasher and let it back out. Before long the same thing happened again. The fish might have stayed on a little longer, I don't remember. Looking at the end of the hookless and hoochie-less leader I could see that it hadn't broken at the knot. It had been cut.

We each got other dogfish all the way in, but we continued to lose quite a few hoochies to dogfish, and didn't catch a single salmon. The "sharks" ceased to be so cool and we decided it was time to move to a new area.

Lingcod

I think ling cod are a great fish. They are aggressive predators, powerful fighters, they are wonderful eating, and they get really big. My first encounter with ling cod left quite an impression.

Colby started at Oregon State in 1992. Our visits during spring break led to adventures on the Oregon Coast, just another hour west of Corvallis, which led to going out fishing on the "head boats" out of Newport and De Poe Bay. It was on my first trip out on one of these charters, where as many as 15 or 20 anglers pay a flat fee for five hours of bottom fishing, that I was introduced to ling cod. The boat supplied the equipment which consisted of a stout rod and reel, a heavy weight to get the line to the bottom, and two or three red shrimp flies tied a foot apart above the weight. Working the weight up and down bouncing along the bottom, we were catching assorted rockfish, none of which were very big. Then someone down the railing from me yelled to the deckhand that he had something big on. His stout rod was bent over pointing straight down. I remember the deckhand or captain quickly telling the guy not to pull too hard; just start slowly and steadily reeling in line. Several of us scooted closer along the rail to watch. It took a while, but he got the foot-long fish he had initially hooked (which I later learned was a kelp greenling) up close enough to the surface that we were able to see it was crosswise in the huge toothy jaws of a ling cod maybe 30 inches long. The hook wasn't in the ling cod at all, but the ling cod wasn't letting go of the smaller fish. The deckhand stood poised with a long-handled dip net and coached the angler to just reel steadily. When the ling cod got close enough to the surface the deckhand quickly plunged the net in the water and scooped up both fish. Impressive.

Since then I've caught some ling cod that way myself fishing for other things. But if the goal is to catch ling cod that method is a bit random, so from that time on I've always taken my own gear and a couple packages of frozen herring when I fish off of the head boats on the Oregon coast. And it has always paid off. I remember one trip in particular out of Newport with Colby and Clark on a flat calm day. The three of us took over the bow so to speak and using our own gear to mooch herring we each handily

Jason Gengerke and his lingcod with the gaping mouth.

183

caught our two-fish limits of ling cod and supplied ling cod for a lot of the people jigging shrimp flies in the back of the boat. Clark in particular had a little swagger in his walk when we got back to the dock.

Ling cod still excite me. In Sitka we catch some huge ones. The year Tom Gengerke from Iowa and his son Jason joined the group they each caught ling cod so big you could shove a soccer ball into the fish's mouth. Fishing out of Port Hardy in 2005 with Paul and Laurie in their boat we found some deep rocky drop-offs near the south end of the Echo Islands where we caught several four-foot long ling cod. We hooked some monsters we couldn't move that had just buried themselves in the rocks. When I retired from Idaho Fish and Game in 2006, Dale Allen and Paul, the fish management team out of McCall, and both fishing companions of mine, presented me with a beautiful custom heavy-duty rod and a very nice heavy-duty Shimano bait casting reel. Paul had made the rod. He had inscribed on it "Al's Ling Zinger."

While you don't catch huge ling cod off the Oregon coast because of the more intense sport and commercial harvest there, without a doubt my most remarkable ling cod fishing experience was a trip I took with Paul to Newport. Paul loved fishing for ling cod as much as I did, and we'd been told the bigger fish moved in shallow in the fall. We talked about how great it would be to be able to go out and fish on our own, without watching the clock and counting down the time left in a five-hour trip on a head boat. So one October we pulled Paul's 19-foot StarCraft loaded with fishing gear to the Oregon coast.

The weather wasn't very cooperative. A front had rolled in with rain and wind, too much wind to motor out on the open ocean in Paul's boat. So we killed some time. We took the boat down to Alsea Bay at Waldport where there was some protection from the wind and did some crabbing one day. The next day the sky brightened some and the wind seemed to slack up a little. There was still a small craft advisory flag flying at the Coast Guard station in Newport harbor, but sitting in the truck at the break-wall watching the swells come in over the bar at the mouth of the harbor, Paul said he thought we'd be OK. So we loaded up gear, launched the boat, and headed out the harbor entrance. And we were OK. It took a while, but we made it out past the big swells at the bar. About the time we thought we had it made, though, we realized that two much bigger boats that had been sitting close together maybe half a mile further out were Coast Guard vessels, and one of them was under power now and was headed for us. We continued to idle out, but I think we knew what was coming. The boat pulled up to within shouting distance and a "Coastie" came to the rail. I don't recall whether he shouted or used a loud speaker, but I clearly heard and remember his words: "There is a small craft advisory in effect. The bar is closed to vessels under 26 feet." And then, about as rhetorically as it gets, he looked over (and down) at us sitting there in Paul's 19-foot boat and asked, "How long is your vessel?" I don't think we even answered the question, we just shouted OK and started to ease our way back in.

Back in our motel Paul started calling fishing charter's to try and get us set up to go out fishing the next day. But it was a weekday in October, not the best weather, and business was very slow. The first two or three told him they needed a certain minimum number of clients to go out and they doubted they would even get close. Then Paul called a charter further up the river on the Newport waterfront that neither of us had ever gone out with, and after hesitating a bit the guy said that sure, they'd take us out fishing.

Typically when you arrive at one of these charter operations at the allotted time in the morning the boat is sitting there at the dock idling and ready to go, but the guy in the small dockside office, the owner of the business, told us the boat was coming down the river. He said Paul and I were the only fishermen going and we should take our stuff and head out to the end of a long dock where the boat would pick us up. I think I asked rather than him volunteering it, but he explained that the boat and crew had spent the night on the boat anchored up-river. Seemed odd.

When the boat pulled up there were two other crew members on board besides the captain. On the way out of the river Paul or I told the captain that we were primarily interested in fishing for ling cod, so he headed to the rock piles south of town. The whole crew was super friendly and even fished right along with us. We caught ling cod and had a great time. We had gone through the herring we'd brought about the time Paul and I figured it was time to head in anyway, but the captain said they had herring we could use, and asked if we'd like to stay out longer. So we did. Quite a while longer.

When we finally headed in at the end of the day and approached the large complex of docks and boat slips extending well out from shore, I noticed a big guy standing alone out on the farthest end of one of the docks watching the boat as we idled past. I remember it seemed a little odd to me at the time. When we got deeper into the complex of docks the captain pivoted the boat and started to back into the slip right in front of the little office. I noticed some guys standing around, guys that seemed just a little different from the ones in brown knee boots you typically see standing around ocean harbor docks.

As the captain backed the boat up closer to the dock his crew were in the back holding the stern lines. The "un-maritime" type guys on the dock moved toward the boat. The crew threw the stern lines to a couple of brown knee boot guys on the dock who worked for the charter business. That's when the chaos began. As soon as there was a move to secure one of the lines onto a cleat there was a big guy there trying to take the rope away. At the same time two other guys jumped on the boat, repeatedly shouting, "Off the (I'm sure there was an expletive) boat." We were so surprised and confused, I'm pretty sure we were actually off the boat and onto the dock before Paul or I said we were just guys who had paid to go out fishing and we needed to get our gear. At any rate I remember I was on the boat when I saw the guy pull out the knife and start sawing on the stern line as a brown knee boots guy was trying to tie it off. And there were two guys up in the cabin trying to shove the captain out but he was fighting back. There was lots of yelling. Then it was only the captain and the two other guys shoving him around that were left on the boat. And then the boat was under power and heading out through the docks.

It hadn't been out of sight too long when the police showed up.

Seems the fishing charter company didn't actually own the boat, but rather was leasing it. The boat engines needed to be rebuilt or replaced, but the owner didn't take care of it so the charter business had it done and paid for it. Then the owner wanted to take back the boat but he didn't want to reimburse the charter company for the engine work. Evidently the owner had been demanding the boat be turned over to him for some time and the charter operator had been demanding reimbursement. I guess the boat owner figured that big guys with knives come cheaper than attorneys.

I've kept fishing logs for decades and over the years I've recorded some interesting things. But that trip fishing for ling cod with Paul is the only one where kidnapping charges were involved and I've had to give written testimony.

Pacific Cod

The only Pacific cod I've ever caught was on the trip with Dan up to Prince of Wales Island. At some point during our stay our host Barb asked us if we'd like to ride along with her in her truck down to Thorne Bay. She needed to pick up her fishing boat that had been being worked on down there. She offered to take us out fishing for the day at some spots she knew and then we could drive her truck back to Coffman Cove while she ran the boat back. We couldn't turn that down.

We did catch a small halibut or two and some salmon that day. At one point Barb pulled the boat up close to the narrow tip of a small island that had some tidal current moving past it. She said it was a good halibut spot. I don't remember anymore what we had on, but it would've been something to catch halibut with. Instead of halibut though, Dan and I both caught cod. They were decent sized fish, maybe six to eight pounds, and had that characteristic single little barbell sticking down from their lower jaw.

Barb's boat tied up in front of a truly unique Alaskan floating restaurant.

There wasn't much more to remember about catching the cod, but the day was very unique for several other reasons. For one, Barb was someone who is just always happy, always positive, and just really fun to spend a day with. She wasn't young and she wasn't old. She wasn't particularly attractive but she was a beautiful person. We heard a lot of stories that day about living in a very small island community in Alaska.

For lunch she took Dan and I to a floating "restaurant." It was essentially a floating shack, the roof partially covered in blue tarps, up in a cove near town. A couple of old "hippies" that loved to cook, tell stories, and laugh lived with their pet Vietnamese pig on this floating platform of logs and plywood (I asked; they claimed the pig was "pig-box" trained). I don't remember their names anymore. He was a big guy with a ponytail and most of the stories; she was blond, rather petite, and very nice. They prepared us a wonderful meal with several courses of fresh sea food and some sweet corn, visiting with us the whole time as if we were having dinner with old friends in their home. When it was time for us to leave either Dan or I asked what we owed them. The guy said that they didn't charge anything for the meals, but we could leave some money if we liked – whatever we thought it was worth. We had a great meal and a wonderful time, and they certainly made out all right financially (with nothing to report to the IRS). They helped us untie and shove the boat off, and waved as we headed back out the bay. What a unique experience.

Kelp Greenling

These fish are never very plentiful, but I've nearly always caught one or two any time I've gone bottom fishing for rockfish, particularly in the shallower areas. They are never very big; 20 inches is a good sized one. But they are pretty cool fish that come in an array of colors and spotting patterns. The females have fairly uniformly distributed reddish to golden spotting and yellow fins, while the males have fewer but larger bright blue blotches concentrated on the front half of their olive-brown body. I like them for a couple of reasons: unlike everything else you commonly catch bottom fishing for rockfish, they don't have any spines; and ling cod love to eat 'em.

Yelloweye Rockfish

The rest of the bottom rockfish that I've caught can easily be lumped into one collected set of memories, but the yelloweye rockfish is different, with its own set of unique memories. For one, they are such a gorgeous fish, uniformly a deep-orange-colored body with big bright yellow eyes. I've caught them along with other bottom rockfish up at Sitka, but not very often. They prefer deeper water and I've most often caught them fishing deep for halibut. Yelloweye get much bigger than other bottom rockfish. And they fight hard. If I caught a lot of them I suppose I'd know the difference when I hooked a yelloweye instead of a halibut, but many have been halibut big and they fought pretty much like a halibut. So my memory of catching yelloweye is the surprise when I see a bright-orange fish coming up instead of the mottled brown one I expected.

Once again though, my clearest and favorite memory of catching a specific yelloweye is of one someone else caught – the one that Paul Janssen caught on his way to Japan. It was on one of the trips to Port Hardy when Marge and I met up with and camped with Paul and Laurie. Marge and I fished out of our boat and Paul and Laurie out of theirs. One day when it was pretty flat we had run north together out through Browning passage to Hunt Rock, off the north side of Nigei Island out at the mouth of the Gordon Channel. It was a great place to cast for big pelagic black rockfish, but I was always a little nervous out there in my 16-foot boat. If the earth was flat, you could see Japan from there.

We did catch some nice three to four-pound black rockfish. But after a while Paul hollered over that he was going to try something different and head out deeper to try bottom fishing. I wasn't going out any further in my smaller boat so we stayed put. Paul got out far enough that his 19-foot Starcraft was a mere dark spot on the horizon. He was out there for a very long time before I noticed him heading in. He idled up to us, reached down, and held up what I think at the time was the first yelloweye I'd ever seen. And it was the biggest I've ever seen, about 15 pounds. Paul was all smiles. Laurie wasn't smiling.

I don't remember whether we heard the story then, floating in our boats next to each other, or whether it was back at the ramp. But it seems that at some point out there a warning buzzer on Paul's boat started going off indicating that the reservoir that feeds oil into the gas to run the outboard had very little oil left in it. At a 50:1 mixture, that reservoir full of oil will let you run a lot of hours. But at some point you have to add oil. With all the running Paul had been doing with his boat he had just forgot (I've done the same thing... on small bodies of water) and he didn't have any extra oil onboard.

Now an outboard will run a while without oil. Not all that far though, and your motor will be totaled. Paul is very much a MacGyver kind of guy. He never seems to get too excited or panic when a challenge presents itself. But he and Laurie were out there by themselves, the boat drifting further out to sea. So what did Paul do? He kept on fishing.

I really don't remember whether he said he caught the big yelloweye before this little emergency or whether it was while they were on their slow drift to Japan, but eventually another boat came in sight and ran close enough for Paul to get their attention. That guy did have extra oil onboard. He gave Paul enough oil to run the boat back into Port Hardy, and to stop and show us his big yelloweye on the way.

Other Bottom Rockfish:
Irish Lord • Cabezon • Copper Rockfish
Canary Rockfish • Vermillion Rockfish
China Rockfish • Quillback Rockfish
Tiger Rockfish

These are the other bottom rockfish that I know I've caught. There are a lot of different kinds (Washington Fish and Wildlife lists 33 different species that occur off their coast). They are all different with their unique colors and spots and stripes and fins. But they are also all the same – generally a couple pounds or less and seemingly all head with a big mouth and lots of spines that will get you if you're not careful. Over the years, with the help of boat captains and deckhands, I've gotten to the point I can pretty much identify what I catch. But I still occasionally get stuck by a spine.

An Irish lord, just one of many odd-looking bottom fish caught in north Pacific waters.

Bottom rockfish were the constant on so many of the fishing trips with Marge and Colby and Clark off the Oregon coast. We first started going there in the early '90s when Colby began college at Oregon State. We had so many fun days together catching bottom rockfish, never knowing what kind it was going to be until we got them in. Our favorite place to fish for them was out of De Poe Bay, where it's a short run to a lot of good rock piles. Rather than go out on the big charter boat that operates out of the bay we would go out with one of the smaller charters. It was a more personal experience. And the boat reminded me a lot of the one Jack Nicholson drove under the bridge and out of De Poe Bay in "One Flew Over the Cuckoo's Nest."

Pelagic Rockfish:
Black Rockfish • Bocaccio • Dusky Rockfish Yellowtail Rockfish • Blue Rockfish

I don't know why these pelagic rockfish are called rockfish. They don't have any of the colors and spots and stripes or the body shape of bottom rockfish. They look like a solid-colored largemouth bass in varied shades of black, blue-black, grey or brown. But they've been a part of nearly all my northwest ocean fishing trips. And similar to my experience with bottom rockfish, I wouldn't have known exactly what I had caught (e.g. bocaccio and blue rockfish) if a deckhand or boat captain hadn't told me.

Twenty or so years ago I was fishing next to an older gentleman on a fishing charter out of Depoe Bay, catching the occasional black rockfish, when he lamented he couldn't believe he was paying to fish for them when years ago he cussed them. He said they had been so abundant along the Oregon coast back then that it was often hard to get a lure down through them to be able to fish for salmon in the deeper water.

It's sure not like that anymore out of Oregon. But I've had some crazy fast action and fun times further north. The blacks run the biggest of all the pelagic rockfish I've caught and can come in pretty big schools. Up at Sitka at the end of a day of salmon and halibut fishing, Guch and the other captains would usually swing in closer to the rocks before heading in so we could catch a boat limit of blacks. Each captain seemed to have his "secret" go-to spot. We switched from the herring we had been using for salmon to plastic grubs for the blacks. It's fast fishing, and the biggest challenge is often for the captain and deckhand to coordinate counting as fish come aboard and yell "that's it!" When you're mooching for salmon all day there can be a lot of time between action, and catching black rockfish is always a really fun way to end the day. It's always hard to stop when you hear "that's it!"

My favorite experience fishing for black rockfish, though, was on the first trip Sue and I made over to La Push, Washington in 2015. Sue had a little go – actually more than a little – with seasickness the first day we tried to go out fishing, so when we did go back out a couple days later we stayed in close and just ran a few miles north from the harbor to fish for ling cod and rockfish. We started out bottom-fishing with herring in the rocks, trying for lingcod but without much action. I think I caught one small one. Sue was enjoying watching the birds and listening to the sea lions barking on nearby "Dog Island", but between not catching anything, and getting hung up on the rocks, and probably a lingering concern over getting seasick, she didn't seem to be particularly interested in the ling cod fishing.

I re-rigged our lines with jig heads and curly-tail plastic grubs and we moved around looking for black rock fish. We found action. We started catching fish on nearly every drop off the north side of Dog Island. It was obvious that getting a 20 fish limit would not take long at all, so to be a little selective for bigger fish we switched over to big two-ounce jig heads and five-inch Flat-Back Shad swimbaits (which unfortunately have been discontinued). I remember watching Sue hit the free-spool on her reel to let the bait start dropping, and fish would be hitting it all the way down, hitting the head or the tail but not getting hooked. And then a big black would inhale it, Sue would rear back, and the rod would bend double. I wish I would have taken an actual picture, but I have a great mental image of Sue just hanging on, trying to keep the rod up while the tip is pointed straight down almost to the water's surface and jerking as a big five-pound black peels off line. She has a smile on her face.

Sue always has and still does enjoy going out fishing with me. Most of the time though, she is more or less along for the ride and a day on the water. But that day, catching black rockfish, she had to admit she really enjoyed the fishing.

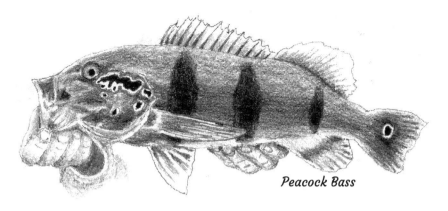

Peacock Bass

PART 3.
Tropical Fresh/Brackish-Water Fishes

The number of different tropical freshwater fish in my species tally surprises me, considering I've only fished a couple of times in tropical freshwater places (there are lots of weird fish in the tropics). I frequently had no idea at the time what I had caught and had to rely on my fishing companion or guide to clue me in, and even then, with the variation in common names for the same species, different varieties, and the difficulty in understanding what I was being told, I wasn't always sure. Checking different fish identification references after the fact still left a little uncertainty in a few cases, but what follows is my best shot.

Snook • Speckled Sea Trout • Oscar Gafftopsail Catfish • Spanish Mackerel

These species are blended together in the memory of my first "exotic" fishing trip. A fishing trip to the everglades is maybe not that exotic to others, but going to a totally different environment than I'd ever fished in and fishing for snook and tarpon was certainly exotic to me. And being invited to go with Keith Kiler, a fish and game colleague and friend who was intimately familiar with the area and one of the most easy-going people I've ever met, made it impossible to say no.

Keith had been taking several extended fishing trips a year to the Everglades for some time and I'd been told that he was considered by some to be one of the top three Everglades fly fishermen. Keith would never acknowledge or agree with that. But the fact that Leigh Perkins, CEO of Orvis, has invited Keith to come fish with him speaks for itself. I was going to be terribly, terribly out-skilled, but Keith was the kind of person who wouldn't care about that.

Unfortunately, a cold front came in just before I arrived at Homestead, Florida, to meet up with Keith and things were a little off. We spent some time looking for tarpon up in different backwater lakes with no success. I caught the speckled sea trout, gafftopsail catfish, and Spanish mackerel in one spot, all small fish less than a pound. I was casting a white Clouser minnow off the bow of Keith's Boston Whaler while we sat at anchor watching for tarpon activity.

The Oscar I caught in a small shallow lake which had road access to it, the introduction of non-native Oscars being the result of easy public access. We saw the only crocodile of the trip, kind of a rarity, on that lake. It lay on the bottom in shallow clear water and just watched us as we floated past within feet of it.

We focused primarily on snook. I actually caught my first snook near our first camp on a small island just offshore before we even got back in the Everglades. We had just been exploring a little in the canoe which we had towed along behind the Whaler and I was doing some blind casting with a spinning rod and caught a snook. I caught it on a Sluggo jerkbait that I use for largemouth bass! Keith was intrigued sort of, but indicated that that didn't really count. We were there to sight-fish snook and catch them on a fly.

The game plan involved leaving the Whaler outside the mangroves and using the canoe to wind up through small channels into remote back lakes which Keith knew about. That alone was worth the trip. Egrets, roseate spoonbills and all kinds of other birds flew out ahead of us, and big somethings boiled the water as we paddled up the narrow channels.

Once we got into a lake, Keith said that catching snook with a fly rod was fairly straight forward: a.) he would stand on the back seat of the canoe and pole the canoe around the perimeter of the shallow lake and try to spot a cruising snook, b.) while he was poling along looking I could blind cast the streamer he had supplied me with up under the overhanging mangroves (yeah, right), c.) once he spotted a fish he would point it out to me and position the canoe, then d.) I would cast the fly to the cruising snook and catch it. There were caveats though: 1.) I couldn't false cast in the direction of the snook or it would spook, 2.) of course if the fly landed behind the fish it wouldn't see it, 3.) if the fly landed more than a few feet in front of the fish it would ignore it, 4.) if the fly landed too close in front of the fish the fish would spook, 5.) if the fly landed beyond the fish and was stripped across in front but too close to the fish it would spook, and 6.) if the fly smacked down too hard on the water pretty much anywhere the fish would spook. It was as easy as that.

I don't remember anymore how many shots at snook I got. I do remember how patient Keith was. He was encouraging and offered a few tips. He never criticized or berated me. But it got to a point where I insisted we switch positions. After all we were on this fishing trip together. And boy is he good. He didn't get every fish he cast to to hit by any means, but his streamer always landed perfectly in the right spot and he caught more than enough snook to humble me.

I finally did catch a snook with my fly rod. On one of the shallow interior lakes that we went back into there was a small but perfect bay for snook. It must have been perfect judging by all the fish that were piled in there which I proceeded to spook. At one point there seemed to be wakes going everywhere around the shallow bay. The silty bottom got stirred up so much that it wasn't long before the water was chocolate and it was impossible to spot fish. That's when I made a blind cast, started stripping the streamer, and bam! Snook on!

That's the way I do it.

I've still got that streamer. And I've got a nice picture of me holding a snook with my fly rod. I've got a better one though of Keith, half turned in the bow seat looking back at me with a big smile on his sun-burned face, his fly rod resting across the gunnel, releasing a big snook over the side of the canoe.

Temensis (Three-bar) Peacock Bass • Speckled Peacock Bass • Orinocensis (Butterfly) Peacock Bass

I was raised by parents who had grown up during the Great Depression and not spending money became a part of me. I think after 70 years I'm finally doing pretty well ignoring that part, but back in 2003 and 2004 when Layne Hepworth suggested that I join him on a trip to the Amazon to fish for peacock bass I just didn't even consider it. He had made a number of trips down there and it sounded amazing, but I couldn't spend that kind of money. However, perspectives change. Layne handled some of my life insurance and retirement fund stuff, and after Margie died in 2005, I was seeing quite a bit of him trying to figure out the best thing to do with the financial fallout of that. He asked me again to join him and some buddies on a January, 2008, trip to the Amazon.

Layne is an upbeat, enthusiastic, funny guy – kind of DeVito-esque in stature. He's a very avid fly fisherman who has fished all over the world. He would be fun to make a trip with. When he asked this time two things came to my mind: I really had nothing but nothing to look forward to; and he was going to the Amazon really on my money, so why shouldn't I go along.

What a trip it was. I got a new perspective on "once-in-a-lifetime" trips. I'd thought of it in terms of only being able to afford a trip like this once, or owing it to yourself to do it at least once. But this trip was so amazing I don't think I would do it again because it could only be disappointing by comparison the second time.

After a middle of the night layover in Manaus, and after killing a few hours in a hotel bar in the continuous company of pretty young hookers looking for work, we flew north for an hour or so in a private plane to a landing strip in the middle of the jungle. Just after daylight the plane rolled to a stop about 50 yards from the fishing resort in a big clearing on the banks of the Agua Boa River. We deplaned and were greeted by the resort manager and two lovely young women balancing glasses of champagne on silver trays.

198

It was a lovely resort with a line of separate air conditioned bungalows, an infinity swimming pool looking over the river, the main building with a gathering place to tell fish stories at the end of the day, and a dining area where we enjoyed great meals on white linen table cloths set with fine china. Forbes magazine had in fact recognized the resort as one of the top ten fly fishing lodges in the world. Layne spends my money in style, I'll give him that.

The resort accommodated 14 guests. There were two of the funniest guys I've ever met – dry wit, sarcasm, funny stories, and heavy accents – from Brooklyn. There was a very engaging older couple, two nice young couples from South Africa, and our group from Idaho and Oregon. Layne was the only one of our group that I knew ahead of time, but the other four were all easygoing and enjoyable guys. I roomed and fished all week with Jim, who among other things was a fly fishing instructor and competitive fly caster. Terribly out-skilled again.

We fished a full week, each day with a different guide on a different part of the river. The Agua Boa, a tributary to the Rio Branco (which flows south into the Rio Negro, which flows into the Amazon) is not a big river. In some places you might be able to throw a baseball across it, but generally you'd need a relay from second base. In the morning we'd step into our assigned boat, one of a fleet of identical lime-green flat bottom aluminum boats, and we'd take off screaming up or down the river, the guide steering the boat from one side of the river to the other to try and stay in the deeper thalweg. January is summer time in the Amazon and the river was very shallow and tricky to navigate in many areas. We covered miles and miles of river each day, and each day just the run on the river was fascinating. On the big sandbars on the inside bends we saw white egrets, out-sized white jabiru storks with black heads and heavy bills, wild Muscovy ducks, many kinds of birds I couldn't identify, and big caiman sunning themselves. The high cutbanks on the outside bends revealed the subterranean profile of the Amazon rainforest, with the entire root systems of the tall forest spread out horizontally in the top few inches of dark, nutrient-laden soil. No roots showed in the cutaway lighter-colored soil below, where nutrients are leached out by all the rain.

We stopped and waded shallow sandy areas of the river and sight cast big streamers to cruising peacocks, and we hiked or poled through winding channels into isolated overflow lakes. The lakes, except for the jungle vegetation and jungle sounds, reminded me of the backwater lakes of the Mississippi where I grew up. Many times when we pulled up to a bank and got out there were tapir tracks in the mud. It reminded me of the awe I felt as a kid seeing my first deer tracks on a muddy bank of the Rock River.

So the peacock bass... Regardless of the name, I hadn't anticipated just how striking in appearance they would be with their lime green body coloration, red ventral fins, and the bold black spot surrounded by a bright yellow halo on the tail. The butterfly peacocks were the gaudiest with three more big black spots outlined with bright yellow on each side.

And they lived up to their sporting reputation. They were ag-

A typical temensis – or butterfly – peacock bass.

gressive, hard fighting fish. We went into a lake a ways off the river the first day and worked the shoreline just like I would for largemouth. There was no need for finesse though. We cast big bright streamers. These fish were predominantly the butterfly peacocks and they seemed almost pissed off at the streamer. They really smashed it. And often they came in big groups, competing to be the first to kill the streamer. Butterfly peacock don't run as big as the temensis, or three bar – the butterflies we were catching were maybe two to three pounds – but they make up for it in numbers and willingness to hit. I didn't even try to keep track of how many we caught that first day, but that night my left thumb was in shreds and sore from grabbing fish by the lower jaw to land and unhook them.

The temensis peacocks were a little bit pickier and not as abundant, but they were big and powerful. Jim caught one that week that weighed 17 pounds. Jim (and our guide using my fly rod one day to show me how it was done) did really well sight casting for the big temensis on the sand flats along the river. It was a little like the snook fishing, requiring casting accuracy a notch or two above my skill level. We caught the biggest ones, though, fishing our largest streamers in the deeper water of the overflow lakes and connecting channels.

I didn't get to see what I think was my biggest fish for the week. We were fishing deeper water where a channel with a little current entered a lake. A fish took my streamer and took off straight away on a really powerful run. I certainly couldn't hold it and was just trying to keep as much pressure on as I could without burning my fingers on the fly line that was ripping out. The line wasn't coming off the reel. It was coming off a pile of fly line lying in the bottom of the boat around my feet (I suck not only in fly casting accuracy, but also in managing my fly line.) It happened so fast. A tangle of fly line shot up off the floor of the boat, through my fingers, hesitated squeezing through the first guide, before jamming on the smaller second guide. I did manage to hang onto the rod, but the fish broke off.

I hooked another really big one back in one of the lakes that I did get to see. It was about five feet long. Jim and I were in the middle of spanking a bunch of butterfly peacock close to shore, we and the fighting peacocks making quite a commotion, when I noticed that we'd gotten the attention of a caiman. A fish that Jim had on was thrashing about in one spot and the caiman swam out from shore to investigate. The guide was gesturing to quick get the fish in, which Jim did. I don't take directions very well though. I hooked a fish and couldn't resist letting it linger at the side of the boat a bit. It was pretty cool to watch that caiman come right at the fish – and the boat – and grab that peacock sideways in its mouth, head and tail hanging out opposite sides. I didn't land that big one either.

Apapa (Coronado)

I caught one of these on the Amazon trip. I don't think they are all that abundant because the guide seemed to be delighted when I caught it. Apapa are kind of tarpon shaped, only thicker. The one I caught was about five or six pounds and fought well, but the thing that stands out was how striking in appearance it was with its uniformly yellow-gold body and fins.

Payara (Vampire Fish)

You don't ever forget catching a payara and bringing it aboard a boat with you. It is the craziest looking fish with a mouth full of long needle-like teeth, and two several-inch long fangs sticking up from an undershot lower jaw. The one I caught was only 18 inches or so. They evidently get up to three feet long with six-inch fangs. When I caught the payara our guide for the day, a very pleasant older gentleman who spoke no English, was very, very respectful of the fish as he unhooked it for me.

Aruana

I caught one aruana on the Amazon trip. Like pretty much all the Amazon fish species other than peacock bass, I didn't know anything about aruana before the trip. They are a primitive looking fish that remind me of a bowfin, with an elongated soft dorsal fin that stops just short of their rounded tail fin and an elongated anal fin just ahead of the tail fin. Unlike a bowfin though, which has a terminal mouth for feeding straight ahead, the aruana has an undershot jaw and mouth near the top of its head for feeding on prey near the

Though this payara is small, our guide was very respectful of the long teeth.

surface and even above the water. I learned later that they are sometimes called monkey fish because of their habit of leaping out of the water to grab prey, sometimes even grabbing birds off overhanging branches.

I heard other anglers at the resort talk about them and Layne mentioned them as one of the highlights of his earlier Amazon trips.

They spend a lot of time holding under overhanging cover, but often cruise near the surface where you can see them and sight cast to them. And that's what happened. We were casting to a shoreline, Jim in the bow and me in the middle of the boat, when the guide pointed out the aruana, actually three together, cruising near the surface a short cast outside and slightly behind us. I turned, cast, and actually landed the streamer just a couple feet in front of the lead fish. I just started to strip the fly and bam. The lead fish was all over it. He didn't have time to think about it. He just reacted.

This fish was probably average size, maybe close to 30 inches, but it was wild and acrobatic. Layne had mentioned that more aruana get off than get landed because they are so acrobatic and their mouths are so hard that a hook doesn't penetrate very well. It was a fight I will remember, and damn if the hook didn't stay in his jaw and we got it in the boat.

There is another thing about that time when I caught the aruana that I will always remember. Shortly after catching the aruana we were back working the same shoreline and the guide again got Jim's and my attention by pointing out to open water ahead of us. We looked, and there cruising on the surface about 75 yards away on a heading to cross in front of us were five otters. But these weren't your cute little North American otters. They were South American giant otters over five feet long. Other than their outsize though, they were behaving just like otters back home. They were swimming across our bow but rising up in the water and turning their heads around to look at us. Then they'd stop and turn to face us and stare. They were curious but not afraid, and they were chattering the whole time. They evidently had business to attend to because they didn't linger, but stayed their course and disappeared in the shoreline tangle of brush.

Wolf Fish • Jacuda • Bicuda • Tetra Plecostomi Sucker • Myleinae Sp. • Characin Sp. • Tiger Catfish • Red Tailed Catfish

These were also all a part of my Amazon experience. Some, like the toothy wolf fish and jacuda, we caught all throughout our trip. I caught one or two of the bizarre looking tiger catfish, with its black vertical wavy stripes, and the boldly colored red tailed catfish. The other species (some I could only identify to genus) were "oddball" ones that I only caught one of, and if it weren't for my notes and being able to compare my pictures against fish identification references for the Amazon, I'd have no idea what all I caught.

Piranha

We didn't catch many piranha, but I suspect we could've caught all we wanted to. One day our guide stopped at a place for lunch where we could catch some piranha just for the novelty of it.

On our last day though, while we were out fishing the staff back at the lodge did some serious piranha fishing to provide a unique final evening meal of fried whole piranha. Our host shared with us over dinner how the piranha were acquired. There was a challenge to it.

The challenge wasn't in hooking the piranha, they were abundant around the docks down at the river. The challenge was getting them in before Oscar got them. Oscar (I can't remember what they actually called him so I'll just call him Oscar) was a several hundred pound caiman that hung around the docks.

The fishermen – and Oscar – had a routine though. The piranha harvesters would take a piranha they had managed to catch and bonk on the head, and throw it out toward the middle of the river, then wait for Oscar, the piranha consumer, to start swimming out away from the docks. The fishermen would then fish like crazy and catch as many piranhas as they could before Oscar came back. You might say they had a symbiotic relationship.

When Jim and I got back to the dock at the end of the day, Oscar did seem a little more attentive. But we thought nothing of it and proceeded on up the ramp to where a young lady was waiting to meet us, as she did at the end of every fishing day, with a refreshing tropical cocktail.

It truly was a once in a lifetime experience.

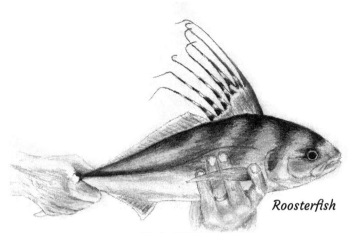

Roosterfish

PART 4.
Tropical Saltwater Fishes

Blue Marlin

Blue marlin: the adversary/nemesis of great Hemingway novels *The Old Man and the Sea* and *Islands in the Stream.* For me as well, there is one particular blue marlin that stands out. It's easy. It's the only one I've ever caught. And it's not really much of a story.

On a 2017 trip to Kona to visit Sue's daughter Anna, we made arrangements to go out fishing with Bobby Cherry, a friend of Anna's, on his charter boat the Cherry Pit II. On previous trips to visit Anna I'd gone out with several different captains. It was always nice to spend a day on the ocean and we would catch the occasional ono (wahoo) and mahi mahi (dorado), but this was different. We were going out for tuna. Anna had touted Bobby as being the second best ahi (tuna) fisherman in Kona. I probably shouldn't have repeated that to Bobby, but it was kind of funny when he seriously questioned Anna about who the hell was better.

Well bummer, but try as we might we couldn't catch any bait around the off-shore buoy where schools of bait fish commonly hang out. Bobby had one live bait left from the day before. We dropped it over some marks on the fishfinder that he thought might be tuna, but a rough-toothed dolphin grabbed it first and cut the line. With the sun getting higher he suggested we put out plugs and troll.

I don't think we'd gone a quarter mile from the buoy when FISH ON! I got the rod and got in the fighting chair and hung on. It was a "small" blue marlin. Bobby guessed maybe 140 pounds. It jumped and jumped and jumped.

It was fun, but what makes it really memorable for me is how that fish beat the crap out of Bobby. After not a terribly long time I got the fish in close enough for Bobby to get ahold of the leader, but he had to let go when the fish turned and ran. Next time I got the leader up Bobby made a couple wraps around his gloved hand to be able to hang on, but almost got his hand ripped off when the fish took off and he had to let go again. Each time the fish peeled out line and jumped repeatedly. I got the leader in again and Bobby was able to get ahold of it and work down the leader toward the fish. He was leaning way down over the side in the port corner of the stern, then all of a sudden he was upright and the marlin was off and running again. I couldn't see it from the fighting chair but he had gotten ahold of the fish's bill with one hand and was trying to get the hook out but the fish jerked and broke Bobby's grip. I got the fish back to the boat a fourth time. Again Bobby grabbed the leader and quickly worked down it, bending way over the side. Then Bobby's shoulders began rapidly pistoning up and down. For a few seconds I thought he was violently jerking at the lure to get it free. But it went on for quite a while, long enough that had he been on a bronc the horn would have blown. Then for a second his shoulders were still. Then suddenly he stood up straight, both arms held up above his head like a rodeo calf roper who just completed his tie-off.

What I didn't understand until I looked at the video that Anna had just shot, was that Bobby had quickly worked down the leader to the fish and got one hand on the bill like before, but when the fish again started to thrash, Bobby grabbed the bill with both hands and hung on. The marlin was on its side and with every rapid flex of its body it was pumping Bobby up and down. When it finally stopped thrashing for a second Bobby let go with his left hand, grabbed the hook and twisted it free. He stood up as the fish turned

Our daughter Anna, who made our Hawaii fishing trips happen.

and dove. Bobby said afterwards that it's not usually that tough to release a marlin, but the smaller blues are generally "hotter" than the big ones. Even so, I can't imagine a rodeo with a 600-pound blue marlin.

Striped Marlin

There have been a few striped marlin fishing memories deposited into my fishing memory bank, and all of them have been bundled up with good times with special people. I caught one small striped marlin, maybe 70 pounds, in Hawaii. In itself it was fun, but catching this one was memorable because it was part of a double with Anna. The two identical-sized fish hit and hooked up only seconds apart and Anna and I were on the two rods almost simultaneously. Many of the trips I've done out of Kona are fishless, so I focused on enjoying and having fun playing the little marlin I had on. I remember looking at Anna in the other corner of the stern and thinking that she seemed kind of intense. My fish was still a ways from the boat

209

when Cyrus, the captain and a friend of Anna's, quickly stepped to the back corner where Anna was, told her to move up the gunnel a little, and reached out and grabbed the leader. He quickly worked down it and unhooked Anna's fish. Anna turned to me, now with a big smile, and did a double fist pump and said, "yeah."

Except for that fish, my striped marlin memories have been made on the Sea of Cortez on various guy-trips and trips with Sue. One experience that I remember, and Sue will never forget, unfortunately, was a marlin that Sue caught. When it got hooked up it didn't jump or show itself like marlin sometimes do but took off on a blazing run while Sue silently hung on. We just watched as line peeled out against the drag. It had been running for some time when a marlin cleared the water over 200 yards out and 30 degrees off to the left of where Sue's rod and line were pointed. Sue nodded toward where the marlin had just jumped and said, "What's that big fish?" She wasn't sure whether to believe me when I told her that that was the fish on her line. The fight went on too long. The last thing boat captains want is someone losing a fish to a broken line, but the drag was set too loose and the marlin kept turning and making runs. Eventually Sue was able to start pumping and reeling down and bringing the marlin in, but it seemed almost like dead weight. Unfortunately, it was. On one of the jumps or runs going away the line got wrapped around the marlin's tail and it drown while being pulled backwards. Sue didn't want to believe that the fish was dead. No matter how much I assured her that there was nothing she did wrong, and shared with her that Virgil had it happen on a trip we had done together, she was pretty upset. And she still is years later when there is mention of that trip and she thinks of the dead marlin. I doubt that she will ever take ahold of a rod with a marlin on it again.

The earlier trip with Virgil, except for the drowned marlin (which we ate and shared with the crew), was in every way just a wonderful time that holds great memories for me. It was a guy's trip; eight good friends on a fishing adventure together. We fished out of Van

Wormer's Punta Colorado resort, which was (it has since closed) out by itself on the East Cape of Baja. It was very nice, but not fancy, and catered primarily to anglers. It was small and intimate enough that we got to know the other guests and the staff and by the second day we didn't have to ask, just handed the bartender some fresh dorado fillets when we came in from fishing, and when we came back after cleaning up a little he had fresh ceviche ready to go with our margaritas. We had a lot of those, and a lot of laughs.

The eight of us split up and fished on two different cruisers. I fished with Bill Goodnight (Sir Buenos Noches to the Van Wormer staff), Hutch, and Steve Elle, all longtime friends. Heading out before sunrise that first day, as the four of us watched the deckhand get the rods ready to go – four with big skirted trolling plugs and a fifth with live bait – I think it was Hutch that said, "Al, you get the first fish." I asked why me, and suggested that we should draw straws or something. The response came from all three that no, I should just go first. That's the kind of thing that good friends do. I accepted.

I don't think we ran more than five minutes after that, we were still watching the resort recede away over the trailing wake of the boat, when the captain excitedly shouted something in Spanish down to the deckhand and pointed ahead off to starboard. The four of us all turned and looked as the captain throttled back. Clearly visible were several dark, slender, pointed things grouped together sticking up out of the relatively calm water. One of the other guys recognized what we were looking at before I did, I'd never seen anything like it. The pointed things sticking up out of the water were the dorsal fins and upper tail fins of three marlin, lying close together, pointed in different directions, not moving at all.

The deck hand already had the rod with the live bait ready and he cast it off to starboard as we got close. The captain steered the boat wide of the resting marlin and then once he was a little past them he started a wide turn to starboard, bringing the bait right past the fish.

The fish hadn't moved at all up until then. Then the one facing toward the bait going by thrust ahead and out of sight and the other two disappeared in big swirls. And, that quick, the deck hand was letting line feed out and jabbering excitedly to the captain. I think he let the marlin have the bait for half a minute before he pointed the rod straight back, flipped the lever on the reel to engage the spool, and when the line tightened he reared back and set the hook. When he did that, the captain hit the throttle, a cloud of black diesel exhaust appeared behind the transom, and the deckhand quickly pumped the rod several more times to drive the hook home. He looked at his four pescadores and a raise of his eyebrows asked who was going to take the rod. I got in the fighting chair and he handed me the rod.

There is really nothing about catching that striped marlin that stands out in my memory beyond that point. It was exciting playing the fish of course and finally getting it alongside the boat, but it is what happened before I even got ahold of the rod that will stick in my memory. All eight of us on the trip ended up landing at least one marlin, all of them the same 140 to 160 pound size. We saw more marlin basking on the surface, which is unusual, but I don't think another one was caught that way on the trip.

The author hangs on as an early morning marlin strips off line and fishing buddies watch.
(Rich Howard photo)

Sierra

This fish made the list during an earlier fishing trip to Punta Colorado with Don Anderson, Bill Goodnight, and Dan Herrig. It was Bill, Dan, and my first trip to the East Cape, but Don had fished there previously. On Don's earlier trip he must've caught a bunch of sierra and had a lot of fun doing it because several times on our trip when nothing much was happening he suggested that we ought to go in closer to shore and fish for sierra. So finally we did.

The deck hand tied old tooth-scarred plugs on two lines and we trolled along within a half mile of the beach. And we caught a sierra. I say "we", because when four guys watch two rods that the deck hand has set up, the deck hand has let the line out, and the captain is trolling behind the boat, it's hard to say "I caught it" just because I was up next in the rotation and got to reel the sierra in.

I will say, though, that reeling that sierra in was a blast. Sierra in general aren't all that big, but these mackerel-like fish are built for speed, and I think the four pounder showed us everything he had.

Sailfish

Dave Cross, a colleague who worked in D.C., told me over lunch at a fisheries conference back in the early 2000's about a trip he'd just made to a place called Crocodile Bay Resort in Costa Rica. He described being picked up at the tiny little local airport and being given a choice of checking into the resort and resting….or going out fishing. He boated seven sailfish before dinner. I never forgot that story.

Then a year or two later I tuned a motel room TV into the middle of an episode of Babe Winkelman Fishing. Babe was somewhere fishing with a guide, and Babe's wife was hooked up to a big fish, and had been for some time. I caught "Costa Rica." Babe's wife was worn out, so the guide helped her hold the rod up right at the end of the fight with what was a monster roosterfish. Babe's voice-over said it would've been a new world record for a female angler, but it didn't get recognized because the guide had assisted her. When the camera

213

panned back to show Babe, his wife, the guide, and the fish, I could read on the side of the boat "Crocodile Bay Resort."

That sealed it. A trip to Crocodile Bay Resort went on my bucket list in ink.

It took many years, years of thinking about it and anticipating how great it would be, but after 15 years I checked it off in February, 2018. And it was a good trip. The resort is located on the remote Oso Peninsula in southwest Costa Rica, just north of the Panama border, in a beautiful jungle setting. The nearby village of Puerto Jimenez has only two blocks of paved streets and is populated by happy, friendly people who offer a smile and "ola" or "buenas dias" to the few strolling tourists.

A Costa Rica sailfish rippin' it up behind the boat.
(Sue Van Vooren photo)

I'd like to say the fishing was great. Maybe in time I will. But how could any fishing trip live up to the years of anticipation and high expectations. I think there's a lesson there.

First day out, fishing with a really fun captain named Anthony, Sue and I boated four sailfish. I was really surprised that for fish that weighed 90 to 100 pounds they didn't pull very hard and came in pretty easily. But what acrobats! It was spectacular, the sailfish launching themselves high out of the water, doing end-overs and twists, and tail-walking back and forth off the stern. Anthony got some great footage on his Go Pro that made it into the resort's February fishing highlights video.

Big tides evidently had the roosterfish put off, and two more days of off-shore fishing resulted in one tuna. We had some other adventures besides fishing though, experienced new things and places, and met some great folks. We really enjoyed Anthony and his stories. One of them, coincidentally, was about a guide years before who got fired the very same day he helped a woman land a 108-pound roosterfish that would've been a world record but was disqualified because he had touched the rod.

Dorado (Mahi Mahi)

Dorado fight hard, are acrobatic, and can get big, but what makes them stand out for me is their affinity for anything floating in the ocean, and how they light up in bright iridescent yellow, blue, and

Hutch with the sleeping-turtle dorado.

green colors when they get excited.

Hutch caught one of the bigger ones I've seen, on a trip we did down to Punta Colorado on the East Cape of Baja. With four of us fishing together on a cruiser we rotated through who would take the next fish. Bill was up. The captain spotted a turtle. Out there in the middle of nowhere, floating along all by itself, is this big sleeping sea turtle. The deckhand threw out a line with a live bait on it, fed it back, and the captain made a wide sweep around the floating turtle. The trailing bait got pulled right past the oblivious turtle. I didn't notice that it was visibly disturbed at all when a big dorado that had been right under it shot out and took the bait.

On a trip to Hawaii, Sue and Anna and I, fishing with Captain Billy and his son out of Kona, got into a mother-lode of dorado (mahi mahi in Hawaii) around a big floating log way off shore. When Billy first spotted the log a ways off he knew it would mean fish. The log had been at sea a long time and had vegetation hanging off of it, which attracted small fish, which in turn attracted mahi mahi. Sue could be content just watching someone else catch fish, but Anna loves catching fish as much as I do. We trolled past the log and immediately had a double hookup with mahi mahi. Billy stopped the boat. The fish Anna and I had on were lighting up as they fought in the clear water around the boat, and at times there were a dozen or more other excited fish darting around and lighting up. After landing those first two fish, Anna and I threw smaller plugs into the fray of darting and circling fish and got hooked up right away. The swirling blues and yellows and greens of all the excited fish in the water made me think of the rapid-fire bursts and swirls of northern lights.

We had already told Billy we were only interested in enough fish for two or three meals. But in Hawaii it's legal for the charter captain to sell sport-caught fish, so Billy saw dollar signs on each fish we hooked. He wasn't about to stop and clean the boat. In the next half hour, before other boats showed up and the school dispersed, we had the fastest mahi mahi fishing and the coolest light display that I've ever experienced – and one bloody boat.

Wahoo (Ono)

Thinking of the wahoo that I've caught conjures up images of spectacular settings fishing out of Kona and trolling nearshore along the west side of the island. I've never gotten tired of being in warm tropical air looking at the blue water, white breaking waves continually washing up against the black lava cliffs, and the nearly always present whales and dolphins. The wahoo I've caught have all been fast, hard fighters, and fun to have on and catch. They've also been the best to have on a bar-b-que grill. Ono, as they are called in Hawaii, means "delicious."

When I reflect on catching ono, two memories stand out in particular. One is of an ono that I caught on one of the trips that Sue and Anna and I did with Captain Bill (not to be confused with Captain Billy). It stands out because I almost caught the fish twice. We were down the west shore south of Kona trolling big colorful blunt-faced skirted lures on one of the breaks that Bill said seemed to attract ono. We got a hook-up, I grabbed the rod out of the holder, got in the fighting chair and had no more than put it to the fish when the line went limp. I was disappointed, but I remember Bill was just not happy at all and grumbled about how expensive those lures were as he re-rigged with a new one and fed it out behind the boat to chug along breaking the surface on the face of the fifth wave back. Bill made a wide turn and headed back in the general direction we'd just come. We got another hook-up after running just a short way. Again I grabbed the rod and got in the chair. Ono cover a lot of water after they're hooked and this fish, maybe 30 pounds, gave me a bit of a workout before I got it to the boat and Bill gaffed it aboard. Bill had a three by five-foot canvas fish-bag with ice in it to put the ono in, but he wanted to get the entrails out first. With the fish lying on the deck, its back up against the stern and its underside facing me, Bill stuck his knife in at the vent and slit the belly up to the head. He reached in, grabbed the entrails, and started to pull them out. And the expensive big-game trolling lure that he had been grumbling about losing earlier slid out of the fish's detached stomach onto the deck.

Sue and I had a good day fishing with Captain Bill on another trip in 2011. We were really hoping to catch an ono to grill up at the little vacation rental on the beach where we were staying up at Puako, and Sue and I each caught one that day. We got back to the harbor after 2:00, later than we had expected, and felt a bit hurried. It was a Friday afternoon and we had to make it to a county office build-

One of two ono caught on a 2011 trip with Capt. Bill out of Kona. We grilled the ono that night...and I married the pretty angler the next day.

ing before they closed for the weekend. The office closed at 3:00. And we didn't know where it was. It was almost 2:45 by the time we found the building and found the office where we needed to go. There were several people sitting in chairs along the wall waiting to be helped by the one clerk. We sat down. I must say we felt more than a little self-conscious being sunburned, weather beaten, and smelling quite a bit like ono.

We sat there for a while before we noticed a small sign that said something about customers not checking in before 2:45 may not be able to complete their business until the next business day. We hadn't noticed a check-in. No one came in after us.

It seemed to be taking an awful long time for the clerk to take care of the other people ahead of us. When the clerk was done help-ing the last of them it was just shy of 3:00. She looked up and started to explain that we would have to come back on Monday, but hesi-tated just long enough when she got a good look at us for me to ask if we couldn't please get what we needed then and not have to wait and come back on Monday. I remember she paused at that point as she thought about it. It seemed like a long time, but was probably only two or three seconds before she said to come on up, and asked what we needed.

Late the next afternoon, March 14th, in our little vacation rental on the beach, the smell of ono had been scrubbed away, I was a little more presentable, and Sue was just beautiful when I gave the completed county form to our new friend Lola Lyons. Then we all walked down to the water's edge and Lona married Sue and me as the sun set on the ocean.

Roosterfish

These are a bizarre looking fish with their outsized dorsal fin-rays sticking way up and curling back almost half way to their tail. And from what I'd heard, they were an exciting fish to catch, chasing bait-fish and feeding voraciously along the beach and fighting hard once hooked up. So one day on a 2008 trip to Punta Colorado on the East Cape, Sue and I chartered a panga to go fish for roosterfish.

The experience of fishing out of the much smaller, open pan-ga is very different than that of relaxing on a cruiser, waiting for some-thing to grab one of the lures chugging along on the surface behind the boat. Pangas are relatively narrow, low-sided boats, but 20 feet or more in length with up-turned bows to handle waves. They are thick-hulled, typically powered by 60 to 150 HP outboards, and very seaworthy. The panga design was actually developed by Yamaha as part of a World Bank project in the early '70s, intended for use in de-veloping countries where the boat could be launched off the beach. They're ubiquitous throughout Mexico and the Caribbean.

Fishing for roosterfish was just as described, with bait fish

Sue hanging on to a hot roosterfish in Mexico.

flying and roosterfish charging all around. We were just off the beach, close enough that we could hear the chatter of adults and squeals of playing children spending the day on the beach in front of the little town of La Ribera.

Sue and I sat side by side on the middle bench seat, each holding a rod with just a hook and a lively sardine on the end of the line trailing behind the boat. Our young guide sat on the stern bench seat manning the outboard, slowly idling us and the baits along. We could actually tell when a roosterfish was close to the bait by the sardine's more frantic swimming and heightened twitching of the rod tip. Sue and I caught several roosterfish apiece, and though small – maybe five pounds or so – they were hard fighters and very fun. But in the process we also caught three pelicans that dove down and grabbed our live bait when it came to the surface trying to escape a charging roosterfish. Pelicans don't fight so much. I don't think the pelicans were hurt in the process, but we felt bad and it took the fun out of fishing for roosterfish for us.

After the guide released the third pelican we told him we'd had enough roosterfish fishing. We went out and caught dorado.

Pargo

In addition to the roosterfish – and pelicans – that Sue and I caught off the beach at La Ribera that day, a pargo took one of the sardines. I don't remember whether it was obvious to me right away that it wasn't a roosterfish that I had on. It was about the same size, maybe four pounds. But when it got close to the boat it was as different in appearance as it could be, a dark red all over with some darker vertical bars on its side.

The thing I remember most about catching the pargo though was how our young guide perked up and excitedly told me not to release it as we had been doing with the roosterfish. He took the pargo and stowed it back behind the stern seat. Evidently pargo are good to eat.

Hammerhead Shark

Fishing was slow on the early-season trip with Don Anderson, Dan Herrig and Bill Goodnight to Punta Colorado. The resort had just opened for the season and the water was still cool. After not having any action one day the captain asked if we would like to stop trolling lures and fish some baits down near the bottom. I don't remember much about it other than we had action catching an odd assortment of smaller fish. What I do remember clearly was hooking into something very big, fighting it for a long while not knowing what it was, and then recognizing as it got close to the surface that I had on a hammerhead about six feet long. Technically I guess I didn't actually "catch" it. The deckhand and captain were deliberating what to do, the shark lying in the water next to the boat, when the fish thrashed and its teeth cut the line.

Yellowfin Tuna

I only have a few experiences catching yellowfin tuna and they have all been memorable. One was in February, 2018, on a long anticipated trip to Crocodile Bay Resort in Costa Rica to fish for sailfish. The sailfish worked out the first day, but the second day we were still fishless at noon when Anthony, our captain, got a call on the radio about tuna almost an hour south. We decided to go for it.

Boats, a cloud of diving birds, and the surface commotion of feeding tuna greeted us when we got to the spot. I tried casting a surface lure ahead of the school with no luck, but Anthony had a fish take a live bait he'd dropped down deeper and yelled for me to take the rod. I love catching fish, but "catching" fish that I don't hook myself just seems like cranking fish in. It's fun. But it's not the same.

I took the rod. And it was fun – for an hour or so. It was the hardest pulling fish I've ever had on, and its only move was diving straight down into the depths. With the fish fighting straight down, sitting in the fighting chair wasn't an option. Anthony strapped a fighting belt around my waist as I stood at the gunnel. I'd pump and reel down and gain a little line, only to have the fish dive and strip the line back off. I was truly whipped by the time Anthony got a gaff in the 90-pound tuna at the end of an hour and forty minutes. So that was certainly memorable, but a couple other things after the catch were uniquely memorable.

One was looking at myself when I showered later on before dinner. A hand-sized area on the inside of each thigh, high in the groin, was bright red, full of little ruptured blood vessels where the fighting belt had dug in and shifted around. It was interesting watching the colors change over several days!

The other thing occurred at dinner that evening. In the four days we'd been there, the dinner menu featured dorado as the fish of the day, every day, for lunch and dinner. This evening the fish of the day was tuna steaks. It was kind of fun watching 40-50 people in the dining room benefiting from my pain. During dinner I caught people at several tables looking over toward Sue and me at our corner table and wasn't sure what that was about, until one group got up to leave and stopped by our table and thanked us for the tuna.

Another favorite experience fishing for yellowfin was on a trip to Los Barilles on the East Cape of Baja in June of 2017. Sue and I went down with Clark and Sofia and our four year old granddaughter Lucia, and stayed at Van Wormer's Palmas de Cortez Resort. It was just delightful. The resort is right on a broad sand beach and has multiple bright-colored swimming pools of different shapes and depths that Lucia pretty much lived in. The best part about Los Barilles is that it is not Cabo San Lucas. It's not anything like it. The resort and the town of Los Barilles are not Cabo kind of places. Los Barilles, while it derives a fair bit of income from tourists I suppose, seems more like a typical laid-back Mexican town. The town school and playground, all the students in their white shirts, is immediately across the street from the resort entrance. Small family-run restaurants, stores, and a small mercado are all within easy walking distance.

There is usually someone who understands and speaks English in the businesses, but the majority of people in Los Barilles are Spanish speaking. On past trips it's actually been fun stumbling through my limited Spanish vocabulary to communicate with non-English speaking locals.

It was different on this trip though. Sofia was raised in Mexico, teaches in a dual-immersion Spanish/English program for elementary students in Boise, and her white-boy, red-headed husband – my son, Clark – has become pretty conversant in Spanish. It made it easy for Sue and I. But what was really fun was watching four year old Lucia interact with people in town and the staff at the resort. She would stand looking up at the person, and often without hearing them speak first, she would ask a question or launch into conversation either in Spanish or English. And boy can she talk. I suspect she sized people up by their complexion or hair color or clothes and just knew whether to speak in English or Spanish.

I'm not an old salt by any means, but this was an all-new type of fishing experience for Clark and Sofia. It didn't matter so much to me what we fished for as it did to have them just be able to catch any of the fast and powerful fish out in the Sea of Cortez, so before we left the dock at daylight I asked our captain, Danny, what he thought our best options were. He said very few marlin were being caught and the dorado that had been caught were 50 miles up the coast and running very small. He said some boats had gotten into yellowfin the day before and, while there is never any guarantee, he thought that was probably our best bet. It was a long run though.

Whether you've never done it before or you've done it dozens of times, running out into the Sea of Cortez as the sun comes up is a pretty magical experience. Magnificent frigate birds soar over the boat, dolphins wake surf behind the boat, seabirds of all kinds skim over the water, and flying fish flutter away, staying airborne an impossible distance before splashing back down to the water. And there is the anticipation.

The first day Clark and Sue and I went out while Sofia stayed in with Lucia. The second day Sofia came out while Clark stayed in. Both days were essentially the same experience. We ran out for two hours to the area where boats had been catching tuna, then trolled plugs as we covered water and watched for a school of dolphin, which signaled feeding tuna below. Except for a couple skipjack one of the days, both days were just covering water, looking, and action-less until mid-afternoon when Danny shouted down from the bridge to reel 'em in and then he poured the coals to it, leaving a belch of black smoke from the diesel engine.

The boat captains are continuously checking in with each other to see what is happening, and both days Danny got a call from another captain who'd found dolphins. That was enough. When we reached the area the day Clark was out, in addition to two squid plugs on the outriggers, the deckhand had a couple of rods, rigged up with smaller wooden darting plugs, which Clark and I held and pumped as we trolled. That's where the action was. Trolling at probably six to eight miles an hour and having a streaking tuna hit and scream off is wild. These were not big yellowfin by tuna standards – probably 12 to 15 pounds – but like most saltwater predators they were hot. When Clark got his first one to the boat he was in total disbelief that it wasn't twice as big. There were some short lulls, but almost always when a fish got on one of the rods that we were working, another tuna took the plug on the other rod. Sue suggested that Clark and I do the fish catching, but we had enough action, including four triples, that we all got a good workout. We ended up boating 17 in about an hour and a half before we had to start the long run in.

The second day when Sue and I went out with Sofia we again made the same long run out to try for tuna, but watching Sofia experience the thrill of running on the ocean for the first time made it seem fresh. Again it was hours of cruising and looking and then the radio call and run out to the dolphin for an hour or so of tuna action. One thing a little different on the second day, though, was that we stopped at some offshore buoys on the way out where the deckhand

Sue had all the fun she wanted with bigger tune on a 2018 return trip.

caught a bunch of baitfish that he put in the live well. When we got into tuna that second day, Danny slowed the boat to an idle and we put out lines with live bait. Sue and Sofia and I each held onto a rod, and the deckhand put a fourth rod with a live bait on the line into a rod holder. And yes, we ended up having four tuna on at once a couple times. It was a circus.

Skipjack (Aku)

Skipjack don't get very big, five pounds or so, but like any tuna these guys fight hard for their size and have been a welcome diversion from hours of watching fishing plugs chug along in the wake of the boat. Boat captains typically consider them a nuisance by-catch. Bill Horton caught a skipjack on our 2006 trip to Mexico. He had never caught one. The captain told Bill skipjack weren't very good to eat. But Bill had to judge for himself. He kept it and had the cooks at the resort fix it for us that night. We all agreed that the captain was right.

Bigeye Tuna

I've caught at least one small bigeye tuna in Hawaii, about the size of a skipjack tuna. There's really not anything remarkable about having caught the bigeye. I wouldn't even have known what it was if the captain hadn't told me.

Albacore (Tombo)

While I did incidentally catch a small albacore in Hawaii, which are called tombo over there, there was nothing noteworthy or memorable about it. My prize albacore memories came out of the great tuna adventure.

Running tuna charters out of Oregon and Washington is common and fairly popular these days, but 20 years ago, going on a tuna charter pretty much meant a trip to California. There was one operator out of Newport, Oregon, that was experimenting with it though. I don't remember his name, but he happened to be a member of the Pacific Marine Fishery Council (PMFC). The PMFC is an organization of sport and commercial fishing representatives and state and federal resource agency representatives who regularly meet to coordinate on marine fisheries issues. Ed Bowles, a colleague who dealt with salmon and steelhead management, was Idaho's representative on the PMFC. Ed and this captain just happened to spend some time talking about sport fishing for albacore at one of the meetings, and Ed came back to our office with a tuna fishing trip lined up.

As I remember, the boat would handle ten or twelve fishermen, and the idea was to recruit enough people to fill the boat with our group. It didn't take long to get a group together. Almost everyone who works in the fisheries field is an avid angler. Joining Ed and I were Virgil, Bill Horton, Paul and Laurie Janssen, Don Anderson, and a friend of Don's. I think that was it. There were two other fishermen we didn't know that had already booked for that day who were quickly assimilated into "our" group.

We made the nine-hour drive from Idaho in different groupings and met up at Newport. After buying licenses and gathering supplies for a long boat ride we boarded the boat and pulled out of the harbor at midnight, heading 50 miles offshore for blue water. There was plenty of time, but I don't think anyone slept. None of us had done anything like this before. New trips and new types of fishing always come packaged with lots of imagination and anticipation.

Sometime just before the first light of day we must've hit blue water, because the captain slowed the boat and the deckhand got busy on the back deck. Ten anxious anglers stood under the floodlight on the wheelhouse and watched. The deckhand lowered long outriggers off the port and starboard sides about amidships. They had a line going out to a pulley on the end and back. He got out coiled lines that had various blunt-faced skirted plugs on them and one at a time fed them out behind the boat, then when they were back as far as he wanted he cinched a heavy rubber band around the line and tied the rubber band to the line running out the outrigger. One by one he did this, pulling the spaced-out fishing lines out along the outrigger. When he was done, there would be three, or maybe it was four lines, out on either side of the boat.

But instead of being normal fishing line attached to a rod and reel, these were heavy nylon cords that were cinched off to heavy rubber shock cords on the gunnel. We were going to be tuna fishing the same way the commercial trollers did: pulling tuna in hand over hand.

The most vivid memory of the entire trip, something that the other guys on the trip and I still talk about, happened when the deckhand was still putting lines out and we stood in the circle of light, black ocean all around. All the lines were out on the starboard side and the deckhand was in the middle of getting them out on the port side when a rubber band snapped on one of the outside starboard lines. The deckhand had just enough time to look that way before

the slack in the "popped" line straightened out and the heavy cord snapped like a gunshot. "What the…?" The captain looked down from the wheelhouse as the deckhand looked up at him. They just looked questioningly at each other. The deckhand finally just shrugged his shoulders. They'd been commercial

Ed Bowles was a little pumped after landing his first albacore.

tuna trolling like this for some time and said that they had never had anything break one of those lines. There was some speculation that the lure snagged on something floating out there. It was dark back where the lures were, but if it was some big floating object, the boat and the light that illuminated the back deck would've passed right by it. And we all thought the line straightened out a lot faster than the boat was traveling. We speculated off and on the rest of the trip trying to come up with an explanation. The captain's best offer was a big shark. Most of us were good with that, but the huge one that broke off in the dark is still a mystery.

The fishing itself was exciting. Bringing in albacore hand-over-hand was closer to work than fun, but we had a rotation for bringing in fish like the batting order for a baseball team. It was almost as much fun being on deck as batting. And the deckhand had two fishing rods on board which we got him to rig up and put straight out the back. We had a separate batting rotation for that and we all got to catch at least one tuna on rod and reel before the end of the day. I don't think anyone in the group had ever had something as hot as one of those albacores on a rod and reel before. There were some big smiles, pumped fists, and tuna held high for pictures when people ended their at bat with the rod and reel.

Ed visited with the captain on the long run in and shared with him that most fishermen were like us and would rather catch one tuna on rod and reel than haul ten in on a handline. The captain acknowledged that, but said he didn't think people would get enough tuna to take home just trolling plugs unless he had live bait to put on once a school was located, as they do in California. He had no source for live bait.

Regardless of how we caught them, we had a great day on the water with good friends and each of us took home three albacore. And within a few years that captain figured out that he could catch fish on frozen baitfish once he got into a school of albacore. Today, there are multiple successful tuna sportfishing charters operating along the Oregon and Washington coasts.

Needlefish

Marge and I and our friends Bill and Vicki Goodnight had researched, planned, and anticipated for months a 2003 trip to Mexico that was a first for all of us. An acquaintance of Bill's raved about a trip he'd made to the small town of Los Barilles on the Sea of Cortez, and even recommended a particular motel just a block off the beach. So it's understandable that as soon as we'd gotten checked into the motel in Los Barilles we headed the rental car, packed with towels, fishing gear, swim suits, snorkels, and a case of Corona, north out of town to find a secluded beach. We unloaded at a nice little beach with scattered rocks jutting out of the shallows which we figured would hold fish. I didn't write down and can't remember everything we caught casting grubs and small spoons around the rocks, but I sure do remember the needlefish. Boy are they aggressive. They would come streaking out of nowhere, hit the lure, and go airborne. Most of the time that was it. Fish on, fish off. But we had some on for a while and they are crazy, streaking, jumping fighters. Bill and I actually got some to the beach.

That first day was a wonderful introduction to Mexico. We laid on the sand by the Sea of Cortez, we swam, we got sunburned, caught some fish, and drank a lot of Corona. Vicki, though, is allergic to alcohol (can you imagine?!). Marge probably had a couple beers, but Bill and I drank the rest of the case. And we drank no water.

Bill was in bed recovering most of our second day in Mexico. I'm sure he remembers that, along with our first day and the acrobatic needlefish.

Bonefish

I'd never been that interested in fishing for bonefish. From what I'd heard and read it sounded like they were more about a mystique than catching fish. But I had to go bonefishing at least once. In 2014, for our winter-get-out-of-the-north-Idaho-gloom trip, Sue

Al Knight scanning the flats for tailing bonefish in Belize.

and I decided to go to Belize, a destination neither of us knew much about other than it was warm, sunny, and had lots of salt water. Rumor had it that it also had bonefish.

We had just a wonderful trip. We spent the first week at a small resort called Turneffe Flats, all by itself out on Turneffe Atoll in the Caribbean Sea. The place had beautiful white cabanas with bright orange roofs spaced out along a beach, each with a deck that offered an amazing palm-tree framed view of turquoise flats. Turneffe Flats had started out as just a fly-fishing resort, but then expanded to offer snorkel trips, scuba diving, kayaking, and eco-tours. Evidently some people like to do things other than fish. That attracted Sue, and I wasn't really interested in just fishing for bonefish day after day.

Sue and I enjoyed all the activities that the resort offered, and I did go out two days with Al, another guest at the resort, to do some guided bonefishing. It was fun, but it wasn't easy. We'd boat to another part of the atoll and wade the flats with the guide and he would point out feeding or cruising bonefish for us to cast a fly to. Suffice it to say that I'm not the best fly caster in perfect conditions and out on the flats there is always a stiff wind. I did manage to catch several bonefish each day out though, and I can see why people like catching them. Once you hook up they just scream across the flats. And it ain't bad scenery; sparkling turquoise water, little palm covered islands with small white beaches, surf breaking on the barrier reef just beyond.

Catching one particular bonefish stands out above any others though. I caught it after coming back from snorkeling the afternoon of our third day at the resort. At the time I hadn't gone out fishing yet, but had joined two guys staying in the cabana next door for a cervesa each of the previous afternoons after they got back from fishing. They had talked about how tough it was to get bonefish to take the little crab flies that are the standard offering. One of the guys was really kind of bummed. He hadn't caught a fish in two days of fishing.

So Sue and I are enjoying an adult beverage on our deck after snorkeling that third day and I see a pod of feeding bonefish just a few yards off the beach right in front of our cabana. They were calling my name. I hadn't even gotten my fly rods out of the case yet, but I went in the cabana, pulled out all my gear, and rigged up as fast as I could. The bonefish had just moved a little along the beach by the time I stepped in the water, made a couple false casts off to the side of the fish to get the range, and then dropped the crab fly on the edge of the group. I waited three or four seconds for the fly to sink to the bottom in the six-inch deep water, and then gave it a very short little strip.

No lie, first cast ever to a bonefish, and FISH ON! I could not believe it. It ran up and down the beach and out toward the open flat and all around me before I got ahold of it, unhooked the fly, and released it. The wife of one of the neighbors watched the whole thing from her deck. The group of fish had dispersed when I hooked up, but I waded around and continued to blind cast with no luck. I don't remember whether the guys from next door came back from their day of fishing while I was still fruitlessly casting or whether I'd already quit, but the eyewitness wasted no time in informing her husband about my first-cast bonefish. She'd even taken video!

We were there another four days, and during that time I made hundreds of casts to feeding bonefish on that flat in front of the cabanas without ever hooking another bonefish.

Yellowtail Snapper • Lane Snapper
Bluestripe Grunt

Wading the flats of Turneffe Atoll fishing for bonefish, we were constantly scanning for "tailing" bonefish, a school of bonefish feeding nose down in water shallow enough that the tips of their moving tails were visible. And we looked for "nervous water," where bonefish actively feeding in water a little deeper cause some degree of disturbance on the water surface.

Probably most bonefish anglers do just that, waiting until they find tailing bonefish or nervous water to cast a fly. But I had to fish while we looked, so I made a lot of blind casts to any little pocket of deeper water or rockier bottom that looked interesting.

Doing that I caught little yellowtail snappers with their bright yellow tails and a yellow streak down their sides, little vertical-barred lane snappers, and bluestripe grunts with iridescent blues and greens. None of them were over six inches, and they didn't offer a lot of fight, but I was catching fish.

Barracuda

Bonefish were really the fishing focus of the trip to Belize, but I wanted to see if I could catch a barracuda as well. I did a little research on-line and ordered a couple of barracuda lures: an 18-inch piece of flexible hollow tubing with multiple treble hooks tied to a wire leader that ran through the middle. I purchased one bright red one and one lime green one. And I took a stiff seven-foot spinning rod and a reel spooled with 30-pound test braided super-line.

The two days I went out with Al and the guide, the guide carried the spinning rod for me as we waded the turtle-grass flats for bonefish. The flats we fished were amazingly uniform in depth, mostly 18 inches or less, but there were occasional areas that were waist deep. When we waded past one of those deeper areas the guide and I switched rods. It was deep enough and the bottom was just dark enough that I didn't actually see barracuda to cast to, even when the guide occasionally pointed one out. But it was pretty damn exciting to fling that big bright hose across the dark water, reel it as fast as I could, and see a big long shape rush it. I felt a couple of them hit, but never got hooked up to one. Most of them rushed the lure and stopped short or just spooked out of the spot.

The second day out bonefish fishing with the guide he suggested that if I wanted to catch a barracuda before we quit we ought to troll the lure in some deeper water just off the flats. Al was good with it so that's what we did. It was high-speed trolling. We only trolled for 10 or 15 minutes before my red hose got eaten and I was hooked up to a powerful speed demon. The guide cut the motor and the barracuda was all over the place, stripping line off my reel on long runs, before I got the three-foot barracuda to the boat. When I saw it I was amazed that it wasn't a lot bigger.

Mutton Snapper

After an action-packed week out at Turneffe Flats, fishing, snorkeling, scuba diving, and atoll exploring, Sue and I scheduled a week at a very small no-frills place on the beach on the southern Belizean coast near the small village of Hopkins. The place, called Beaches and Dreams Seafront Inn, was owned by Tony and Angela who had escaped Alaska, where they had operated a restaurant fifty miles outside Fairbanks. Tony's culinary skills were such that even with a location an hour out of Fairbanks, people couldn't expect to get in without a reservation. Tony brought those skills to Belize and created a menu and a restaurant at Beaches and Dreams, that Fodor's described as "one of the best eateries on the Southern Coast."

In addition to enjoying Tony's fabulous dinners that week, we did some tourist things as well. Most notably we visited Xunantunich, an amazing Mayan site near San Ignatio along the Guatemalan border. But mostly we just relaxed.

Tony did have kayaks sitting there on the beach just waiting to be used though, and I did have fishing gear with me. Sue and I took a kayak out several times. A two-pound mutton snapper took the Rapala I just happened to be dragging behind the kayak one of those times. Tony had to tell me what it was

Jack Crevalle

Winters in north Idaho are not especially severe, but they are long. And the sun becomes a stranger. Fortunately, Sue and I have had the retiree luxury of being able to take a little break from it all in January or February, and going someplace sunny and warm (there is always saltwater involved).

I'd caught a few jack crevalle casting off the beach in Mexico, but our most recent winter escape and the role that "jacks" played in it overshadows any previous experience with them. Sue and I had had such a wonderful, relaxing time in 2014 at Beaches and Dreams that we decided to revisit the same place in February, 2019.

One of the major appeals for Sue and me, was the experiences we had had with the Garifuna people of Hopkins. The Garifuna are a people of Carib culture with a history of exile, isolation, and survival. They were discriminated against because of their exceptionally black coloration, and were even restricted by the Belizean government to the southern coastal area until well into the 20th century.

Historically they survived by looking to the sea and native plants for sustenance, and by sharing whatever they had with one another. They embody the Joh Heywood quote "Enough is as good as a feast." While fiercely proud of their culture, their tradition of community and sharing also make them some of the most open and easy going people I have ever been around. Grabbing a Belikin beer at a beach-side shack in Hopkins, or a just a bike ride into the village always meant warm smiles and friendly greetings. That prevailed at Beaches and Dreams, the staff being from the village.

During our most recent trip we arranged to spend a day fishing the nearby Sittee River and its adjacent mangrove-lined sloughs and channels with a local Garifuna fisherman, Levi. Sue and I were driven out to Levi's place, a modest house on stilts situated on the bank of the river in an opening cleared out of the jungle. (Levi said it was not uncommon for him to see a jaguar in the yard at night). We climbed in his panga parked on the river bank behind his house and headed downriver.

Levi was not especially talkative compared to the typical Garifuna, but he had a little smile that came easily. Most Garifuna speak three or four languages and it may be that he wasn't the most comfortable with his English. But he was quick to get our attention and point out in the first fifteen minutes a half dozen different three-foot iguanas lazing in the sun on tree limbs hanging over the river. Further down we saw several crocodiles from three to six feet long, an inhinga (cormorant like bird sometimes called a water snake bird), a large jabiru stork like I'd seen on the Amazon, and lots of small birds new to Sue and me.

But the fishing and the jack crevalle. I have to say the fishing was a little disappointing. We trolled plugs along the mangroves along the river bank without any results, then wound through a narrow tunnel of mangroves into a large open slough where we drifted along off the mangroves and cast plugs and soft plastic lures. But it wasn't until Levi started us trolling plugs (six-inch Rapala-like lures) into a long channel through the mangroves that the real action started. When we first started the first pass, Sue had only just let the lure back when her rod bent over and line ripped off the reel. When she finally got the fish in after a lot of coaching and a little help, it was a jack crevalle with its bright yellow tail and bottom fins. It wasn't nearly as big as I would've thought – maybe 18 inches – but jack crevalle are like all saltwater fish, their fight really belies their size.

We made a couple of passes through the channel and landed several more jack crevalle, some a little smaller and some a little bigger. While landing one of them, a jack that truly dwarfed anything we had caught swam slowly by just under the surface. Then Sue hooked something really big that she just couldn't control and it buried itself in the mangroves and tore off the hook. Levi thought it was probably a big black snapper.

Sue would tell you, though, that the part of those trolling runs through the mangrove channels that she liked the most was passing over all the jellyfish. It was something. They weren't big, about the size of a tennis ball, but there were thousands of them. They were floating in the water just under the surface and down as deep as we could see all through the mile-long channel. At any one time you could see dozens of them. They were so thick that as we trolled our rod tips would bend back a few inches and straighten back out every few seconds as our lures bumped into a jellyfish.

One of the things I liked best about the day, beyond the jacks and iguanas and crocodiles, was the fresh jack crevalle fillets that we had back at Beaches and Dreams that evening for dinner.

Silk Snapper • Black Snapper Schoolmaster Snapper • Porgy

Relaxing and being in warm sunshine for a couple weeks was the main objective for that most recent winter-break, but I just had to take advantage of going out on what was referred to as a "reef and troll" fishing trip. These four species were added to my life list on the "reef" part of the trip (the "troll" part produced two dandy barracudas and a variety-platter of grilled, blackened, and lemon-garlic barracuda steaks, compliments of the chef at Beaches and Dreams).

Part of the appeal of going out on the reef and troll trip was also just spending the day with Steven and Jeremy, two fun, laid-back young Garifuna guys on the staff that we had gotten to know.

Part way out on the 14-mile run to the Belizean barrier reef, Jeremy swung the boat into the shallows adjacent to a mangrove-covered Caye. He idled the panga along while Steven stood on the front deck with a cast-net at the ready. They both peered into the water for sardines. Scores of brown pelicans and white terns soared above, and occasionally folded their wings and dove into the water. It was a sign that sardines were around. Steven's first throw landed in kind of a figure eight, but after that he threw perfect circles. The weights around the edge of the circle of netting dropped quickly to the bottom and trapped the sardines. A sharp pull on the main line that Steven hung onto pulled the weighted perimeter together and pursed the net. We had enough sardines after a half dozen throws.

Jeremy ran on out to a spot where there was a break and a deep channel through the barrier reef. Steven dropped anchor in the shallow water upwind of the break and let out rope until the panga was positioned right above the drop-off.

We fished like we do when we drop-shot for lake trout in Idaho. But the action on the barrier reef is a whole lot faster. We baited with chunks of sardine, and as soon as the weight hit the bottom something tried to eat the bait. It was non-stop for the first 30 minutes.

All the porgys and silk, black, and schoolmaster snappers that we caught (along with yellowtail snappers and bluestripe grunts which I'd previously caught) were small – less than 12 inches. But everything that came into the boat (except the bluestripe grunts) was kept regardless of size. Snapper fried whole, head and all, is one of the more common Garifuna dishes, and Steven and Jeremy said they had lots of friends and neighbors who would be happy to get some fish.

After Steven realized that we were perfectly fine baiting up and taking fish off ourselves we lost him. While laid-back by nature,

Steven throwing the cast net for sardines.

both he and Jeremy were even more so this day after one of the departing guests bought them beers until the wee hours the night before. Steven stretched out on a padded bench seat, put a towel over his face to block the sun, and took a little recuperative break.

Before too long Sue had had enough fishing and set her rod aside and sat down. Steven stirred. Then, with the help of a joint and a cold Belikin, he rallied, took up the rod Sue had been using, and started fishing.

Steven and I were standing back to back fishing off opposite sides of the boat so I can't say how it happened, but a loud expletive caused me to turn and see Steven madly pulling line up out of the water hand over hand as fast as he could. I didn't see a fishing rod. It was suspended in the water straight down under the boat, kept from sinking out of sight only by the friction of the line stripping off the reel and through the guides. Jeremy scrambled up from the back of the boat with a long-handled gaff hook, leaned way over the side, and managed to hook and recover the rod.

Possibly Steven's little break hadn't been sufficient to provide complete recuperation. But Sue and I – and I'm pretty sure Jeremy and Steven as well – sure had a fun and memorable day.

Black Grouper

Colby, Clark, and I had our very first saltwater fishing experience on a trip to visit Margie's mother in Florida back in the early '90s. We drove over to the Gulf coast and went out bottom-fishing on a "head boat."

Head boats are typically 40 to 50 feet long or larger that charge by the head, thus the name. They take out as many anglers as the boat can reasonably accommodate. Fishing in a floating crowd is not a fishing experience I'd prefer, but it was an easy and affordable way for the boys and I to share a day together on the water doing some fishing that was new to each of us.

We were greeted at the dock by the captain, and as the "heads" (there were 25 or so of us) shuffled around getting ready to board, a second guy who I took to be a deckhand approached everyone in turn and asked if they wanted to put some money into a pool for biggest fish of the day. Though it smacked a bit of competition – something that for me doesn't go with fishing – I figured that with everyone on the boat using the same gear and bait that was provided, catching the biggest fish would just be a random act. And the random chance that one of the boys would come off the boat with bragging rights was worth a few bucks, so I gave the guy some money. I don't remember, but I suppose it was probably five bucks a person. I do remember he already had quite a wad.

By the time the boys and I got aboard there were people already stationing themselves at the spots where fishing rods were waiting in rod holders along the stern rail and up both sides. We headed up the port side toward the bow where there was no one. But right in the point of the bow there was a big yellow plastic tub filled nearly to the top with water and some other gear, so we took up stations just back from the bow.

After the captain made the short run out into the Gulf and parked the boat at "spot X", and the boys and I started fishing. Right about then, the guy who had collected the money and I had taken as a deckhand came up and stationed himself – and his fishing rod – in the bow.

We were dropping our weighted hooks baited with chunks of cut-up squid straight down to the bottom, and proceeded to catch a variety of fish that were all new to us. I don't know anymore, and I'm sure I didn't even know then, what all we caught. I do know that Colby actually caught a remora, the cleaner fish that attaches itself to the sides of whales and sharks. And I caught a black grouper that was a little bigger than the rest of the fish we caught, maybe three pounds.

The boys and I had a blast that day catching fish, not knowing what was going to take our chunks of squid next. It was pretty steady action.

The guy who showed up in the bow didn't act like he was particularly having fun. He was working. Not being a deckhand, but working to win the pool for big fish.

Rather than fishing with cut-up squid like everyone else, he was fishing with live four to six-inch bait fish that had been in the yellow tub. He didn't catch as many fish that day as the boys and I did, and he sure didn't have as much fun, but he did catch a grouper that easily won the pool.

At the end of the trip, as we got off the boat back at the dock, I saw him huddled with the captain shuffling bills between them.

White Grunt

These fish are kind of like crappies. They don't look like a crappie, and they sure don't live in the same places, but they are abundant, cooperative biters, and you can end up with a lot of small fillets. I was introduced to them by Doug NeMeth. Doug was a fisheries research biologist who I had worked with in Idaho, who moved to the funky little town of Cedar Key on the Florida Gulf Coast. I stopped to visit Doug and his wife and two boys while I was on my 2006 walkabout.

Doug took me out fishing in his smallish open fiberglass boat and we parked in one spot and caught white grunts. One after the other. We had a lot of white grunts to clean when we got back to Doug's house. The space under Doug's house, which was elevated on stilts to help protect it from tropical storm surges, provided a perfect shady spot with a light breeze off the gulf. We stood in the shade under Doug's house for a long time filleting white grunts at a makeshift table while his two young boys rinsed the fillets and told me about what good fishermen they were. And I'm sure Doug Nemeth's sons are.

Sardine

Sardines? Who sport fishes for sardines? Probably no one, but they were added to my life list of sport-caught fish while down in Costa Rica, fishing out of Crocodile Bay.

One morning Anthony stopped the boat where some birds were working before we headed out to blue water. He pulled out a light rod with six tiny flies spaced out along the line above a heavy weight. "Wanna get some bait." I watched him drop it over, jig it, and pull up wiggling sardines just a few times before I said I can do that. After all, I was the one paying to go fishing and, while there wasn't much sport to it, technically it was fishing. I made some sport out of it attempting to bring up six sardines at a time. Five was the best I could do. The real sport, though, came hours later when one of the sardines became dinner for a 90-pound tuna. But that's a story I've already told.

AFTERWARD

"You start your life as a collector of precious moments and end it clinging to them."
- Kirk Landers: Alone on the Shield

This project has been at once fun and enjoyable, reminiscent and emotional. To pull up and record so many wonderful memories from the well-full I've collected – memories of people and fish and places and experiences – both revitalizes them and enables me to cling to them in a tangible way.

In the process, a couple of things became apparent. One is that the richest and most meaningful experiences were shared experiences. I've fished quite a lot by myself. I appreciate solitude. If the time was right and I had the time I never hesitated to go fishing alone. But the experiences of fishing by myself, by and large, generated indistinct memories. In retrospect, I wish I'd have placed more importance on sharing fishing experiences with friends, and less on just catching fish.

That leads to another thing that became apparent to me: my limited ability to find words that come close to describing the mental images, emotions, and events that I hold dear. Adjectives in particular seemed to become more diluted in meaning the more I used them. Nowhere was my frustration greater than in trying to describe the friends I shared fishing experiences with. *Good, special, true, longtime, new, close, dear,* or any other adjective, by itself or in a string, can't fully communicate what we mean when we refer to someone as a friend.

New might come the closest. When someone says that they met or made a new friend, it's understood that they are referring to someone they recently met who seemed to share their interests, values, or beliefs; someone that they felt they might enjoy spending time with. In describing someone as a *new* friend, adjectives like *short, tall, red-headed,* or *bald* might as well be thrown in. At that point we are just referring to the characteristics of the person.

Nearly always when we refer to a friend, however, there is a relationship which exists. And relationships – friendships – are grown over time. Which friend do we call at 3:00 am when we are in a jam. Likely not the new friend we just recently met. Friendships are nourished and grown with shared experiences, each friendship a product of a unique set of experiences. Fishing might be one, but other shared life experiences – shared hardship, shared celebration, shared support, shared kindness, just day to day interaction – really forge and temper friendships. Friendships that endure.

In the Yuptik Inuit language there are 53 different words for snow. To refer to softly falling snow, the Yuptik word is *aquilokog.* In English, the word is snow. To refer to crystalline powder snow that looks like salt, the Yuptik word is *pukak.* In English, the word is snow. Wet snow that can be used to ice sleigh runners is *matsaaruti.*

Friends, at the end of a day of fishing. Left to right Steve Elle, Bill Horton, Hutch, me, and Virgil. (Bill Goodnight photo)

The English word is snow. We have to put a series of words together to describe different kinds of snow using the English language. But even if we had 53 distinct words in English to describe friends, and friendships, I doubt it would suffice. I would likely still struggle to come up with adjectives to attach to the words. Sharing a story is often the best I can do.

The shared experiences over the years with my family are especially cherished. Times fishing with my boys, Colby and Clark, from their first experiences to more recent big adventures, are particularly treasured. And Clark and I teaming up to help his little Lucia, my five year old granddaughter, catch her first fish was priceless. It's the beginning of her personal collection of fishing memories and in some way kind of seems to complete the big circle.

But I'm not done. I'm still hell bent on collecting. There are a few more kinds of fishing that I really want to experience: throwing top water lures for bluefish off Cape Cod, throwing a swim bait into a school of feeding striped bass off Nag's Head, stripping a fly to a cruising Louisiana bayou redfish, and fishing for tarpon by any means in any place. I dare not think about giant trevally off a remote South Pacific island beach.

And there are friends – old friends, and ones I've not met yet – that I want to make new memories with. Because in the end, whenever it comes and "the deal goes down," as Bob Dylan refers to it, all we have of any real value is our family and friends and our collection of memories. I'm already a rich man.

INDEX OF FISHES

American eel......................106
Apapaa............................202
Arctic char 60
Aruana 203
Barracuda.........................233
Bass
    Largemouth 113
    Smallmouth 120
    Spotted 119
    White 108
    Yellow 111
Bicunda............................205
Black grouper 239
Bluegill............................140
Bocaccio 192
Bonefish...........................230
Bowfin..............................26
Bullhead
    Black 101
    Brown 101
    Yellow 101
Burbot.............................108
Cabezon 191
Carachin sp........................205
Carp 85
Catfish
    Channel...........................95
    Flathead 100
    Gafftopsail 153
    Redtailed 205

Tiger...............................205
Chain pickerel 79
Chiselmouth........................90
Crappie
    Black 132
    White 132
Creek chub..........................91
Dolly Varden 59
Dorado.............................215
Flounder
    Arrowtooth.......................179
    Starry 180
Freshwater drum...................158
Goldeye.............................28
Goldfish............................89
Grayling............................67
Great sculpin 180
Grunt
    Bluestripe........................233
    White 241
Halibut............................175
Hammerhead shark 221
Hogsucker..........................84
Irish lord 191
Jack crevalle.......................235
Jacuda 205
Kelp greenling 189
Lingcod............................182

⌁ INDEX OF FISHES ⌁

Longnose gar 27
Marlin
   Blue................................207
   Striped...........................209
Mooneye 28
Muskellunge 69
Myleinae sp. 205
Needlefish...........................230
Northern pike......................70
Northern pikeminnow.........92
Oscar...................................195
Pacific cod 187
Paddlefish...........................25
Pargo..................................221
Payara.................................203
Peacock bass
   Butterfly 198
   Speckled..........................198
   Three Bar.........................198
Peamouth 90
Perch
   Yellow 145
   White 111
Piranha 205
Porgy..................................237
Ratfish................................181
Rock sole............................168

Rockbass.............................139
Rockfish
   Black................................192
   Blue 192
   Canary.............................191
   China...............................191
   Copper 191
   Dusky 192
   Quillback.........................191
   Tiger................................191
   Vermillion........................191
   Yelloweye.........................189
   Yellowtail.........................192
Roosterfish 219
Sailfish 213
Salmon
   Chinook 159
   Chum 175
   Coho 168
   Kokanee 31
   Pink 173
   Sockeye 172
Sardine...............................242
Sauger................................157
Schoolmaster 237
Shiner
   Common 94

⌲ INDEX OF FISHES ⌲

Golden................................91
Sierra....................................**213**
Smallmouth buffalofish.......**82**
Snapper
    Black..............................237
    Lane..............................233
    Mutton 234
    Silk...............................237
    Yellowtail....................233
Snook...................................**195**
Spanish mackerel...............**195**
Spiny dogfish......................**181**
Steelhead **46**
Sucker
    Bridgelip........................84
    Largescale 85
    Mountain 84
    Plecostomi 205
    Redhorse 84
    White 84
Sunfish
    Green...........................140
    Pumpkinseed................144
    Redear 145
Tadpole madtom................**105**
Tetra....................................**205**

Tiger muskie..........................**78**
Trout
    Brook 50
    Brown 49
    Bull 57
    Lahontan cutthroat............41
    Lake 52
    Rainbow 42
    Snake River finespot 41
    Speckled sea 195
    Westslope cutthroat 34
    Yellowstone cutthroat 38
Tuna
    Albacore 226
    Bigeye 226
    Skipjack 226
    Yellowfin 222
Wahoo..................................**217**
Walleye.................................**151**
Warmouth **138**
White sturgeon......................**19**
Whitefish
    Lake 62
    Mountain 63
Wolffish...............................**205**

ACKNOWLEDGMENTS

My thanks to all those who helped make these memories over the years. Collectively, they made it impossible to merely compile a simple life list of fish caught. My appreciation goes to Bill Hutchinson and Clark Van Vooren for their manuscript review, encouragement, and content suggestions. My deepest gratitude goes to my wife, Sue, for her many days of line editing and her suggested revisions, which greatly improved the readability and flow of the manuscript. And a special appreciation to Sue for her understanding and acceptance of my frequent absences during this process; both my physical absences working on the project in my office, and my frequent mental absences when I was with her but thinking about the project.

ABOUT THE AUTHOR

Author Al Van Vooren
(Bobbie Dennett photo)

The author was born and raised in Moline, Illinois, a city sandwiched between the Mississippi and Rock Rivers, where he became obsessed at a young age with fish and fishing. He earned a degree in fish and wildlife biology from Iowa State University in 1968 and went on to a 38-year career researching and managing fish populations in Ohio, Iowa, and Idaho. Personal and professional travels took him to far reaching locations where sampling the local fishing was always on the agenda. He has written technical and popular articles on fish and fishing, and wrote a regular fishing column for the bi-monthly *Idaho Wildlife* magazine. This is his first – and likely only – book. He is retired, and, between fishing trips, lives on Lake Pend Oreille in northern Idaho with his wife and fishing partner Susan.

49515526R00144

Made in the USA
San Bernardino, CA
22 August 2019